Rising
from the Rails

RISING

FROM THE RAILS

Pullman Porters and the Making of the Black Middle Class

LARRY TYE

Henry Holt and Company

New York

Henry Holt and Company, LLC
Publishers since 1866
115 West 18th Street
New York, New York 10011

Henry Holt® is a registered trademark of Henry Holt and Company, LLC.

Copyright © 2004 by Larry Tye
All rights reserved.
Distributed in Canada by H. B. Fenn and Company Ltd.

Library of Congress Cataloging-in-Publication Data
Tye, Larry.
  Rising from the rails : Pullman porters and the making of the Black middle class / Larry
Tye.—1st ed.
    p. cm.
  Includes bibliographical references.
  ISBN 0-8050-7075-3
    1. Pullman porters—United States—History. 2. Brotherhood of Sleeping Car
Porters—History. 3. African Americans—Social conditions. I. Title.
HD8039.R362U68 2004
331.88'1138522—dc22   *2003067573*

Henry Holt books are available for special promotions and premiums.
For details contact: Director, Special Markets.

First Edition 2004

Designed by Fritz Metsch
Frontispiece photograph courtesy of William Howes

Printed in the United States of America
1   3   5   7   9   10   8   6   4   2

To Pullman porter Lawrence "Happy" Davis

and dining car waiter Robert McGoings,

who enthusiastically shared their stories

but did not live to see them told

▓

CONTENTS

PREFACE

THE MOST INFLUENTIAL black man in America for the hundred years following the Civil War was a figure no one knew. He was not the educator Booker T. Washington or the sociologist W. E. B. DuBois, although both were inspired by him. He was the one black man to appear in more movies than Harry Belafonte or Sidney Poitier. He discovered the North Pole alongside Admiral Peary and helped give birth to the blues. He launched the Montgomery bus boycott that sparked the civil rights movement—and tapped Martin Luther King Jr. to lead both.

The most influential black man in America was the Pullman porter.

For millions of whites who rode the sleeping cars west toward San Francisco or south to Florida, the porter was the African-American man they mixed with more than any other—yet understood not at all. They did not know that scores of men like the North Pole pioneer Matthew Henson and the blues legend "Big Bill" Broonzy had worked on sleepers until they earned enough money and confidence to try something else. They saw porters serve as props in hundreds of films, but few realized porters' starring roles as patriarchs of black labor, or in financing and orchestrating the civil rights struggle from Montgomery right through the 1963 March on Washington. And no one calculated porters' most lasting legacy: activists like NAACP boss Roy Wilkins, political leaders like Los Angeles mayor Tom Bradley, artists like jazz great Oscar Peterson, and all their other children and grandchildren, nephews and nieces, who run universities and municipalities, sit on corporate and editorial boards, and helped spawn and shape today's black middle class.

If whites did not grasp that, they can be excused. Few blacks did, either. In his earliest years the Pullman porter was seen in the black world as a figure whose very presence captured the romance of the railroad, a traveling man with cosmopolitan sensibilities and money in his pockets. But by the 1960s he had come to personify the grinning servant, an Uncle Tom transplanted from plantation to locomotion. Neither image was complete. Behind the porter's constant smile and courtly service lay a day-to-day struggle for dignity that anticipated black America's bloody crawl toward equity. If race is the story of America, the Pullman porter represents one of its most resonant chapters.

Yet while the nation's racial history is an unwieldy story, one that convulsed the country from its most remote corners to its most public spaces, the tale of the Pullman porter unraveled within the narrow confines of a railcar and thus can serve as a kind of historical prism. It was a capsule of space and time where all the rules of racial engagement came into succinct and, at times, painful focus. Sometimes they were suspended altogether—as long as the train was moving, that is. The porter's story extends from the end of the Civil War to 1969, when the Pullman Company terminated its sleeping car service, which lets us see how those close contacts between the races evolved over a complete century.

I came to this story by accident. Ten years ago, when I was a Nieman fellow at Harvard University, Professor John Stilgoe used the Pullman porters to help explain the shaping of America's landscape and culture. Porters were agents of change, we learned, much the way Jewish peddlers had been in the shtetls of Europe and small towns across the United States. They carried radical music like jazz and blues from big cities to outlying burgs. They brought seditious ideas about freedom and tolerance from the urban North to the segregated South. And when white riders left behind newspapers and magazines, porters picked up bits of news and new ways of doing things, refining them in each place they visited, and leaving behind a town or village that was a bit less insular and parochial.

What they saw and read changed them, too. It made porters determined that their children would get the formal learning they had been denied. Whom they met was even more transforming. Most people who rode Pullman cars have only vague memories of their porters, albeit pleasant ones. The porters, by contrast, were keen observers of the politicians and movie stars, businessmen and leisure travelers, who boarded their trains. They shined their shoes and marveled over the careful stitching and soft leather. They took their orders and noticed the meticulous phrasing and mannered expressions. Through their time on the train these black porters learned the ways of a white world most had only vague exposure to before, coming to know how it worked and how to work with it. All of which helped fill in their expanding sense of self-esteem and power. "I don't know if you ever heard about the three Ls, because L stands for so many things," explained Jimmy Clark, who worked as a chef on the Pullman cars from 1918 to 1950. "But these three Ls was 'look,' 'listen,' and 'learn.' And those things imbedded into my mind to the point where I lived with it, and it helped me all through this world, and it's helping me to this day."[1]

Professor Stilgoe's preoccupation with such porter stories quickly became mine. It stayed with me when I returned to the *Boston Globe* and understood in a new way how critical race was to so many issues I wrote about, from Pentecostalism's becoming the fastest-growing religion in the world, and especially in the black community, to why Boston still cherishes its forty-year-old program for busing inner-city blacks to largely white suburban schools. My first book, *The Father of Spin,* taught me how biography can tell a bigger story, specifically how spinmeisters like the public relations pioneer Edward L. Bernays help determine America's commercial choices and public discourse. My second book, *Home Lands,* on the renewal under way across the Jewish world, helped me see how religion and race can furnish identity and hope.

Pullman porters embrace all that. They are men whose compelling biographies tell bigger stories of racial dynamics, democracy, and the building of African-America. Not only are they a singular tale of history; they are one that is living and breathing today. Behind almost every successful African-American, there is a Pullman porter.

Or so it appeared as I cross-checked porters against lists of prominent black scientists and artists, political and business leaders. One in every few had a porter father or grandfather, uncle, cousin, or in-law. Others had worked on the sleepers themselves. The theory that porters fueled black advancement seemed true beyond what I had imagined. But it was equally clear that such progress came at an enormous price. For every inch the porter gained there was a humiliation to endure. The very definition of his job was roiling in contradictions. He was servant as well as host. His was the best job in his community and the worst on the train. He could be trusted with white passengers' children and safety, but only for the five days of a cross-country trip. The Pullman porter shared his riders' most private moments, but, to most, he remained an enigma if not a cipher.

To fill in that puzzle I had to find and talk to porters, which was a challenge. Every source I consulted said there were only a handful left in the country, which made sense since the Pullman Company had been out of business thirty years and had hired very few porters for the thirty before that. I tried to track them down using every technique I learned during twenty years as a journalist in Boston, Louisville, and Anniston, Alabama. I posted ads in black papers, railroad journals, and retirement magazines. I scoured retirement records the company left behind in Chicago, then wrote to every porter there was a chance could still be alive. High-tech detective agencies ran searches at ten dollars a shot, Amtrak scoured its files and collective memory, authors who had written about porters or their union offered up contacts, and interns helped me contact black politicians, ministers, civil rights leaders, and nursing home administrators across the United States.

It worked. All told I found nearly forty porters and other black railroad workers, along with dozens of their daughters, sons, and other relatives. I reached Babe and Virgil Smock, two survivors in a family of Pullman men that traced back three generations, with a fourth opting out after a brief experiment. I talked to a 102-year-old porter named Ernest Porter. Ernest had difficulty recalling the name of his grandson who left ten minutes before I arrived at his senior center, but this grandson of slaves recounted in detail how he had learned to get by sleeping just four hours a night in cramped quarters and eating warmed-over food in the blacks-only section of the dining car. Each porter I met led me to another. By the end I found there were a handful not in the nation but in most every city that had been a railroad terminus, from Washington to Los Angeles, Boston, and Chicago. The youngest were in their 80s, the oldest their early 100s. I also found and talked to black dining car waiters, chefs, and bartenders, and to porters who had worked directly for the railroads. The Pullman porter is a metaphor for them and tens of thousands of other African-Americans who worked the railroads, including such celebrated figures as the former Supreme Court justice Thurgood Marshall and the activist Malcolm X.* This book tells their story, too.

Every time I showed up on a porter's doorstep, or a waiter's, we went through a similar dance. They greeted me politely, but their facial expressions suggested I had dropped in from another planet. "What's a white man like you got to do with my story?" one long-time porter asked. Fair question, and one I asked myself as I wondered whether I would be able to tell a black man's story the same way I had written about my Jewish community and the familiar world of public relations. Fifteen minutes into every interview that

---

*Not only are the busboys, laborers, and other black railroad workers as much the real McCoy as Pullman porters, their numbers include the original real McCoy. Elijah McCoy was trained as an engineer, but, because he was a Negro, one of the few jobs he could land on the railroad in the mid-1800s was as a fireman shoveling coal and oiling the engine. He quickly realized the inefficiencies of using a tiny oil can like his and having to stop the engine to lubricate it. So he devised, then patented, a system that provided continuous oiling of the gears on trains as well as ships. While his invention worked brilliantly, its many imitators did not; hence would-be purchasers insisted on knowing whether they had the "real McCoy."

porter's doubts—and mine—began to dissipate. What mattered was not that I was white, but that I was there, and he was old and worried his story would die with him. All the black railroad workers I talked to despaired at how little their children and grandchildren knew about what they had been through, the suffering or the triumphs. In their younger days they felt it essential to shield their families from that, not wanting to burden them or brag, but now these porters were determined that the new generations grasp their roots.

After tracking down every African-American railroad worker I could find, I spent weeks listening to dozens of tapes other interviewers had made of workers no longer alive. I pored through memoirs, letters, and articles left by early porters. I reviewed twenty-five hundred cubic feet of management, labor, and employee records that the Pullman Company bequeathed to the Newberry Library in Chicago, along with the Brotherhood of Sleeping Car Porters' files at the Chicago Historical Society, Library of Congress, and New York Public Library. Scores of habitual Pullman passengers told me what they knew about porters, as did scholars, archivists, and civil rights leaders. I watched Pullman porters in movies, documentary and commercial, and read everything written by or about them in fiction, nonfiction, poetry, and songs. I also made a tactical decision after consulting with black railroad workers and seeing how they had described themselves over the years: I opted to call them *Negroes* in the period when that was what they called themselves. I switch to *black* and *African-American* in writing about eras when those terms began to be used.

The story that emerges from my conversations with and research on porters has a cast of full-bodied characters—from George Pullman, the visionary and ruthless Caesar of the sleeping cars, to Robert Todd Lincoln, the Great Emancipator's son who presided over the Pullman Company during one of its most oppressive eras, to A. Philip Randolph, the firebrand founder of the porters' union and a father of the civil rights movement. Yet the real stars are the Pullman porters themselves, men like Jimmy Clark and the Smock family, whose narratives have been scarcely articulated, with the popular press and historians treating them as footnotes, and Hollywood portraying them as featureless step-and-fetch-it characters.

The tale of those Pullman porters is, most of all, a story of America—of how one group, disadvantaged and powerless, learned to triumph in the sometimes brutal arena of American democracy. It is a story of black men not just riding along the rails but rising from them.

*Rising
from the Rails*

1

Out of Bondage,

All Aboard

⁛

HE WAS A black man in a white jacket and sable hat. Having stepped out of the cotton fields barely two years before, he now was stepping onto one of the locomotives that had long symbolized freedom to slavehands across America. He lit candles that illuminated the passenger carriage, stoked the pot-bellied Baker Heater, and turned down hinged berths that magically transformed the day coach into an overnight compartment. He was part chambermaid, part valet, shining shoes, nursing hangovers, tempering tempers, and performing other tasks that won tips and made him indispensable to the wealthy white travelers who snapped their fingers in the air when they needed him. It was the only real traveling he would ever do.

That much is known about the first porter to work on George Mortimer Pullman's railroad sleeping cars. What is not known is his name, age, birthplace, date of employment, or just about anything else about him. Historians will say the reason is that a fire in Chicago destroyed the early archives of the Pullman Company. But, curiously, it didn't destroy the names of those first two primitive Pullman cars back in 1859, remodeled day coaches 9 and 19 of the Chicago, Alton & St. Louis Railroad, or the provenance of the first three paying passengers, all from Bloomington, Illinois. Or even the name of the original conductor, Jonathan L. Barnes, who like all conductors was white and whose narrative is preserved in telling detail.

The pioneering porter, in fact, was not expected to have human proportions at all, certainly none worthy of documenting. He was a phantom assistant who did not merit the dignity of a name or identity of any sort. That is precisely why George Pullman hired him. He was an ex-slave who embodied servility more than humanity, an ever-obliging manservant with an ever-present smile who was there when a jacket needed dusting or a child tending or a beverage refreshing. Few inquired where he came from or wanted to hear about his struggle. In his very anonymity lay his value.

And so it was that the polished passengers who rode the plush velvet-appointed night coaches over the first half century of Pullman Palace Car service summoned him with a simple "porter." The less polite hailed him with "boy" or, more often, "George." The latter appellation was born in the practice of slaves being named after slavemasters, in this case porters being seen as servants of George Pullman. It stuck because it was repeated instinctively by successive generations of passengers, especially those below the Mason-Dixon Line, and by caricaturists, comedians, and newspaper columnists. If the more socially conscious among riders perceived the grim irony of the moniker, they did not say so publicly. They certainly did not object. The only ones who protested, at first, were white men named George. They were sufficiently annoyed by the slight, or more probably amused, that they founded the Society for the Prevention of Calling Sleeping Car Porters George, SPCSCPG for short, which eventually claimed thirty-one thousand members, including England's King George V, George Herman "Babe" Ruth, George M. Cohan, and Georges Clemenceau of France.[1]

Whether George Pullman knew his passengers were calling his porters "George" is unclear. That he would not have cared is certain. It was not that he was mean, or more coldhearted to black employees than to white. He believed he owed workers nothing more than a job, and when business slackened, even that was not ironclad. He hired more Negroes than any businessman in America, giving them a monopoly on the profession of Pullman porter and a chance to enter the cherished middle class. He did it not out of sentimentality, of which he had none, but because it made business sense. They came cheap, and men used to slave labor could be compelled to do whatever work they were asked, for as many hours as told.

There was another reason George hired only Negroes, one that had to do with the social separation he thought was vital for porters to safely interact with white passengers in such close quarters. Women, after all, were disrobing on the other side of a thin curtain. Riders were stumbling into bed drunk, slinking into compartments of someone other than their spouse, tumbling out of upper berths. Such compromised postures called for a porter whom passengers could regard as part of the furnishings rather than a mortal with likes, dislikes, and a memory. It had to be someone they knew they would never encounter outside the closed capsule of the sleeping car, someone who inhabited a different reality. It must be a Negro.

Recruiters started signing them up shortly after George launched his fleet of sleeping cars. The Pullman Company built the sleepers and rented them to the railroads, complete with everything from fine linen and sweet-smelling soap to a service staff whose center-piece was the porter. George's first choice for that job was Negroes from the old slave states. The blacker the better, passengers told him. If some riders were rude in return, so be it. That was outside his control and concern.

All of which was okay with most porters, at least at the beginning. They were, as George suspected, grateful for a steady salary, for being out of shackles and able to hurtle across the landscape in his luxurious sleeping carriages. They cherished the job and stayed a lifetime, with many passing it down to sons and grandsons. Work on the train was rigid and hierarchical, but they were accustomed to structure. No hierarchy could be more confining or cruel than that of slave and slavemaster. Little by little, however, some porters asked for more. They wanted the human dimension that slavery had taken away and without which they could not feel fully free. They needed a heritage and ancestors worth knowing. If the Pullman Company could not or would not tell them who their patriarch was, that first porter, they would frame their own gilded image.

They called him Daddy Joe. He was a Bunyanesque figure tall

enough to pull down upper berths on either side of the aisle at the same time, agile enough to prepare uppers and lowers simultaneously, and so appreciated by riders that his pockets were weighed down with silver and gold. Once, when marauding redskins besieged his Central Pacific train at a water stop, Joe climbed atop the sleeper and spoke to the Indians in their own idiom, charming the chiefs into accepting a pile of Pullman blankets in place of passenger scalps. Another time he convinced passengers panicked by a rising river to stay seated 'til floodwaters subsided. Daddy Joe may or may not have been real, but the way porters told and retold his stories it was clear he reflected their aspirations as well as their need to know whence they came.[2]

GEORGE PULLMAN KNEW his own roots enough to know they did not matter. Like most true believing entrepreneurs in the making, he saw history as mere curiosity, preordaining nothing. He was determined to become a player in the new financial and political orders, an age defined by the iron horse, shrinking frontiers, and the war brewing between the states. Industry was eclipsing the old land-based economy. Men who grasped those trends, men like George Pullman, were free to shape their future and, when needed, reshape their past. They were self-made.

The third of ten children, George set out in 1859 from the village of Albion in upstate New York to seek his fortune in Chicago, a city, like him, about to bloom. He was nearly twenty-nine, which was old for a pioneer and for a bachelor. Standing just over six feet, he had dusky hair he hoped would stay thick and glossy through regular application of a hair invigorator. His beard then had none of the fullness, or gray, that would become his trademarks, and in the style of the day it did not include a mustache. Just as he was not quite handsome, so his three decades in New York testified more to what he could not do than could. He was less drawn to God than two brothers who became Universalist ministers, less capable a craftsman than his father and other brothers despite having grown up with a carving knife and wood block by his side. He served long enough as apprentice in his father's cabinetmaking and building-moving businesses to learn both, and know he loved neither. That might explain why, after calling himself a cabinetmaker in the 1850 U.S. Census, in 1855 he told New York census takers that his occupation was "gentleman." Gentleman or not, when his father died two years earlier George, just twenty-two, had taken over as breadwinner for his mother and youngest siblings, a role he dutifully performed for seven years.

It felt liberating leaving Albion, a town of three thousand known for its snap beans and sandstone. He took with him more than he realized. Having experienced the grind of manual labor at his uncle's general store, then the family furniture shop, George decided he preferred the hours afterward when he could scrub clean, then promenade in high top hat and long-tailed coat. He had watched the newly widened Erie Canal fuel commerce in shorefront communities like his, but realized that the more agile railroad was displacing inland waterways as the preferred mode for carrying cargo and people. Most of all, he had learned that while making a sound product was important, even more critical to the riches he sought was a proficiency in peddling that product.

He already had cashed in on that understanding by convincing the owners of Chicago's Matteson House that, though he may have been from upcountry New York, he was the man most qualified to lift their hotel the eight feet needed to install a sewer system. George had learned a novel technique for moving buildings from Lewis Pullman, his father, who nearly twenty years before had patented a device to roll huge edifices away from the banks of the Erie so the canal could be broadened to handle bigger barges. In Chicago's case the commercial district had been built on poorly drained lowlands. The challenge was to elevate downtown buildings above the level of Lake Michigan, letting workers fill in muddy streets and flooded cellars with sand and concrete, then add sewers and lay gas and water pipes.

George and his minions were glad to oblige. They began with the Matteson House, which stood on the priciest section of downtown and was the largest building ever raised in Chicago. Next they lifted an entire block of clothing stores and print shops, banks and book-binderies. The process was artful: workmen dug underneath the existing foundations to insert timbers and blocks, set in place six thousand jackscrews, then, at the sound of George's whistle, each of six hundred laborers gave their screws a quarter turn. Pilings under the buildings were reinforced daily to fill the widening gap; within five days, thirty-five thousand tons of buildings had been lifted nearly five feet, all without breaking a pane of glass, interrupting a shopper, or tipping a teacup. Chicago, which thirty years earlier had been a stinking swamp of wild onions, was getting the solid foundation a world-class city required. And George was proving to himself and anyone watching that he could bring off what seemed like the most fanciful of public works projects—levitating, then reconstructing, a major slice of downtown Chicago.[3]

His next fantasy was even more improbable: putting a hotel on wheels.

The notion of a railroad car comfortable enough to let passengers sleep seems unremarkable from today's perspective, but at the time it was revolutionary. The earliest version of what might be called a train hit the tracks in the middle of the sixteenth century, when English mine owners realized that horse-drawn carts could be moved more easily along wooden rails than rutted roads. The first steam locomotive was tested in Britain in 1804. In 1827, a rudimentary railway was opened in America to cart granite the four miles from a quarry in Quincy to the Boston site where workmen were erecting a monument to the Battle of Bunker Hill. It wasn't until 1825—three centuries after British miners set up their pseudorailroad—that the public there began riding trains, and it took six more years to launch the first fully equipped, steam-powered passenger service in America.

The passengers rode, but they seldom rested. "Without a proper place to stow away one's hat, with no convenience even to repose the head or back except to the ordinary height of a chair, with a current of cold air continually streaming in and rendered necessary by the sulphurous heat of the furnace, and with the constant slamming of the doors at either end of the car as the conductor goes in or out, or some weary passenger steps onto the platform to have a smoke, the passenger must indeed be dead beat who can sleep or even doze in a railroad car," one rider recalled of a night trip to Wheeling, West Virginia.[4] Another chronicler said the narrow, stiff-backed seats made travel so uncomfortable during the early years of steam that "it is difficult to understand how any passenger could have fallen asleep amid the horrors of the journey. Nevertheless, many travelers—fatalistic, steel-nerved, or exhausted—did indeed succumb to a sort of limp, half-conscious hibernation. Their heads lolled sideways on the wooden benches, their hats fell off, their mouths drooped open, and their eyes closed on the waking nightmare."[5]

That nightmare included the havoc those first locomotives left in their wake. A British traveler traversing the United States in 1840 kept a journal of his uneasy experience. Feeling a "violent jolt, accompanied by a loud crash" as his train pulled past a crossing, he asked the engineer and conductor what had happened. "'Well, it was in going over a chaise and horse,' replied one of them, very coolly. 'There was no one in the chaise?' asked I, anxiously. 'Oh, yes, there were two ladies.' 'Were they thrown out?' 'I guess they were, and pretty well smashed, too.' 'Good God! And why didn't you stop the train? Can't you send back to know what state they're in?' 'Well, mister, I reckon they're in the State of Delaware; but you'd better jump into the steamer there, or you're likely to lose your passage.'" The man caught his steamer but later read that one lady had been killed, the other badly wounded, the horse "smashed," and the chaise broken to pieces.[6]

Seeking to soften such bad dreams, or at least let riders sleep through them, officers of Pennsylvania's Cumberland Valley Railroad in 1838 launched regular sleeping car service for the fifty miles between Harrisburg and Chambersburg. Calling those primitive cars sleepers did not make them such. Beds typically consisted of bunks stacked three high, with cast-iron platforms and no sheets. There was no fresh air either, and about as much privacy as in an army barracks. Wooden floors creaked, windows rattled, wood-burning stoves roasted passengers who sat too close and froze those who kept their distance, and tallow candles offered up noxious fumes and little illumination. Any washing had to be done in a narrow basin at one end of the coach. Eating was on the run during station stops. A row of brass spittoons lined the wall with signs imploring, "Gentlemen Are Requested Not to Spit on the Stove," but the floors flowed with saliva and tobacco juice. Innovations over the next twenty years, from swivel couches to cane-bottomed berths, were insufficient to induce grumbling men to shed pants or even muddy boots as they bunked down for the night. Or to entice any but the bravest women to venture in at all. Most who did remained fully clothed, clutching hatpins through the night to repel wayward men.

"We all 'retired' at ten o'clock, with a fair allowance of open windows and virtuous resolutions," Horace Greeley, America's most celebrated journalist, recalled in a memoir of his trip on an Erie Line sleeper in the summer of 1859. "But the rain poured, the night was chill and damp; and soon every orifice for the admission of external air, save the two or three humbug ventilators overhead, was shut, and a mephitic atmosphere produced. . . . After gasping a while, like a netted fish on a hot sandbank, I rose to enter my solemn protest against all sleeping-cars not provided with abundant and indefeasible means of ventilation." Not easily deterred, Greeley tried another sleeper two nights later, this one on the Michigan Southern. The air grew "absolutely poisonous" after just twenty minutes, he reported. "The builders of cars have no right to be ignorant of the laws of life with which they tamper; and two or three presentments by Grand Juries of the makers of unventilated cars, especially sleeping-cars, as guilty of manslaughter, would exert a most salutary influence. I commend this public duty to the immediate consideration of jurors and prosecutors."[7]

Greeley was not the only one horrified by the insufficiency of ventilation, space, or anything else likely to induce sleep on early trains. George Pullman rode often enough in and around New York in the mid-1850s to become conversant in the discomforts. One trip in particular stuck in his mind, and his company's lore. It spanned just fifty-eight miles, between Buffalo and Westfield, where his mother's family lived, and the train included one of the new sleepers. Pullman paid the extra dollar for a berth, intending merely to examine the accommodations, not test them. What he found when he did were ceilings so low a long-legged man like him had to stoop, ventilation so lacking it was difficult to draw a breath, and bedding so uninviting he felt obliged to keep on his pants and shoes. As for his triple-tiered bunk, he slept not a wink.

While the trip to Westfield might have left fellow passengers cranky and tired, George took it as a challenge, dreaming of a sleeping car where passengers actually could sleep. The fact that others shared that vision, but had not seen it through, he took as his opportunity as he headed to Chicago in the spring of 1859. He already had discussed railroad sleeping cars with his friend and neighbor in Albion, the state senator Benjamin C. Field. Once in Chicago, George found his building-moving business neither reliable enough to ensure his prosperity nor entrepreneurial enough to engage his energies.

Pullman and Field soon convinced the Chicago, Alton & St. Louis Railroad to let them convert two old passenger carriages into sleepers, known simply as Numbers 9 and 19. The cars, which cost two thousand dollars to remake and went into service the night of September 1, 1859, became part of railroad history partly because they were George's first. They also introduced a magnificently clever upper berth whose sleight-of-hand construction allowed it to be closed and lifted to the ceiling during daylight, when it stored the mattress and blanket, then dropped halfway to the floor at night. Heat came from box stoves, light from candles, and small toilet rooms with tin washbasins were situated at either end of the car. There were no sheets to start with. The nightly fare was fifty cents for the upper berth, one dollar for the lower, and passengers had to be instructed to remove their boots and spurs before climbing into bed. One early rider—a lanky lawyer with whiskers from Springfield named Abraham Lincoln—was intrigued by the conveyance and, after quizzing George on its features, curled himself into an upper berth for the night.

George was captivated by the sleeping car business that would define his career and life, and transform the industry, but these crude cars serving frontier settlements represented more a dipping of toes than diving in full body. Sleeping car titans like Theodore T. Woodruff and Webster T. Wagner had tied up the profitable eastern routes, not to mention patents on innovations. George was feeling the burden of supporting his mother back in New York, along with younger sisters and brothers. So he set out again in the summer of 1860, this time to the goldfields of Colorado for about three years. It was long enough to earn a small fortune by supplying miners with provisions, wagons to carry them, and other merchandise. That money, along with new expertise in marketing, let him return to Chicago and resume his passion to revolutionize overnight train travel.

The timing was perfect. With the Civil War entering its decisive stage, the nation was about to be stitched back together. Railroads had proved themselves during battle, moving hundreds of thousands of troops to the front, and work was beginning on a Pacific line that would be the last link in a transcontinental network. The crazy quilt of track widths on different railways was about to be replaced by a standard gauge that would let a car pass continuously from New York to Chicago, and would make trains the only sensible way of traversing the country. Passengers were demanding more comfortable accommodations. And Chicago, America's crossroads city, was the focal point of the ferment, with George having just the right contacts, finances, and know-how to cash in.

The immediate result was the *Pioneer,* the planet's most celebrated sleeping car. It was George's love child. He set up the workshop where it was built, hired the laborers, purchased the raw materials, and kept a father's prideful watch over the installation of every shag of Brussels carpeting, French plate mirror, ceiling mural, marble washbasin, and carefully encased upper berth. Gone were the flea-ridden, paper-thin cushions of old, replaced by mattresses stuffed with soft animal hair, sheets of silky linen, and enough plush blankets to warm the *Pioneer*'s fifty-two passengers. Heaters were hidden under the floor. Windows in the clerestory roof ensured endless fresh air. An engineer warned that his scheme was too ambitious, that "there isn't space to fit your idea." George remained resolute: "Then make space to fit my idea."[8] Eking out space and implementing all those ideas cost a whopping $20,178.14, four times as much as a conventional sleeper. But the *Pioneer* was anything but conventional. It was the most opulent overnight train car ever constructed, a palace on wheels. It nullified night and blurred the separation between destinations. It marked a watershed not just in the history of railroading but in the history of travel and, thus, in the history of America.

Or so said George as he recited the tale over the next thirty years. The sleeper that emerged from his Chicago shed in the spring of 1865 *was* a triumph, but his crescendo of ballyhoo made it difficult to distinguish axiom from embellishment. He originally referred to his creation simply as "Car A," suggesting the modesty of his enterprise and the expectation that he would build fewer cars than there were letters of the alphabet. Its christening as *Pioneer* came later, when George and others were cementing its image as a trailblazer and building an empire with so many sleepers that it would have taken nearly four hundred alphabets to name them all. It *was* sumptuous, but so were sleeping cars built back then by Wagner and Woodruff, Eli Wheeler, Edward Collings Knight, and Colonel William D'Alton Mann. George's raised roofs and sixteen-wheel trucks were different only in degree. Ditto for his hinged upper berths, which had been used thirty years earlier in the cars that Richard Imlay designed for the Cumberland Valley Railroad. Even the *Pioneer*'s price tag required an asterisk: it *was* many times what other first-class sleepers cost, but that was mainly the result of Civil War inflation that had nearly tripled the price of railroad equipment.[9]

The truth is that George was not the originator of the sleeping car, nor even its most inventive interpreter. What he was was sharper and shrewder than his nearly three dozen rivals, building more sleepers than they did, standardizing them, and striking lucrative deals with rail lines to lease his cars and crews. He bought out competitors who were open to wooing and busted the rest. He knew the public wanted overnight trains that were not just snug but luxurious, and gave them the first topflight dining service on a train, the first Pintsch gaslights from Europe, and the first sleepers to deliver precisely the same fluff of the pillow, fold in linen, and bouquet in wine regardless of which railroad happened to be hauling their Pullman Palace Car. When being first was not possible, George insisted on being best, and he usually was. The rich were used to being pampered, and appreciated a train with the amenities they had at home and on their yachts. The middle class loved feeling rich.

So sure was George that the public would pay for that indulgence that he put it to the test, running his elegant cars with their two-dollar tariff side by side on a Michigan Central line with older, drabber sleepers costing just a dollar and a half. The decision came instantly. "Not only did the patrons of the road utterly refuse to look at the old cars so long as any two-dollar berths were available, but those who were crowded out of the Pullman complained so loudly at being compelled to put up with dollar-and-a-half berths, that within six weeks the cheap cars were taken off altogether," wrote the rail historian Charles Frederick Carter. "Instead of driving traffic away, the more expensive palace cars drew travel from the other roads, so that competing lines were forced to make terms with Pullman."[10]

George also grasped the importance of the as-yet-unnamed profession of public relations, masterfully wielding its tools of spin and puffery. He escorted visiting kings and dukes on his personal car and added "palace" to his company name, knowing royalty was the vogue in those Victorian days. He unveiled each new feature on his sleepers as a breakthrough, no matter how minor or borrowed. And never did he fret about vainglory, as he showed in 1870 while escorting Mayor Alvah Crocker and assorted nabobs out of Boston on the first chartered transcontinental trip and the first train composed entirely of Pullman cars. The baggage compartment was fitted with a printing press used to publish a dozen editions of a self-congratulatory journal. One issued a prayer for "no delay in placing the elegant and homelike [Pullman] carriages upon the principal routes in the New England States." Then there was this song from George's press agent: "Hurrah for a ride without jostle or jar! Hurrah for a life on the iron bar! Hurrah for a ride in a Pullman car! *Vive la compagnie.*"[11]

Whatever the Boston Brahmins thought, stunts like those did impress a Scottish-born immigrant who arrived in America at age thirteen and went to work as a bobbin boy in a Pennsylvania cotton mill. George Pullman "was one of those rare characters who can see the drift of things, and was always to be found, so to speak, swimming in the main current where movement was the fastest," wrote Andrew Carnegie. Carnegie saw in George not just a reflection of himself but of their Gilded Age. It was a time for speculating in stocks and erecting monopolies. Cornelius Vanderbilt, James Jerome Hill, and John Insley Blair were masters of the railroad. Carnegie was the man who mattered in steel. And in that era of the robber baron and Texas-sized tycoon, the only name history would remember when it came to overnight travel was that of the young man from Albion. So enchanted was Carnegie by the palace car prince that he went from being George's arch-competitor to his partner and the Pullman Company's biggest stockholder.[12]

George's greatest exercise of wile, of reshaping reality in a way that would have wowed the circus mandarin Phineas Taylor Barnum as it did Andrew Carnegie, centered once again on the *Pioneer.* The story, as Pullman executives told it, was that the acclaimed sleeper had been built a foot wider than any contemporary car and two and a half feet higher, which let it accommodate its hinged upper berth yet meant it could not fit onto railway bridges and under station platforms. Critics dubbed the costly colossus "The folly of the Pike's Peak lunatic," a reference to George's hiatus in Colorado, and the carriage gathered cobwebs in a Chicago storage barn. But George was not worried, so confident was he that the railroads would embrace his novel creation. Luck—along with the Lincolns—proved him right.

His good fortune began shortly after John Wilkes Booth assassinated President Lincoln in April 1865. Organizers of the Lincoln funeral train decided the *Pioneer* was just the vehicle worthy of bearing the president's body the last leg from Chicago to Springfield,

Illinois, where he would be buried. The Chicago, Alton & St. Louis Railroad, anxious to oblige, dispatched an army of workers to widen viaducts and whittle away platforms, completing in two days a project that otherwise might have taken a year. The result: on May 2, 1865, the *Pioneer* and the rest of the train passed in grand procession to Springfield. The *Pioneer*'s presence in the Lincoln funeral cortege, and the railroad's Herculean efforts to make it possible, generated nationwide publicity for the sleeper and gave a huge psychological boost to George. It also got him the railway clearances he needed, on the Chicago & Alton, then on other lines across the United States and Canada.

The narrative became more majestic with each recounting, and it was told repeatedly over subsequent generations in newspapers, magazines, and one railroad treatise after another. One version centered on Mary Todd Lincoln, the president's widow, who spent twelve days and nights escorting her husband's corpse on its circuitous route from Washington. After witnessing four thousand mourners an hour file by the open casket, while thirty-six young women representing the thirty-six states offered up tributes, Mrs. Lincoln finally collapsed upon reaching Chicago. She begged to be taken to Springfield ahead of the funeral train, at which point George volunteered his sleeper and a single engine whisked it and the former First Lady home.[13] Another rendering picks up on the Lincoln family's long fascination with sleeping cars—from Abe's use of them during his precedent-setting whistle-stop campaign for president against Senator Stephen A. Douglas, and on the way to his inauguration, to Mary Todd's supposed enchantment with the *Pioneer* when she got a peek months before her husband's death. According to this version, it was *she* who suggested the *Pioneer* for the sad trip from Chicago to Springfield, and rather than the sleeper chugging ahead of the funeral procession, it was part of it, with a pilot train clearing the way and the engine bell tolling at every station.[14]

All those renditions shared one more thing: not quite fitting the facts. Following her husband's death, Mrs. Lincoln is known to have ensconced herself in the White House, not emerging for thirty-eight days and missing all the obsequies. Newspapers nationwide chronicled every detail of the funeral cortege, including the inclusion of more than one Pullman sleeper, but none mentioned pruned platforms or elevated arches, which would have been among the grandest construction feats of all times. And no press account of the *Pioneer*'s maiden voyage said a word about its exaggerated proportions. The first published reference to the *Pioneer* as too thick and tall came twenty-three years after President Lincoln's demise, in a *Boston Daily Globe* account attributed to J. W. Stockton, an assistant superintendent of the Pullman Company. Several months later *Scribner's Magazine* ran a similar story penned by a Pullman vice president. A third telling of the tale appeared in an official history of the company published in 1917; the last came fifty-two years later, in the Pullman Company's final annual report.[15]

What really happened? George did provide sleepers for the funeral procession to Springfield, although it is unclear whether the *Pioneer* was among them. It is pretty certain that the *Pioneer* was neither as fat nor as statuesque as claimed. Pullman sleepers probably were invited to join the cortege because of George's ties to Colonel James H. Bowen, who was in charge of funeral arrangements in Chicago and the president of Chicago's Third National Bank, where George was a director and, later, the largest depositor. Over the years Pullman officials must have thought the real story pallid, and potentially embarrassing, so they applied a bit of luster—linking their firm's early history to the martyred president, then painting their founder as a man so daring he defied the very scale of the railroads. It worked, for more than a century, as their version was repeated and even varnished by reporters and authors. "It made a better story" the way Pullman executives told it, concluded Charles Long, a railroad historian who unspun that embroidery in the spring of 2002, 137 years after the fact.[16]

What part did George Pullman play in any hyperbole? Stockton said he got his story straight from the Pullman president. So did the author of the "On the Tip of the Tongue" column in the *New York Press,* who wrote about the Pullman link to the Lincoln funeral train in December 1897, two months after George's death. This unnamed columnist recalled that, a few years earlier, he was part of a small party that rode with George Pullman in his private car. After dinner, over cigars and coffee, George regaled his guests with the story of how he had built a sleeper "so broad and high that it couldn't run a mile on any road without smashing everything along the line." Then came President Lincoln's assassination, and "the officials of the Vandalia road, over whose line the party was to enter Chicago, were anxious to make a display and impress the Eastern men. They borrowed my car, turned out all their wrecking trains, worked day and night pulling up platforms and widening bridges and cuts, and in two days had things in such shape that the car could run safely from one end of the road to the other. It did duty as the funeral car, and its description was published throughout the country."[17]

One heroic link was hardly enough. "The war came to a close, and General Grant, the conquering hero, came Westward on a triumphal tour," George told the columnist. "The Michigan Central had to have my car. Again the wrecking gangs did their work, making straight the road to Detroit for my sleeper. So it happened that what was once spoken of as 'the folly of the Pike's Peak lunatic' became the car of state, observed of all observers, and without effort of my own the value and importance of my invention became established among railroad men and known to the general public."[18]

Even without the added romance, George already had in place by the late 1860s nearly all the elements to make his sleepers the "observed of all observers" and crown him the titan of overnight train travel. Dozens of overstuffed sleeping cars were on track, with beautifully grained black walnut interiors, berths carefully concealed by painted screens and royal blue curtains, double windows for enhanced ventilation, and all the other flares he knew would make Pullman stand for luxury. He had secured a charter for Pullman's Palace Car Company, along with $100,000 in financing, and secured for himself the posts of president and general manager. His former partner Benjamin Field was retired now, and a wealthier and more influential Field, department store baron Marshall, had become an investor and confidant. In 1867 George introduced the first hotel car, the *President,* a sleeper with an attached kitchen, wine cellar, and scullery. It offered seatside service of sugar-cured ham, Welsh rarebit, and 131 other culinary offerings that for the first time made female passengers feel at home. A year later he inaugurated the *Delmonico,* the world's first railcar dedicated exclusively to supping and a worthy namesake to one of Manhattan's finest eateries.

Trains offering manna worth savoring were almost as revolutionary as those providing the possibility of sleep. Before the *President* and *Delmonico* came on the scene, culinary options were but two: a shoebox lunch packed at home or purchased trackside, and a railroad eating house where a mere twenty minutes were allotted to digest fare that typically included bitter coffee brewed the previous week, eggs fried in rancid grease and stored in limed water to preserve their color, and biscuits so leaden they were dubbed "sinkers."[19] "The bell rings for departure," one traveler wrote of such early-era refreshment rooms, and "in they all hurry with their hands and mouths full, and off they go again until the next stopping-place induces them to relieve the monotony of the journey by masticating without being hungry."[20] There were exceptions, most notably the Santa Fe Line's Harvey Houses, where conductors wired ahead to fire up the fare and "Harvey Girls" greeted passengers with mouthwatering steaks and chops. In general, however, dining cars represented the long-awaited last relish that made Pullman trains, in the words of a later admirer, "the most sumptuously upholstered landfaring in the history of human movement."[21]

But George was a realist. He knew that while luxury accommodations were critical to his appeal, even more essential was service. Being treated like royalty was something passengers would remember long after they had grown blasé about majestic furnishings and appetizing edibles. Service was the way to get railroads to give up their own overnight trains and give in to George's sine qua non that they lease not just his sleeping cars but Pullman staff as well. The Pullman division that ran sleepers would prove considerably more profitable than the manufacturing one throughout the 1800s, and

George knew from the start that service had to be the gospel to keep profits coming in and customers coming back.

All of which begged this question for him in 1867: where could he find a single worker willing and able to act as hotelier and waiter, chambermaid, butler, electrician, entertainer, and all the other things required for his five-star rolling hotels?

ABRAHAM LINCOLN HAD the answer, this time for real. In 1863 the president began the process of liberating slaves by issuing the Emancipation Proclamation, although it could not deliver on its promise since it covered only states at war with Lincoln's Union. The South's surrender in April 1865 signaled the end of slavery, even if Lincoln would not live long enough to savor it. The formal and final abolition took another eight months until, in December 1865, the last state ratified the Thirteenth Amendment to the U.S. Constitution.

It was a fantastic moment. Suddenly 4 million Negroes were out of bondage and able to taste their first freedoms. They could work where they chose at whatever wage they could negotiate. They could live anywhere, travel everywhere, and be masters of their own homes and universe. Then reality set in. Fewer than one in ten ex-slaves could write their name. Fewer still were able to read a labor contract. They had no money to buy land, no skills beyond those learned in the fields or plantation house, no experience overseeing even their own lives. General William Tecumseh Sherman had promised Negroes who joined his triumphal March to the Sea "forty acres and a mule"; like other promises from the federal government, it proved ephemeral, and nearly all who got land had to give it back. Politics was in the slippery hands of that motley collection of Yankee adventurers and reformers contemptuously referred to as carpetbaggers, along with their scalawag fellow travelers from the secessionist states. As for those who had wielded power in the old Confederacy, they were intent on reinventing the realm in its old image.

Their cry of "come home" was aimed at rallying southern whites who felt aggrieved by everything from their wartime defeat to their loss of racial dominance and the high taxes imposed to pay for Reconstruction. They lashed out at Negroes, tearing down as many of the new freedoms as they could, including even the liberty to learn to read and write. The Fourteenth Amendment's due-process protections were undermined by a series of "Black Codes" that authorized unemployed Negro adults to be hired out as forced labor, unattended Negro children to be bound over to white employers, and other opportunities for Negroes to be severely curtailed. It is true that freed slaves could no longer be bought or sold, which was huge progress. Their marriages were legally recognized, they were able to organize their own churches and hold revival meetings, and the Fifteenth Amendment gave them the right to vote. But again, rebel reality trumped even the U.S. Constitution as Mississippi disenfranchised Negroes in 1890, followed by South Carolina, Louisiana, North Carolina, Alabama, Georgia, Virginia, and Oklahoma. Even as Congress was laboring to ensure equality of the races, southern states were erecting a segregated system called Jim Crow—after a crippled slave in an 1830s minstrel show. In 1896 the Supreme Court sanctified the setup by arguing that separate accommodations for the races were okay so long as they were roughly equal.

The result was that while the freed slaves no longer were chattels, most of the 4 million remained in the South and stayed bound to wealthy landowners as part of the oppressive systems of sharecropping and tenancy. Their days were nearly the same as before, separating silky tufts of cotton from skin-piercing stems, lugging seventy-pound sacks as they crisscrossed the dusty fields from sunrise to sunset, and earning about three dollars a week. Sometimes their bosses were their former owners, and generally their wives and children worked alongside them. Even with those extra hands, at year's end sharecroppers owed the landowner most of their earnings to pay for bacon and molasses bought on credit, along with tobacco, tools, fertilizer, and work animals. The new system panned out for southern farmers: by 1880 King Cotton was back, with the region producing more than before the war. For the liberated Negro, however, the end of more than two centuries of slavery in America looked less like freedom than serfdom. He was "free from the individual master," the former slave Frederick Douglass observed in his autobiography, "but the slave of society."[22]

Nat Love was ten years old and the property of Tennessee planter Robert Love when the Civil War broke out. Nat's mother oversaw the kitchen in the Big House; his father supervised other slaves in the fields. His earliest memory: "pushing a chair in front of me and toddling from one to the other of my Master's family to get a mouthful to eat like a pet dog." While General Robert E. Lee surrendered on April 9, 1865, "it was quite a while after this that we found out we were free," Love wrote decades later. He recalled how quickly visions of freedom became clouded. "While a great many slaves rejoiced at the altered state of affairs; still many were content to remain as before, and work for their old masters in return for their keep. My father, however, decided to start out for himself, to that end he rented twenty acres of land, including that on which our cabin stood, from our late master. We were at this time in a most destitute condition, and father had a very hard time to get a start, without food or money and almost naked, we existed for a time on the only food procurable, bran and cracklins."[23]

Some freed slaves headed North. Burgeoning industry there offered an escape from the plantation and promises made, then broken, by opportunist southern politicians. What they found on the floors of iron mills and textile factories were hours as long and work as punishing. Pay scales were higher than on the farm, thanks to labor unions. But they met unexpected hostility from their unionized white coworkers, who resented Negroes' frequent role as strike-breakers, yet barred those same Negroes from joining unions where they might have forged a black-white front against management.

The railroads, by contrast, had been anxious for "colored labor" since before the Civil War. Most of the jobs, and the best ones, were in slave states. That was easy to understand in the early 1800s, when the Wilmington & Raleigh, Montgomery & West Point, and other southern lines exploited slaves, twenty thousand of them, to lay and

repair tracks. Sometimes the railroads bought their own bondser-
vants or bartered for them using stock in the railroad; more often
they rented slaves from plantation owners, who were grateful for the
extra cash when cotton prices were low and charged usurious fees
when cotton was high. After the war southern railways were even
more desperate for laborers to repair battle damage and expand
existing lines. Again they turned to Negroes. Many freedmen will-
ingly abandoned sharecropping for the lucrative railroad jobs. When
more workers were needed, railroads paid states to use convict labor,
most of which was colored.

It was not just as laborers that southern railroads relied on
Negroes. They worked as firemen, riding alongside the engineer and
shoveling coal into the boiler, as well as brakemen, who did the dangerous jobs of setting hand brakes and coupling together cars. They
helped load baggage and freight and, on occasion, drove the train.
They held those jobs when they were indentured servants, and after
the war were hired in even greater numbers as brakemen, firemen,
and yard switchmen on the Gulf Coast, Seaboard, and other lines in
the South.

In the North and West, Negroes held few railroad jobs, responsible or otherwise. At first it was because there were fewer of them
to draw from, but as more moved there after the war, opposition to
hiring them grew on the part of management as well as unions representing white railroad workers. Racism fueled the resistance, along
with unionists' legitimate fear of being replaced by Negroes from
the South. In the South, railroads believed they had compelling reasons to hire Negro workers, starting with their earning 10 to 20 percent less than whites doing the same work. Management also was
determined to keep out trade unions. Negro workers helped keep
militant whites in line and, when needed, served as strikebreakers.
Finally, southern railroads knew that workers used to performing
slave labor were less likely to complain regardless of the rigors of
their work or length of their day.

Those last qualities, the willingness to work long as well as
hard, were eternalized in the former slave John Henry, a six-foot,

two-hundred-pound railroad hand from North Carolina. With a heavy hammer and steel drill, Henry bored holes for explosives used to carve tunnels and smooth terrain so trains could pass. But in the early 1870s the steam drill threatened to displace Henry and his co-workers. In a classic showdown between man and machine, John Henry challenged a steam drill operator to see who could sink more steel. The two were set up at the Chesapeake & Ohio's Big Bend Tunnel in West Virginia, Henry with a twenty-pound hammer in each hand, the drill and its handler to his right. The ballad bearing his name tells of the outcome: "The men that made that steam drill thought it was mighty fine. John Henry sunk a fourteen-foot hole and the steam drill only made nine." Much the way Daddy Joe would later stand tall for Pullman porters, so John Henry, whose legendary life was cut short by his superhuman exertions, stood as a marker of Negro contributions to early railroading.[24]

Those accomplishments did not escape the notice of George Pullman, who was making his own contribution to railroad lore by raising the bar for ornate overnight travel. He already had the makings of his sleeper in the form of the two-tiered *Pioneer*. He was bringing dining aboard. And years ago he had begun hiring conductors, starting with Jonathan L. Barnes, who was twenty-two when he made that first trip from Bloomington, Illinois, to Chicago on September 1, 1859. "I remember on the first night I had to compel the passengers to take their boots off before they got into the berths. They wanted to keep them on—seemed afraid to take them off," Barnes recounted later. Passengers also seemed afraid of the new sleeping car service, or at least skeptical, convincing George he could not afford his own conductors. But as rider reticence abated Barnes was brought back, along with scores of other specially trained Pullman conductors, all of whom were white.[25]

The conductors were masters at ministering to needs of the Pullman Company, from collecting tickets to selling berths and dispatching wires. As with managers in a hotel, their duties could include anything from doctor to diplomat, policeman to undertaker. Even at their best, however, these Caucasian men were neither trained nor disposed to do the humble work of valet, bellhop, maid, and janitor that any front-rank hotel relied on. Brakemen helped out in the early days, periodically passing through the sleeper to make beds and open or close windows. Adolescent entrepreneurs were part of the sleeping car scene, too. Water boys sold ice water and lemonade. News butchers, including a school-age Thomas Alva Edison, hawked newspapers and dime-store novels, maple sugar cakes, peppermint drops, sweetmeats, and salted peanuts designed to fuel later sales of ice cream and soft drinks. All that sated certain passenger needs, but it did not help George honor his pledge not just to match but to better America's best hostelries, no matter that his happened to be moving at sixty miles an hour.

That meant hiring personnel whose sole devotion was to unhesitating service. He baptized them Pullman porters. George did not invent the term *porter*. It was applied in the thirteenth century to doorkeepers, in the fourteenth to human bearers of burdens, and in the early 1800s to stewards who fed, filled with rum, and otherwise tended to passengers on boats that plied winding U.S. waterways like the Mississippi River and Erie Canal. Nor did he coin its use on railroads, where porters had been carrying passengers' luggage and otherwise easing their journey for decades. But as with so many of his offerings, George Pullman's porters set a standard for the hospitality industry. They came to define the vocation of railroad attendant and, for most Americans, made *porter* synonymous with *Negro*.

The first porter came aboard a Pullman sleeper as early as 1867 and was a fixture by 1870. Who he was is not known, due to the destruction of Pullman Company records in the great Chicago fire of 1871, but a lot can be surmised. He surely was a Negro and almost as certainly was one of the 4 million slaves President Lincoln helped free. He came from the plantation house rather than the fields, which better prepared him for working in close proximity to wealthy white passengers. He probably was from Alabama, Georgia, or the Carolinas, which were among the biggest slaveholding states and where George and his successors most often turned for the right blend of training and acquiescence. He would have been tall enough to pull down upper berths and slim enough to maneuver in narrow corridors of the sleeping car. One last thing: his skin probably was black as pitch, which would have been a drawback in many workplaces but was an asset to Pullman managers.

Why did George prefer dark-skinned Negroes, and why turn in the first place to ex-slaves to wait on his passengers? He never explained himself. He did not have to. His actions on other matters, at work and home, made clear what he was after.

The first thing was a bargain. The Pullman Company needed to cut costs anywhere it could in those days, when capital was limited and competition was fierce from Wagner, Woodruff, and a dozen other sleeping car magnates. George loved hunting for bargains, an instinct that would grow to an obsession. So he was parsimonious with workers who manufactured his sleepers, including craftsmen he brought over from Germany, Sweden, and England. Same with his conductors, ticket sellers, and, later, with his twin sons, whom he resented for their lavish living and left just trifles in his will. His philosophy on wages was the maxim of the marketplace: as little as necessary. Which, in the case of ex-slave porters, meant just enough to keep them fed, clothed, and disinclined to sample their other limited employment options.

"We pay them good salaries," George told a newspaper reporter in the early 1890s, explaining, in a statement that defied reason as well as reality, why porters need not look to the public for tips. But he probably was accurate when he added, "We can get all the good porters we want at the price we pay them."[26]

Pliancy also mattered to George, in how his sleeper staff responded to passengers and to Pullman Company bosses. This, too, was part of his evolving credo in life as in work. He demanded deference from the younger brothers he helped raise, and who rebelled against his overbearing authority. He insisted on fealty from his four children, only one of whom met his Victorian standards. He was fanatical in demanding loyalty from his factory workers and known to fire, on the spot, managers who second-guessed his edicts.

Negro porters seemed the ideal choice to deliver obedience bordering on obsequiousness. Who better to anticipate and cater to passengers' every caprice, from fetching a sandwich at sunup to mending torn trousers in the middle of the night, than men whose entire upbringing had been a long lesson in vassalage? How better to sell white riders on the slavish service on a Pullman car than to greet them with a smiling ex-slave? Despite his denials to the press, he knew his low wages would force porters to rely on tips to survive— giving them yet another incentive to provide the best service imaginable and raise as few protests as possible. That submissiveness also ensured, for at least the first half century of George's enterprise, that his Negro porters would follow orders the way he wanted, resist unions he detested, and be grateful for the jobs he dispensed.

The practice of recruiting Negroes from the Deep South in the hope they would be more compliant persisted long after George was gone and most old slaves were dead or too old to work. Pullman managers reconstructed it each time labor troubles heated up. In 1915, company officials were called before a congressionally chartered commission and questioned about those hiring policies. L. S. Hungerford, the general manager, explained that "the old southern colored man makes the best porter on the car." Asked why by the commission chairman, Hungerford recounted the reasoning used by George decades before: "He is more adapted to waiting on the passengers and gives them better attention and has a better manner." As for what training the company preferred in ex-slaves it hired, Hungerford said, "We get mostly house servants."[27]

George Pullman's most compelling motivation for hiring only Negroes, however, had to do with his conviction that for passengers to truly feel comfortable on his sleepers, they had to see the porter as someone safe. Ideally it would be a man you could look at but not notice, as if he did not exist. An invisible man. Which, given the social divide between Negroes and whites in those years after slavery, meant an ex-slave. To underline that otherness, Pullman managers favored swarthy-skinned applicants over those with creamier complexions. No danger, then, of a porter ever being mistaken for a passenger. In the words of one porter, the Pullman Company wanted "the blackest man with the whitest teeth."[28]

Did that make George a racist?

Undeniably, by today's standards or those of much of the last century. He paid freed slaves and their descendants embarrassingly small salaries, worked them as hard as they could stand, encouraged and exploited their submissiveness, and denied them—based solely on the blackness of their skin—promotion to conductor or any other meaningful management job. He barred most Negroes and all porters from the industrial town just south of Chicago that he founded and named after himself. While he was tough on all his workers, porters worked longer hours and earned considerably less than conductors and other whites in his employ. They were the only ones forced to fall back on tips to earn a living. And at the hint of unrest, George made clear that Negro porters could be replaced. Without hesitation or remorse.

His callousness stung more than just his porters. So high was the Pullman profile, and that of his sleeping car attendants, that over the years the Pullman porter came to personify the groveling Negro— and to reinforce the notion that the whole race was like that. Such stereotypes proved especially damaging in America's West and North, where porters were the only Negroes many whites knew. George's success in tapping for financial gain the image of the servile ex-slave, meanwhile, became a model for other employers, from managers of big buildings to hoteliers and restaurateurs. The Pullman Company "does more than any other organization in the world to make the negro a beggar and a grafter," the *New York Press* wrote in 1911. "More negroes are demoralized each year by the Pullman Company than are graduated by Tuskegee, Hampton and some other negro educational establishments."[29]

All that is true, but it also is hindsight. In the 1800s, George's record on race made him a moderate if not a reformer. He hired a Negro coachman and black domestics at a time when fellow aristocrats on Chicago's Prairie Avenue would only consider English servants. His will included five thousand dollars for Arthur A. Wells, the Negro porter who rode herd over his private sleeping car and was a trusted assistant. He sold Pullman tickets to Negroes in the South despite accusations that he was selling out the white race.*

George relished defying conventions that way and embracing what seemed like contradictions. He had broken every rule in transforming himself from cabinetmaker to sultan of the sleepers but was so proper that throughout Chicago's sweltering summer he wore a heavy Prince Albert topcoat, vest, and silk hat. He charmed the Scotsman Andrew Carnegie and doted on his own rheumatic wife but had little use for four of his seven surviving siblings, three of his four children, and, most especially, his mother-in-law. He contributed generously to charities like the building fund for a church in Albion but insisted that the church be called Pullman Memorial Universalist, that company gifts be made in his name, and that he be listed first in the donor registry of any charity he gave to. He never did anything merely because it was right. But he did more than most.

So it was with his porters. George did not pioneer the use of Negro workers on the railroads or the sleeping cars. Earlier railroad magnates understood that slaves and former slaves made good workers and could be had cheap. It has even been suggested that President Lincoln first broached to George using freedmen as sleeping car menials. And well he might have, since it would have solved his problem of putting them to work. While George's children denied a Lincoln link, over the years it became a mantra among porters that "Abe Lincoln freed the slaves and George Pullman hired 'em." Whoever planted the idea, it is clear that George appropriated as his own the formula that Negroes constitute the ideal sleeping car servant. He then translated it into a science, the way he

*The *Mobile Daily Register* denounced George Pullman for letting his conductors "admit to the sleeping car blacks and whites without distinction." Calling the sleeping car titan an "extreme Republican" who "made his money from the patronage of white men," the newspaper, in its March 25, 1875, edition, called on him to "sympathize with our white citizens who abhor the contact of the vulgar and filthy creatures who compose nineteen-twentieths of the negro race. . . . We hope that the Southern people will at once, from the Potomac to the Rio Grande, denounce the conduct of the Pullman sleeping cars, and that the Southern press will represent the dangers to which our white travelers are exposed from the fanatical efforts of Mr. Pullman to transport foul odors, vermin, and disease."

had with the sleeper itself. It worked so well that by the early 1900s the Pullman Company was the largest employer of Negroes in America and probably the world.

That is the sleeping car czar's most consequential legacy, to his porters and the nation. Social commentators of his era applauded George for his beneficence. His motives mattered little to them and could not have been worse than those of his fellow robber barons, most of whom hired no Negroes at all. George never disguised his intent in bringing on only black-skinned porters. It was to earn cash, not accolades. It was meant to bless his company's bottom line, not the colored race. Whatever the reason, the results were arresting: thousands of Negro men freed from the dead-end choice of farm or factory, riding the nation's most ornate railroad carriages and relishing their adventure. He was the first northern industrialist to employ large numbers of Negroes—and his porters, in turn, helped prod the northward migration of tens of thousands of other southern Negroes as the nineteenth century drew to a close. President Grover Cleveland acknowledged those achievements at the 1893 World's Fair in Chicago, commending George for hiring more ex-slaves than anyone else.

Porters themselves rendered a similar verdict in those early years. Most were former chattels cautiously testing their liberties and sizing up the constraints. Making the job of Pullman porter a Negro monopoly let them trade in overalls for bow ties and starched pants. A job on the train meant nothing less than a chance to escape both Reconstructionists and Klansmen, along with fields of cotton, laws of segregation, and their own well-meaning parents whose experience as slaves blinded them to what the brave new world might offer. *Opportunity* was the operative word. To be sure, theirs was a Faustian bargain, one that meant earning next to nothing and working eternal hours as caretakers to almost unbearable luxury. But most cherished the position and made it a career, and many passed it down to sons and grandsons, brothers and nephews. They were grateful for their jobs and thankful to George.

"It was my pleasure to meet and chat with George M. Pullman, the father of the sleeping car, several times," recalled Nat Love, who began his work as a porter twenty-five years after he ended his bondage on a Tennessee plantation. "I found him to be a fine man, broad-minded in every sense of the word, always approachable and with always a kind word for every one of the large army of his employees that he met on his travels, and he always tried to meet them all."[30] Henry Pope Jr., a porter based in Nashville, never knew George but credited him with giving ex-slaves "not only employment and a way to support themselves and families, but also that which they most needed: namely, an opportunity to educate themselves by travel and by contact with the more intelligent classes of travelers."[31]

George Henry Smock worked for the Pullman Company, same as his father, grandfather, and two brothers, and like them he had rough times on the sleepers along with easy ones. "Regardless of all the hardships, there was something to be gained, and it took care of our families and brought our families to a start that we were able to take care of them," Smock said. "There's good and bad in everything. There was more good in the Pullman porter and more good stated by passengers and people alike about the Pullman porter than there's been any other profession the black man's had. I don't care whether he was a doctor, a postman, a preacher—none of those: a Pullman porter, it stands out."[32]

Stand out he did. There were gripes, too, legitimate ones that would grow over the years and fuel a relentless drive for a trade union. But in the beginning the Pullman porter knew the confines of his choices. The prospect for Negroes like him who stayed close to home was sameness; porters experienced change. Staying meant rural simplicity or city ghettos; riding the trains let them see the country that had just granted them their first taste of independence. On the rails they met Americans of money and influence—presidents and starlets, Wall Street wizards and university chancellors—which was simply stunning to think of for men who had lived most of their lives as someone else's property. Most of all, Pullman porters understood that riding the sleeping car they were king, even if that regal standing ended when they pulled into the last station.

2

Rough Rides,

Intimate Encounters

⁛

THERE WAS AN edict for everything, starting with how to make a bed. The head had to point toward the engine, to align the passenger with the train. A third sheet was slipped *over* the blanket so the sleeper's face was not chafed. Pillows went crosswise, closed ends dovetailing in the center. (Teeth marks or chin creases on pillowcases were verboten.) An emerald curtain was draped across the berth for privacy; ladies got two. Fresh linen accidentally unfolded was sent straight to the laundry.[1]

A single sheet soiled, pillow askew, or seam out of alignment and the man could be out of a job. It happened often enough that porters carried the compact Pullman Company manual in their hip pocket.

Then there was Sanitary Regulation No. 8, on the correct way to jettison airborne insects: "Darken car by lowering shades at all windows except in rear section, in which window and screen should be raised to allow flies to escape." A corpse had to go even quicker than the rogue fly: it was put off at the next stop, undertaker or not. As for waking a passenger, "Under no circumstances shall berth curtains be parted in so doing. In most cases desired result can be obtained by shaking curtains and calling passenger in low tone of voice."[2]

What of the rider who stirred in the middle of the night in need of a good spit? The porter was prepared, having situated a spittoon "under front edge of berth, near the head."[3]

The pint-sized brown rulebooks, which filled fifty pages for sleepers and more for dining and beverage services, reflected George

M. Pullman's credo that nothing be left to chance. The first manual was published not long after he launched the business in the 1860s, the last not long before it folded in the 1960s. In between there were entire catechisms on how to clip a passenger's hair and pour an Old Fashioned Kentucky Colonel Mint Julep. What to do if a rider required surgery or the heating system did. Along with a list of things *not* to do on duty: chew tobacco or gum, carry a toothpick in your mouth, discuss politics with passengers, or wear a frown. All set in type by a Pullman printer, and all reflecting careful calibrations by Pullman efficiency experts. George's system was grounded in the twin theologies of quality and conformance. They guaranteed each passenger equally meticulous service no matter whether his sleeper ran on the Union Pacific line or the Baltimore & Ohio. More important, they sent railroads a message that, tempted though they might be to operate their own overnight service, there was no way any carrier could match the precision of the Pullman Palace Cars.

Along with the dos and don'ts, George's rulebooks carried a series of implied messages. The porter was part of the equipment, with his conduct able to be broken down to 217 simple rules. No need for social or psychological skills to keep the passengers happy. This Negro also needed more guidance than the conductor and other white workers, which is why rulebooks for porters were longer and more encyclopedic. Never mind that many porters could neither read nor write and thus relied on the conductor or a fellow porter to decipher the reams of regulations; George had no clue.

The rulebook in effect established a racial wall of separation. It ensured that white passengers never had to share bedding with a Negro man by spelling out that "blankets provided for passengers must not at any time be used by porters." (That risk was further reduced by giving porters blue blankets and passengers brown ones.) Even worse was for them to use combs or hairbrushes furnished to riders. Porters were forbidden from helping a white woman into an upper berth unless there was no conductor around, or she explicitly asked. And on the rare occasions when porters got to sleep in a bed, the rulebook mandated that "in no instance should porter occupy a berth over lady passenger."[4]

WHERE TO FIND the man who could do all this? Not, perhaps, in eastern colleges, whose graduates would never take to the role of menial. Nor in the center of cities like Chicago, where Pullman managers feared the "younger colored man" would not be sufficiently accommodating.[5] As for the "sheik" and "high-pressure" types, a company memo presumed they were easy to pick out and made clear they "do not make good servants and should not be considered."[6] Best to go South, where a large pool of former slaves was seasoned in serving, or to swank hotels, restaurants, and private estates. George's best recruiters were his early porters, who left a lasting impression every time they went to church or walked the neighborhood. It was an image outlined by midnight-blue tailored jackets and crisp visored caps, filled in with tales of exotic destinations and celebrity passengers, and completed by the sound of coins jingling in the pockets of these veteran porters. Before long young Negroes were lining up.

The question then was how to winnow candidates. Some criteria were clear-cut: porters should be of a certain age (not younger than twenty-five, nor older than forty), height (tall enough to reach upper berths, which meant at least five-foot-seven, but under six-foot-one so they could clear the car door), and weight (slim enough to slip through narrow corridors). It was the only Pullman job to require pictures, which confirmed that applicants met height and weight prerequisites along with the preference for jet-black skin. They must have enough money to buy a uniform and cap, about fifteen dollars. Education mattered, too, with graduation from grammar school the goal if not always the result in the earliest days, and more high school graduates beginning in the 1920s.

Measuring character was more elusive, but, as ever, it was exhaustive. Police files were checked and employment records perused. The slightest blot on either could eliminate a candidate. Then there were the personal interviews. With no way to confirm the accuracy of paper records, George dispatched inspectors on surprise home visits to see where and how an applicant lived and to interview neighbors "as to the character of the applicant." And he required would-be porters to furnish testimonials from influential members of the community. Existing Pullman men were best to vouch for you, which helps explain how so many porters brought on brothers and cousins, uncles, fathers, sons, and friends. Old bosses also carried clout, as did ministers, doctors, and politicians. Better still if the patron were white.

"They turned me down at first because I was too light. They said, 'You might get too friendly with our wives,'" recalled John R. Merritt of Baltimore, who ended up spending nearly forty years with the Pullman Company and Pennsylvania Railroad.[7] James Burke Johnson was recruited out of Atlanta to work in Boston, and he wondered "why they came South to get [a] porter when there was so many porters around." So he asked the Pullman manager who hired him. "He said [that] guys up in New York, Chicago and Boston, they didn't want to say 'Yes sir, no sir.' They thought they was too good to say that."[8]

Years later the Pullman president Carroll R. Harding put a more positive spin on his firm's recruiting philosophy when addressing a convention of Pullman porters: "You people were carefully chosen for such an enviable position from our large list of applicants. Emphasis was placed upon your family background and character—as exemplified by the applicant's attitude toward wife, mother and father, sons and daughters. Those were chosen who had the background of good homes, faithful at church, and good recommendation from the minister."[9]

Character did count, but what mattered most was whether a candidate could handle the work. So they put him to the test. First there was a written exam to see if he had "absorbed" the inch-thick rulebook. Then retired porters used a sidetracked car to demonstrate the Pullman technique for everything from applying bedding to laying out the step box when greeting passengers. Thoughtful trainers would add their own advice: stay away from whiskey at work, get along with passengers no matter how hard they push, and do not let even the prettiest woman rider talk you into something you will regret. Recruits then got a trip on an actual train with a longtime porter. Those who survived the six days of training collected their first paycheck and began a six-month probationary hire.

The whole process seemed militarylike, and was. The railroads had been organized on a military model, and Pullman naturally followed suit. Precise rules, careful recruitment, and perpetual training were the only ways to ensure seamless operation of a dispersed organization, civilian or martial. Top managers could not be on the trains overseeing operations the way they could in a factory, so they relied on rigid regulations and detailed documentation.

The real indoctrination into being a Pullman porter happened on the road, in stages. The first inkling of how the job would swallow up their lives, in hours and attitude, came when new hires were cut loose from home and family. It was not just leaving on the train, without itinerary or hint of return, but having to pack up and move. Thousands of men hired in Georgia, the Carolinas, and Alabama were made to work out of railroad hubs like Chicago, New York, and Boston. The climates were icy, the accents hard to decipher, and there was a whole new set of racial rules to absorb. The transfer was temporary at first, so the men went on their own and stayed in a rooming house or with another porter; when they had enough money, and a certainty the job would last, they fetched their wives and children.

Albert Flake was a lucky one. After a year working from his native Memphis he was told he would be transferred, but he got to pick the city. He was glad to leave Memphis "because of the discrimination and all of that going on down there," and picked Boston "because as a student of history [I] always heard they were so liberal."[10] His wife followed him to Boston, then came brothers, nieces, nephews, and cousins. He rented a room to start, then an apartment big enough to fit his furniture from Memphis, and ended up buying a home.

New homes and communities were great. But work was the main thing in the 1870s and 1880s, when the Pullman Company was picking up steam and porters were spending four hundred hours a month on the job, covering upwards of eleven thousand miles, for as little as ten dollars. What they did depended on demands by particular passengers, but some things were standard.

A Pullman porter was, before anything, a man who made beds. Or, as they said, *made down* beds, since the most taxing part was popping the upper berth from the ceiling. The lower was formed by folding down opposing seats, fastening curtains, affixing the headboard, and adding blankets, pillows, and linen. An experienced porter could do all that in three to five minutes, with hands working independently of toilworn bodies; some claimed to finish in just ninety seconds, which would be handy since they had to do it dozens more times a night. Porters also learned touches that never made it into the rulebook. Like knowing just the spot and angle to lay folded sheets so the bed essentially made itself. Or keeping linen loose enough on the lower berth that a restless passenger could wriggle and toss, but taking no chances with the upper, where a wrong turn could send the sleeper into free fall.

A porter's biggest worry was not the bed-making itself, but when to do it, as retiree Robert E. Turner recalled: "A wise porter will begin making some of his beds just as soon as some of his passengers begin going to the dining car for supper. If he has a heavy load, sometimes he may be lucky, and his passengers may be in good humor and ready to go to bed. Then again he finds one ready for a fight, and if the porter can keep his teeth in sight he may win them over to his side or at least be able to feel that the passenger will forget the whole matter. Several uppers may want to go to bed before the lowers are ready, and they keep looking at the porter, wondering why he doesn't make their beds down so they can go to bed. They feel that the porter should ask the lowers to vacate their seats so that the porter can make their uppers."[11]

Most passengers were indifferent to how or when their bed was readied as long as it was, although some who paid attention were impressed. "The 'bed boys,' or coloured attendants, who acted as chambermaids, began to make up the beds soon after nine o'clock, and by eleven everybody was fast asleep," the British patrician William Hardman wrote in 1883 of his trip on a Pullman sleeper. "It was a very strange sight to watch these darkies at their bed-making. Their rapidity and dexterity were marvelous. Their civility and attention too, were beyond all praise."[12] Not all British back then held America's master bed-makers in such esteem. "The porter service is very imperfect and unhealthy," the *Independent* newspaper wrote in 1883. "Generally the porter is a man who does not take a bath. His mode of living is irregular. He covers up dirty garments. We would like to examine about fifty of those attendants in the presence of the company."[13]

Once beds were made and passengers climbed in, a new preoccupation set in: keeping them there for the night, safe and content. They might yen for a drink or need to empty their bladder. The car could seem oppressively warm, no surprise with the windows shuttered and the Dixie-born porter wanting to stay toasty while keeping watch, or too chilly, as it often did to older passengers. Sometimes just the novelty of having a servant a call bell away stoked an urge to ring. A porter's night was spent shuttling between berths, setting up a ladder so the cherub in Upper Seven could climb down after a bad dream, adjusting the heat for the octogenarian in Lower Two, and answering endless inquiries—"What time is it, porter?" "How long before we pull in to Wichita?"—for the restless sleeper in Upper Eleven.

Nocturnal fidgeting was so much part of life on a sleeping car that porters and conductors penned names for passenger types. There was the Chronic Kicker, who never settled in or took his finger off the bell. The Man from out West had an insatiable thirst for whiskey matched only by his disinclination to part with his boots, even at bedtime. Captain Smorker alternated between picking his teeth with a pocket knife and wiping his oversized brow with a handkerchief retrieved from his hat. Best of all were the Farmer and his Wife. They took an hour to corkscrew their corpulent carcasses into bed and replace street clothes with nightshirt and cap. During the night they would snake their way back from the toilet down corridors echoing with midnight snores, often ending up in a stranger's berth. Their ultimate fate was to join mothers-in-law, country cousins, and the Saturday night bath as peerless prototypes for funny papers and burlesque shows.[14]

It was no joking matter for passengers to be roused in time to make their stop. Conductors gave porters a call card showing each rider's destination and indicating who wanted to be woken early for breakfast. A savvy porter knew to give ladies ten extra minutes in the bathroom, and with a jiggle of the curtain or whispered call could stir the soundest slumberer without waking anyone above or below.

Berth attendant was one among many hats worn by the Pullman porter. He was official greeter, helping passengers climb aboard and lugging up their baggage, then doing the reverse when they left. He was a chambermaid, endlessly dusting cinders from window ledges and seats, always with a wet cloth to keep embers down, then using mop and whisk broom to sweep grime off washrooms, passageways, and platforms. Spittoons had to be polished, ladies' hats boxed, letters mailed and telegrams wired, heaters stoked, lights lit and extinguished, "Quiet" signs posted then removed, card tables set up and broken down, and coolers stocked with ice. In the old days a porter helped the crew load wood for the engine and sometimes had to traipse into the forest to find it; later he kept the air conditioner humming. He was a flesh-and-blood lost-and-found, helping passengers retrieve misplaced dentures, diamond bracelets and wedding rings, mink coats and golf bags, and children. He brought food and drinks from dining and hotel cars, and sold cigarettes, candy, and playing cards everywhere Pullmans ran.

Other duties were too indelicate to discuss. Like mopping up after liquored-up men who urinated in the washbowl or vomited in their berth. Or improvising when a passenger ripped the seat of his pants. "He was a big man, 260 pounds, and it showed his big butt. He was walking around with a sheet around him. He couldn't have gotten off the train," recalled Eugene E. Bowser, a Pullman attendant for twenty-two years. "I took two sections out of his wife's umbrella. I knew how to sew and stayed up all night working on it. He said, 'Oh, man, you did a beautiful job.'"[15]

How could a porter be expected to keep track of all that needed doing, and do it? Only one way, according to an instruction book from 1888. The conductor must be constantly on the lookout for "any disorder whatever in the car," at which point he should "call the attention of the Porter to the improper condition of things." The porter, meanwhile, "should be almost constantly on his feet and working upon the car."[16]

While on his feet, he was expected to do everything a health inspector or doctor would have, without being sworn in, trained, or protected against illness. He tried to keep off anyone with smallpox, yellow fever, cholera, typhus, or the plague; people with other contagious diseases could ride, but only in later years, in a private compartment, and the room had to be fumigated afterward. He tended the sick and invalid, warmed bottles for newborns, babysat toddlers, and was midwife to premature moms. All available twenty-four hours a day, just as in a hospital. Eradicating expectorating was inconceivable, but the porter urged men to aim for one of the spittoons situated at strategic intervals and pleaded with riders of both sexes to forswear flushing until the train left the station.

"They didn't want toilets flushed onto the platform," recalled Kenneth Judy, who went to work as a porter shortly before World War II. "Toilets just flushed on the railroad tracks, you know. People would smoke cigars and put them in the cuspidors and we'd empty those into the toilet. We'd flush when the train was running and when it hit the roadbed it would just fly all over everywhere. Same with everything you put in the toilet. Like I say, that was really a steadfast rule: when you were coming into a station you had to keep your vestibule closed so no one would use the toilet."[17]

There were no rules for how to treat a passenger's flaming hemorrhoids, so, as any attendant would, George Henry Smock extemporized. "I had a passenger who was suffering from hemorrhoids one time on the Lark, and he asked me, 'Porter, could you help me? I don't have a medication, and my hemorrhoids are down,'" Smock recalled. "I said, 'Well, let me go back and get you some bacon grease, and I'm sure that will take care of it, until you get to a doctor.' The next morning he gave me a $50 tip."[18]

A porter's own hygiene and fastidiousness also were company concerns. An annual doctor's checkup mattered so much that Pullman paid. Fingernails had to be clean. No sideburns or mustache. No torn or soiled jackets. Making beds called for a white coat, with a separate one to serve meals. Black cap and blue jacket were worn receiving and discharging passengers; the cap was not allowed on the train during the day and its silver plate with the engraved "Pullman Porter" had to sparkle, while the jacket must be buttoned to the top. Black shoes were essential, always polished, never adorned with spats. Shirts had to be white, with a stand-alone white collar and blue four-in-hand tie "without figures, stripes or patterns." A lightweight white coat could be substituted for the bulkier blue, but only in sweltering weather and with the conductor's okay. While passengers were sleeping, porters could don a hat and slip on slippers.

The customs officer was another government agent the porter was supposed to stand in for. That meant rooting out gambling and, during Prohibition, purging Pullman compartments of alcohol. It also meant enforcing peculiar laws particular to the states. In Maryland it was illegal to throw anything from a moving train. Iowa outlawed the sleight-of-hand game three-card monte, while spitting on the train was a crime in Mississippi, Oklahoma, Pennsylvania, Texas, Virginia, Kansas, Louisiana, South Carolina, and Wisconsin. Wisconsin had a separate statute that made it unlawful to sweep a car unless the floor had been watered to prevent dust kicking up. A third Wisconsin law, eventually overturned by that state's highest court, gave extra stretching space to Pullman passengers as large as its legislative author by ordering porters to close upper berths if no one was sleeping there. The Pullman Company vehemently protested, afraid that would foil its strategy of opening vacant uppers so passengers would be sufficiently pinched for space that they would buy the upper berth just to close it.

The porter's true home on the train was the smoking room, and that is where he best earned his title as World's Most Perfect

Servant. Shoes were shined there every night—only black and tan ones, the rulebook said, and only one pair at a time to avoid mix-ups. Pants and jackets were pressed. And since the smoking room doubled as a men's bathroom, toilets, washbowls, and dental lavatory needed to be scrubbed, mirrors polished, soap dispensers filled, and towels replaced. Then it all had to be done again. The *Louisville Medical Journal* was impressed enough to write that hygiene in a Pullman sleeper was better than in nine of ten American homes.[19]

For most of the Pullman years the porter did one more thing in the smoking room: sleep, or at least try to, on a sofa behind a dark curtain. It was not easy, on a wafer-thin mattress, with passengers in and out using toilets and cuspidors. Or stopping by to light up a cigar or cigarette, then staying for a card game and storytelling that could go on till dawn. The smoker had long been the most social of rooms in gentlemen's clubs, a place to catch up and cool down, and that custom thrived on George Pullman's sleepers. Few noticed the Negro porter trying to sleep behind the screen. Few who did cared. And the company rulebook mandated that "under no circumstances will porter request passengers to vacate smoking-room so that he may retire," although it did let conductors assign him an empty upper berth in special circumstances and it reserved cramped Upper One for him on tourist cars with no smokers.[20]

Porters quickly crafted a custom of their own to reclaim their bedroom: politely ask everyone to leave the smoking room, explaining you had to clean up and go off duty. "If they didn't go, I would come in there with some formaldehyde on the mop," porter Leroy Graham explained from the living room of his Washington, D.C., home, black shoes and pants, white shirt, and green-striped suspenders making clear he was just back from church but the intensity of his gaze suggesting he was back aboard that Pullman sleeper. "Once I mopped the room, you couldn't stay there. You couldn't stand it. It burned your eyes and choked you almost." The only way Graham and other porters could stand the burning stench was by sleeping with a handkerchief covering their mouths.[21]

That was one of a bag of tricks porters used to maintain their sanity and dignity. Mark the soles of shoes with soap so you know whose they are, then ignore the one-pair-at-a-time rule on shining. Bang out a tune on the steam pipe with your keys, then tell the old lady in Lower Two you have turned up the heat. Stick a bucket of oysters way down in the cooler so they will last on the trip back from the West Coast; so what if the company says not to. Fill the coffee cup just three-quarters full to avoid spilling any as the train sways.

Dodges like those did defy George Pullman's rulebook, but mainly at the edges. "A trainman should, and does, depend more on his judgment than on any set of rules," the pioneering Negro film-maker and former porter Oscar Micheaux wrote in 1913. "And [he] permits the rule to be stretched now and then to fit circumstances."[22] A porter also learned that dexterity, physical and mental, was criti-cal to surviving on the rails. So was the recognition that no matter how taxing the work, it was easier than their fathers' as slavehands and their neighbors' in the fields or factories. A sense of humor helped, too, along with the ability to read passengers' personalities and plenty of patience. "My mother taught me never to quarrel with a fool but to humor him," said James Bennett Newsome, a porter who started on Pullman cars way back in the beginning, in 1870, and stayed for fifty-five and a half years. "That's what I do; I study my man and I know him."[23]

M. Kincade, a porter from St. Louis, lived by a comparable creed: "You just gotta haul folks as they come. Some's good, some's bad, some's nice and some's crabby."[24]

THAT RELATIONSHIP WITH folks they hauled was *the* defining feature in the life of Pullman porters, for better and often for worse. To understand why, it helps to understand who it was inside the chocolate brown, steam-driven sleepers that roared across the prairies and shortened the separation between America's great metropolises in the late 1800s.

The popular image was of J. P. Morgans, Cornelius Vanderbilts, and others of George Pullman's own set, which was accurate in the very earliest days and was understandable since George's cars offered urbane, sophisticated touches the Newport crowd was accustomed to. Manicurists and maids were ideally suited to the leisure class, who at home were catered to by a furnace man, carriage attendant, nanny, cook, butler, and maids for each floor. Tables of linen, crystal, and cut flowers begged for evening dress. But it was those very trappings, together with George's moderate charges, that persuaded teachers, clerks, and others of modest means to abandon unbearable coach cars and make their trip a true escape. Riding a sleeping car across the country meant five days of adventures, encounters, and, if they were lucky, libidinous liaisons. Boarding a Pullman meant going topflight. "The bulk of the Pullman Co.'s business always has been with the great American middle class," *Fortune* magazine wrote in 1938. "More specifically its typical customer is the businessman in a rush to get from Omaha to Kansas City, from Chicago to Oshkosh at a price that will not stick up like a sore thumb on his company's expense account. Two-thirds of Pullman's business is with customers who do not pay more than $2.50 for their night's lodging."[25]

Thousands of Negroes could afford that fare but could not get on a Pullman or other first-class carriage, at least below the Mason-Dixon Line. The Civil Rights Act of 1875 assured Negroes full and equal use of rail transport, but the U.S. Supreme Court ruled that the law only barred segregation by states, not by individuals or corporations. And only on interstate travel. One southern state after another passed Jim Crow laws requiring separation of the races on the rails, and railroads decided that it was simpler to segregate all riders than change state to state. The result: despite George's early efforts to open his cars traveling South to Negro passengers, they were banished to separate carriages just behind the engine, where they suffered the full effects of noxious fumes. That also required riding *with* stored baggage or whites who wanted to smoke, gamble, and drink, and *without* heaters, washbasins, flush toilets, water coolers, and upholstered seats. Such second-rate accommodations lasted through the 1930s, while segregation that reeked of racism persisted for another thirty years. Consequently, for most of the

Pullman era, Negro passengers missed out on the legendary service proffered by their fellow Negro, the Pullman porter.

Benjamin Elijah Mays dangerously defied those restrictions during a trip South from St. Louis in 1923. At first the white Pullman passengers responded with "dagger" looks and an occasional "additional glare of hatred." In Tennessee, when Mays decided to take the conductor's advice and move back to an empty car with the porter, two white men paid him a visit, aiming their pistols in his face. They escorted him to the Negro coach. Mays, who had worked as a Pullman porter to help pay for college and later became president of Atlanta's Morehouse College, was still shaken by the experience almost half a century later: "Neither the Pullman conductor nor the train conductor did a thing to protect my person and my right to ride as a free man in a so-called free society. Not one white passenger protested my treatment. It is my considered judgment that if I had been killed or thrown off the running train, absolutely nothing would have been done about it. The conductors would not even have lost their jobs."[26]

That a porter's dark skin would make him unwelcome on his own Pullman car, and in scores of other places his white passengers took for granted, made the close contact between porter and passenger especially curious. And particularly precarious. That called for special rules, and not just the formal kind that George and his managers included in their thick instruction manuals.

An entire treatise could have been written on the canons of touching, or not. In general it was hands off, with men almost as much as women, which is what George had in mind when he ordered porters to tug the curtain rather than the person of a sleeping passenger. When touching was unavoidable, as when helping a rider onto the train or into a berth, the elbow was the proper point of contact. A normal mortal found it impossible to avoid grazing someone coming the other way in the long narrow passageways of a Pullman sleeper, but the porter was the paragon of body English. He merely flattened himself against the wall, beckoning the approaching passenger to "come ahead, come ahead."[27]

The template on talking was even simpler: shh! That was the rule at night, when sleep was paramount and noise impermissible. Even more dangerous was gossip. The porter simply saw and heard too much for any tattling to be tolerated. So he became the most close-mouthed of men.

Pullman travel also necessitated suspending the normal rules of racial engagement so long as the train was moving. That let parents entrust to the porter for an entire trip cross-country the care of children traveling alone. Grown children did the same with invalid parents. Disconsolate riders unburdened themselves to their porter, sometimes under the influence of alcohol but often sober as a judge, because they knew they never would encounter him in a setting where their indiscretion would prove embarrassing. No matter that if they passed this same Negro man on the street those passengers would escape to the other side, especially if they had children in hand. Or that many were Negrophobes, and most neither knew nor cared about the porter's life off the train. That was the point: this was a Pullman Palace Car, and contact with the porter would end when the trip did.

What the porter got in return was a tip. The contract seemed straightforward: you take care of my child, and I will make it worth your while. Over a century of Pullman travel, however, tipping took on an elaborate web of customs and hierarchies. It measured the tippee's agility and artfulness. It tested the tipper's grasp of rules of the rails. It reflected the company's strategy of keeping wages low to ensure slavelike service. It was the perfect lens through which to observe not just the porter-passenger interplay but the evolution of relations between patron and servant.

Tipping was not invented on a Pullman sleeper, nor is it an exclusively American habit. It was imported from Europe and may date to an eighteenth-century custom at London coffeehouses where customers handed waiters coins with a note marked "To Insure Promptness." Over time the message was abridged to "T.I.P." There have long been equivalent customs in France (*pourboire*), China (*cumshaw*), the Middle East (*baksheesh*), and most every other nation on Earth. But as the *St. Louis Republic* noted a century ago, "It was the Pullman company which fastened the tipping habit on the American people and they used the negro as the instrument to do it with."[28]

The average tip on a Pullman car started as a nickel, although pennies were handed out, too, usually two at a time. By the end of the century the standard was a dime, and in the 1930s it rose to a quarter for men and fifteen cents for women. Giving shoes a lasting shine was what porters called their "hustle," the ministration most likely to elicit a reward. Next were delivering a telegram, mailing a letter during a station stop, running a bath, serving food or drink, delivering a card table or aspirin, and carting baggage. Making down a bed was less clear-cut, unless you were about to climb in with someone you wanted the attendant to quickly forget. A plea to "take care of my child" always came with a sawbuck or two, with another tip likely upon safely handing her or him off to grandparents down the line.

Not quite sure when to tip, or how much? Emily Post, the princess of punctilio, was ready with a road map. Dining car waiters in 1922 got 15 percent of the bill, just as in a restaurant, and "never less than a quarter." Same for waiters or stewards in the bar, with an extra quarter if they toted the setup to your Pullman car. As for porters, it was "fifty cents to one dollar for each person on an overnight trip—more if he has given additional service other than making up the berths."[29] The easiest way to judge whether a tip was enough was to study the porter's response: a nickel brought silence or a scowl; a dime a clipped "thank you"; a quarter "thank you" along with a hand salute; fifty cents "oh thank you," a low bow, and a broad smile; and for a dollar most porters would fall dead.[30]

But porters were not about to leave matters that vital to chance, or even to Emily Post. Although they knew asking for money was taboo, they had their ways. Sometimes it was simply remembering a returning traveler's name, favorite brand of Scotch, or preference for a lower berth. The technique was slightly different upon departure: best to administer the whisk broom to jacket or hat just as the passenger was leaving, to separate companions in hope of separate tips, to compliment the feather in her hat or silk in his suit. The way to a soldier's pocket typically was through his sergeant, who not only would pass the hat but might order his men to make their own beds. As for passengers who tried to slip out the back door without whisk or tip, "we finally found a remedy," porter H. N. Hall wrote in 1931. "We got wet towels and placed them in the doors. When those heavy steel doors swing on a wet towel it's a job for a half dozen men to open them."[31]

The best tippers ("fish") and the worst ("snakes") were well known to porters, by occupation and name. Grooms were fish, to impress their blushing brides. Musicians were skinflints, actors marginally more philanthropic, journalists sugar daddies. Baseball players— especially Babe Ruth and Jackie Robinson—were cheapskates. They let off steam by punching the stuffing out of their pillows or lathering windows with shaving cream—and left the porter not a penny. Ditto for boarding school brats. Valets held on to money their masters intended for tips. Drunks and hookers were almost as generous as mobsters. So were salesmen, moms with kids, Jack Dempsey, and nearly everyone who rode the *Twentieth Century Limited*. Sammy Davis Jr. would hand over twenty dollars "as soon as he looked at you," agreed porters who waited on him, but pals Peter Lawford and Jack Benny were snakes who snuck out the back door. George M. Cohan, Morton Downey, "Diamond Jim" Brady, and Humphrey Bogart were grand, Jay Gould miserable. Old man Rockefeller would hand over a mere penny; his wife discreetly added a dollar. Japanese were the most generous foreign businessmen, followed by Englishmen, Frenchmen, Italians, and Russians. Adhering to the adage "watch what I do, not what I say," porters themselves tipped big after eating in the dining car.

No one tipped bigger than Mrs. H. J. Heinz, heiress to the ketchup kingdom. Soon after boarding she laid out her demands: wrap my coat in cloth before hanging it in the closet, apply my silk bedding, find four bottles of Poland Spring water, and bring me twenty towels. That sounded simple enough to Garrard Wilson

"Babe" Smock, George's youngest brother. He suspected his ward
was special when a fellow porter offered twenty dollars to switch
assignments. But he was crushed when, after a weekend of special
service, she left him tipless. A month later Smock's wife, Bertha,
called with the explanation. "She said there was a man at the house
with a truckload of groceries from the Heinz Company," Babe
recalled. "There were six cases of Heinz ketchup, along with cases
of peas, corn, baby food, and the rest of the 57 varieties Heinz had.
I gave food away to neighbors up and down the street."[32]

That was one in a series of unusual rewards Smock got during
twenty-seven years with the Pullman Company. A washer and dryer
came courtesy of the vice president of Bell Telephone in Chicago,
who was grateful that Babe tried to help his son stop stuttering. A
horse was the tip from a TRW executive, while a furniture store
owner in Kansas City told him to pick out anything he wanted for
his living room. It was a thank-you, Babe said, for "having me do
certain things for him. He had diarrhea and he poo pooed all over
everyplace. I had to clean it up."[33]

A different sort of cleaning up was required with American presidents who rode Pullman cars, and not all showed their gratitude.
Ulysses S. Grant and Calvin Coolidge were renowned tightwads.
Rutherford B. Hayes would give a dime or, if the porter persisted, a
quarter. Chester Arthur, by contrast, was "one of the freest tippers
in the East." As a senator, John F. Kennedy commuted by rail between
Washington and Boston and was known as a half-dollar guy, especially if the porter remembered to put a board under his bed to ease
his aching back. Ronald Reagan was "the cheapest of them all,"
even after his shoes were shined to a spit, but his traveling companion, the actor Robert Young, compensated by being doubly generous. In the fashion of Boston politics, U.S. House Speaker Thomas
P. O'Neill and Mayor James Michael Curley tipped liberally to gar-
ner votes of porters, along with their families and friends. Tops in
the political set was First Lady Eleanor Roosevelt, who in 1939 was
crowned "most generous" by the Dining Car Employees Union.

Some porters found the bizarre rituals of tipping exhilarating, testing their skill and offering big jackpots. Others admit it made them do things that, looking back, give them chills. Lying about tips was common—either underestimating what they got on lucrative runs to preempt interference from other porters, or exaggerating tips on trains they were eager to get off. They also regret having neglected riders who could not afford to tip—women and old people, immigrants, and even pastors—while doting on those who could. It was degrading to have to ingratiate themselves to win tips, they say, and more degrading not to get any.

That ambivalence about the tipping system, and what it says about warped relations between passengers and porters, was captured in a 1978 talk at the Smithsonian Institution by William D. Miller, last president of the Washington, D.C., branch of the porters' union. A distraught passenger summoned Miller, saying he needed to talk. Spinning his tale, the white rider paused repeatedly to give Miller money for listening. "It's my daughter," the man said, handing over a tip. "You don't mind my talking about it?" he continued, pulling out more money. "She ran away to New York. Are you sure you don't mind my talking about it?" Another pause, another tip, as he explained that the girl ran to New York to get married. "What's so terrible about that? You should be happy," Miller interrupted. "No," the passenger replied. "She married a Pullman porter."[34]

Episodes like that made clear that "it was the tipping system itself that allowed passengers to be so rude and insensitive to porters in the first place," wrote Jack Santino, the folklorist who assembled Miller and other porters at the Smithsonian and expanded their recollections into a book called *Miles of Smiles, Years of Struggle*. "If he had not depended on tips, the porter would not have needed to put up with such behavior. The line between selling oneself and maximizing tips— that is, between slavery and economic freedom—was very thin. Perhaps it can be seen as one of the porters' finest achievements that they walked this delicate tightrope with grace. It was a line that the porters were constantly aware of and always attempted to maintain. Whether they were always successful is something that they work out with each other, and internally, in the solitude of their own thoughts."[35]

Malcolm X, the Negro activist who worked on a train briefly during his troubled teens, said the teachings of tipping helped shape his views on racial relations: "It didn't take me a week to learn that all you had to do was give white people a show and they'd buy anything you offered them. It was like popping your shoeshine rag. The dining car waiters and Pullman porters knew it too, and they faked their Uncle Tomming to get bigger tips. We were in that world of Negroes who are both servants and psychologists, aware that white people are so obsessed with their own importance that they will pay liberally, even dearly, for the impression of being catered to and entertained."[36]*

Every porter knew that he had earned whatever tips he got, and not just by shining shoes. He was like a mother hen guarding her flock. During his night shift he sat on a stool, draped in a blanket, protecting his car from thieves, degenerates, and other threats from within or out. During the day he rocked toddlers on his knee, anticipated passengers' needs before they rang their bell, and decided whether to intervene or assist when a male rider propositioned a female. He also had to fend off advances on himself, from passengers of both sexes.

"One man came up through the car near closing time. I'm doing my reports because I have to tell what I sold in each seat," recalled Robert McGoings, a light-skinned Negro with a face full of freckles who worked on Baltimore & Ohio dining cars for thirty-five years. "He comes up and sits across from me. I said, 'I can't serve you anything yet because we're in West Virginia or Pennsylvania,' and he said, 'Can you bring it back to my room?' I said 'yes' and when I went back there, he slid the door open, then locked it again. As I poured the drink, he stands up and starts kissing me. What am I

*In addition to his time as a dishwasher and sandwich seller with the railroad, Malcolm Little, as he was known then, worked for the Pullman Company. Briefly. He cleaned sleeping cars at the Dover Yard in Boston from June 25 to June 27, 1941—for a grand total of twelve and a half hours. Neither Pullman records nor his autobiography indicates why he left so soon, but it is likely that the work bored him and he knew he would not be able to abide by Pullman's endless list of rules.

going to do? I knew the cars, it was a Pullman car, so I felt behind me and found the button to call the porter. Sure enough the Pullman porter and Pullman conductor come up. Soon as they knocked on the door I turned the lights on, turned around, and got out of there without him even paying the check."

Another time it was the woman doing the propositioning. "I made her a drink and she told me to bring it back to her room. I brought it back and she was stripped, nothing on," said McGoings. "I just poured the drink and gave it to her. She said, 'Won't you have one?' I said 'no.' In a sense that was a temptation, in another it wasn't. I had too big a mortgage."[37]

Temptation apparently got the better of Undersecretary of State Sumner Welles after he boarded a Pullman sleeper on a sweltering September day in 1940. The graduate of Groton and Harvard had proved his diplomatic skill by drafting the Good Neighbor policy with Latin America. He had forged a friendship with Franklin Delano Roosevelt that garnered him a role in the president's wedding and patronship as he progressed through State Department postings. He was now odds-on favorite to succeed the aged, infirmed Cordell Hull as secretary of state—or he was until he summoned veteran porter John Stone to his Pullman compartment. Coffee was not all that a highly intoxicated Welles wanted. Stone told his colleagues that the statesman offered money for sex, and that he refused. Other porters reported indirect advances made to them by Welles. The FBI and Secret Service authenticated the charges, but with a national election just seven weeks away the scandal made it no farther than the president's desk. Welles quietly resigned. The full story was not told until 1997, thirty-six years after Sumner Welles's death, when his son Benjamin published a telltale biography of Sumner.[38]

Porters did not always say no. And when white passengers offered themselves to a Negro attendant, it often was as much a matter of racial experimentation as sexual. Porter Taylor Gordon understood that, and later wrote about it. His sleeping car was taking a just-wed couple from southern Ohio to their new home in the wilds of Saskatchewan, but when the train arrived the bride decided not to get off. Watching her husband ride off in a covered wagon, she struck up a conversation with Gordon: "'You—you know: you're the first Nig-nigger I have ever talked—talked to. Can I? I?— believe all—believe all my mother and father have told me about you people?' she inquired hesitatingly, with a peculiar smile. Her remarks flashed through my mind, bringing with them things the boys had told me that white people say about niggahs, and I realized what she was suggesting. It's sure hard to make white people believe that what they say might be true about some of us, but not about the whole race. Still, as the legend is to our advantage, I left my work for an hour, so that it shouldn't die with me."[39]

There are other ways porters put themselves on the line for passengers, and which the company applauded. In 1924, John Robert Davis had a tubercular patient board his train in Kansas City. Davis stayed up all night bathing the delirious passenger's head, bringing him water, and spending his own money to buy medicine and food when the train stopped. Another passenger, Harold Parish, was so impressed by porter Davis's efforts that he sent a report to the Pullman Company, and so curious about what happened to the invalid that he called on his family. The man died several days after his train trip, Parish reported, adding, "His mother told me her son said 'that porter was sure black, but Mother, he had a pure, white soul.'"[40]

Sometimes a porter's sacrifice included his very life. That was the case with Oscar Daniels when his train derailed near Rockport, New Jersey, in the summer of 1925. The front door of the car flew open, letting in scalding steam, but Daniels managed to push the portal shut. He was carried out of the car and a doctor tried to examine him, but he insisted that a seven-year-old girl be treated first. By the time the physician returned, Daniels was dead. The Pullman Company honored him by renaming his sleeper the Oscar Daniels, the first time a porter was so honored.[41]

Their work also made porters targets for criminals. A passenger described as "violently insane" shot and killed porter Samuel Williams as their train passed through Newark in 1910. A year later one porter was killed, another wounded, when bandits held up their train in Utah. And in 1930 porter J. H. Wilkins was lynched in Locust Grove, Georgia, in a field a quarter mile from the tracks where his Atlanta-bound train had passed hours earlier. His attackers hit him over the head, fracturing his skull in two places, then used his white Pullman jacket to string him up. That assault drew outrage from Pullman porters everywhere, who had never heard of such a thing happening to one of theirs. It also offered a reminder that however otherworldly Pullman sleeping cars might seem, they could not insulate porters from the violence and thuggery that threatened Negroes across America.[42]

ONE WAY PULLMAN porters coped with such stresses was to lean on one another, the way people do in any high-pressure work. Yet few workplaces could match the stress of the sleeping car. There were the close and closed quarters. The long days, or even weeks, together with no break. And the us-versus-them relationship between the train crew—particularly Negro porters, waiters, and maids—and white passengers.

Their bonding was apparent to anyone who knew what to listen for. Porters had their own lexicon, reflecting their take on the railroad, Pullman Company, riders, and fellow workers. Most passengers never knew because porters never used it with them, and even if they overheard, they would not have understood. Which was the point. It was meant so porters could talk about passengers without their overhearing, the way immigrant parents used Yiddish, Polish, or Italian to keep things from their English-speaking children. Or children use pig Latin, and jive, to keep things from parents. For the Pullman porters, their language was about more than just secrecy. It fostered intimacy. It was a shorthand for making their world make sense.

Some expressions they brought from the Negro community and small-town South. *Blue hen biddy* was someone special. *Handkerchief head* was a close relation to *Uncle Tom.* So was *white folks' Negro,* a term often associated with Booker T. Washington. *Uncle*

Tom, meanwhile, had become a verb: *tomming.* Porters preferred *Negro* to *colored,* and later to *black,* much the way they favored *lady* over *woman.* A *liquor head* was a drunk. A *pail of coffee* was a thermos-full, good on the night shift to wash down your *midnight lunch.* A *suit and necktie man* was a stuffed shirt, a *rocking chair guy* a retiree. Count on a *hundred-proof guy,* and check out a *pretty brownskin with a shape on her hittin' ninety-nine.* Beware of *nasty types* or anyone slick enough to have *oil on his bottom*; both are *as unwelcome as an undertaker at a marriage breakfast.*

Sleeping and dining cars were whole new contraptions and required a specialized vocabulary for the equipment and crew. *Coffin rack* captured the look and feel of the first all-male coaches. An observation car was a *rubberneck,* the buffet car a *tin can.* When the train was ready to load passengers, or unload them, the attendant *decorated the platform* by putting in place a set of stairs. The kitchen staff was hierarchical: the chef was a *big man,* with the *lizard scorcher* overseeing food preparation. The *pantryman* made salads and stocked the kitchen, *silver man* kept knives, forks, and spoons sparkling, and *upstairs man* carried the food to a sleeper or anywhere beyond the diner. Low man was a *pearl diver,* whose only underwater activities were with suds and dirty dishes.

The most telling language was what Pullman porters used only with one another. The earliest porters, the first Negroes to see America, were *travelin' men,* and during stopovers they were *foreign porters.* Ones a bit too loyal to George Pullman were *company porters,* while doctors, lawyers, and other Negro professionals who lined up against the union were *parlor stool pigeons. Grinning* was what company porters did; those with pride stuck to *smiling.* Crooning porters constituted a *quartet,* be they four or forty. Porters good-naturedly called one another *pillow punchers,* but it was no joke when a passenger or journalist said it. *Red, white, and blue* were Negro rail workers—redcaps, porters in their white coats, and blue-jeaned laborers who laid the tracks. *Getting a set of keys* meant a man had achieved the status of Pullman porter. At the other end of a career he prayed for a *pension run* with fewer berths.

Porters got to practice their in-house idiom at Pullman clubs that sprouted in New York, Chicago, Boston, and other railroad hubs. Retirees gathered there, and foreign porters stopped by. They also were choice spots for the Baker Heater League to convene, although that could happen anywhere with more than one porter. Pullman porters had leagues for everything, from baseball to balladeering, but none had a richer heritage than the one formed around the coil-tube boilers that heated the early sleepers. Porters gathered to trade stories and tell jokes, and kept doing it long after the old stoves were mothballed. That may be where the legend of Daddy Joe was born, and certainly was where it got embellished. The only rule was taking turns. Popular topics were outrageous passengers, heroic porters, and prurient ladies. Tones were hushed, the pace rapid-fire, the dialect all theirs.

A favorite was the tale of Lester Simmons and the Death Train. Lester had been a Pullman porter for thirty years, and in his retirement he shined shoes and spent evenings at the porter club on Compton Avenue in St. Louis, exchanging stories and playing cards. Lester told every rookie porter who dropped in about the death train, known as the 11:59. "Any porter who hears the whistle of the 11:59 has got exactly twenty-four hours to clear up earthly matters," Lester whispered. "All us porters got to board that train one day. Ain't no way to escape the final ride on the 11:59." Walking home one night Lester felt a biting pain in his side, then heard the doleful whistle of a train. He checked his watch: 11:59. The next day he desperately tried to evade his own prophecy, but that night a ghostlike train magically appeared in his apartment and a specter dressed in Pullman blue welcomed him aboard. "I'm ready," Lester said as the engine ripped through his home, shattering the walls as it collapsed his heart. Two days later friends found Lester on the floor of his apartment, eyes fixated on his gold retirement watch that had stopped at precisely 11:59.[43]

Language and stories were not the only bond porters forged. There also evolved a code of how to handle jams the job perpetually put them in, from the awkward to the outright hateful.

One quandary was where to find lodging during long layovers. In most big cities the Pullman Company provided beds, for free or a nominal fee, in rooming houses, old or empty sleeping cars at the rail yard, or the YMCA, which was more welcoming to Negroes than hotels. In Omaha in the early 1900s those quarters consisted of three double-decker beds on the ground floor of the Pullman office, which the men said was damp and had no bath. Salt Lake City had two rooms at the Wellington Hotel, one with four single beds and the other with chairs, while nearby Ogden used a dismantled Pullman car in the middle of the freight yard. In San Francisco, the company assumed porters could go across the bay to Oakland, where it had beds, or that San Francisco hotels would put them up for free in the hope that porters would send passengers their way.

In his first novel, the 1928 *Home to Harlem,* Claude McKay drew on his days as a porter to describe the Pullman quarters in Pittsburgh: "They were double beds, like Pullman berths. Three of the waiters had not come in yet. The second and fourth cooks were snoring, each a deep frothy bass and a high tenor, and scratching themselves in their sleep. The chef sprawled like the carcass of a rhinoceros, half-naked, mouth wide open. Tormented by bedbugs, he had scratched and tossed in his sleep and hoofed the covers off the bed," wrote McKay, a leading figure in the Harlem Renaissance of the 1920s. "Ray was sitting on a lower berth on his Negro newspapers spread out to form a sheet. He had thrown the sheets on the floor, they were so filthy from other men's sleeping. By the thin flame of gaslight he was killing bugs."[44]

Housing so cramped and decrepit almost compelled porters to get along, and gave them common ground in railing against their skinflint employer. Some looked for other places to stay, including homes of local porters. Most who used company quarters did so solely for sleeping, with the rest of the stopover spent taking in sights or seeking out entertainment. In Vancouver it might be the Swedish baths, in New York a Broadway play. All were brilliant adventures for men reared in isolated outposts and not used to cash in their pockets. Nice, too, to have someone waiting on *you.* Over time they learned that movies were cheaper in the morning, and that each town had at least one bar catering to railroad men. They knew where to find the friendliest pool hall, most savory beef stew, and ripest prostitutes. Often at the same stop.

Women were a preoccupation for Pullman porters. They spent days or weeks at a stretch away from wives or sweethearts and had it drilled into them that white passengers were untouchable. Few chanced the automatic firing that came with fraternizing on the train. The rest waited until they got home, or tried to. "I remember one night on the road I had a girlfriend up there, and it was cold, and Bertha called up," Babe Smock said of his first wife. "Bertha kept asking questions, but I couldn't talk back, and she said, 'Is there something wrong?' I said, 'No.' She said, 'Do you love me? Give me a kiss.' I did. The woman who was with me said, 'I like that, I come up to visit you and you throw her a kiss on the telephone.'"[45]

Others actually had second wives or whole families on the road. "There was a theory that porters always had some money," said the ex-porter Kenneth Judy as he contemplated the matter of bigamy. "Whether that happened any more among porters than anyone else I'm not sure. It probably did happen a little bit more because Pullman porters were away from home a lot. When you got a long time away from home your marriage ties kind of loosened up, you know. Those things did happen. . . . But you had to take all that with a grain of salt because men liked to boast about their conquests with women. A lot of fellas claimed things that they absolutely didn't do."[46]

Boasting like that is common anytime men gather. It makes even more sense with Pullman porters. They spent their lives making beds and scrubbing toilets, dusting, ironing, and polishing. Back then wives and mothers did "women's work" like that at home. Maids and washerwomen did it at hotels, offices, and manor houses. Did porters see their work as unmanly? Demeaning? They insisted not, to others and themselves, then and even now. But they knew the whispers, and that provided an extra drive to demonstrate their manhood. Or at least talk as if they had.

What did their wives think of such carrying on? Some reasoned that even if the conquests porters bragged about were real, that would be all the more reason to want a settled life at home. "They knew," one wife philosophized, "what was on the other side of the rosebush, so they weren't so easily turned astray. My own husband was always glad to get home after being on the road."[47] Other wives worried—about what their husbands were doing and, more pressing, the responsibilities that fell on them as the sole parent at home. "That's part of the reason, after babies started coming, that I gave up the railroad in 1962," said Jimmy Kearse, a longtime dining car waiter. "Our youngest son, André, was a baby. My wife would drink between eight and twelve cups of coffee, brewed coffee, every morning before twelve o'clock, and she'd smoke a lot of cigarettes. I didn't know when my wife was going to get nervous and throw one of my kids out of a window. That's just what I felt."[48]

Porters' safest and most constant activity at home and on the road was playing cards. Decks were perpetually being shuffled and hands dealt at company lodging houses, porter social clubs, and, when time allowed and no bosses were watching, on the sleepers. The game almost always was the same: bid whist, a shortened form of bridge and direct descendant of whist. Some trace the game to slave days and suggest bondsmen were imitating bridge and spades played by plantation owners; others place its roots in seventeenth-century England. Wherever it started, porters made bid whist popular much the way they did tipping, and by the 1950s it was the rage in Negro homes across America.

Bid whist ideally suited a porter's lifestyle. It was quick enough to be played on the run, competitive enough to be engaging, and straightforward enough to be learned by men without much formal schooling. It uses a standard deck of cards, plus jokers. Four people play, in teams of two. Points are tallied by bidding for, then winning, what bridge calls tricks and bid whist calls books. Porters sometimes played for money but more often for fun. And bragging rights. They might take a break by dealing a few hands of poker, knock rummy, or pinochle, or pulling out a checkerboard, although most never tired of marathon sessions of bid whist.

The games generally stopped when the train pulled below that imaginary line in southern Pennsylvania that signaled entry into the segregated South. Finding a restaurant willing to serve them was a challenge at every layover, so they brought along tins of sardines and Sterno stoves to warm them. Hotels for Negroes were even more elusive, so some nights they slept on benches in the park or station. Until they learned to navigate a community's particular pastiche of Jim Crow, just walking down the street could land them in jail or worse, as Joseph Strowder discovered on his first trip to Florida as a waiter for the Seaboard Railroad. "We asked the rest of the waiters and cooks how to get down to Second Avenue in Miami, and they told us to catch a trolley that went past the station, go so many blocks, get off, and we'd find the black neighborhood. Evidently we didn't listen good. We got on the trolley and went in the wrong direction," said Strowder, who now lives in Washington, D.C.

"When we got off, just about that time a cruiser shows up and says, 'Where you niggers going?' We said we were going to Second Avenue, and the officer says, 'This is not Second Avenue; where you from, boy?' He and his partner interrogated us. One of our fellas told him he was from Georgia, told him the county and everything. The cop said to go down this street about four blocks and he'd find the railroad track, make a right turn, and keep going till he came to the nigger quarters. The officer came to me then and said, 'Where you from, boy?' I said I was from Florida. I was, but I'd moved to Omaha when I was five and didn't know nothing about Florida. He told me the same thing, to run down the railroad tracks and turn right. Our other fella was a little guy named Bill, a westerner, and he didn't like nobody calling him 'nigger.' When he told the officers not to call him that, they beat him good; his face was all bruised, and he had two black eyes. He didn't come back to Florida anymore.

"Every time you got off the train in the South you had to be very careful. Even if you were just jumping off to buy twelve bottles of Coca-Cola, you had to make sure you didn't bump nobody, that you gave respect to every person. It was like walking on eggshells."[49]

The former porter Charles H. Mitchner Sr. stepped on one of those shells at the station in Jackson, Mississippi. His train was bound for Mobile, and he was hungry. The stop was brief, so he took the quickest route to the food counter—through the whites-only section. "Boy," a voice bellowed, "do you know where you are?" It was a white policeman. Mitchner produced his Pullman badge and explained about the train. "I don't give a damn where you got to go!" the policeman replied. Then, as Mitchner recounted in his memoir, the officer "took out his pistol, put it squarely up against my ear and walked me around that whole block to get to the colored side of the station! While we were walking he said, 'If you run, I will blow yo' damn brains out.'" By the time the policeman let him go, Mitchner's train had left, and he had to wait seventeen hours for the next one to come through for Mobile. "When I arrived, the superintendent at the station said, 'Where the hell you been?' When I told him what happened to me in Jackson, Mississippi, he said, 'You're telling me a G--damned lie, Nigger! You know you niggers get tied up with those black whores and don't want to work!'"[50]

To Lawrence "Happy" Davis, the Mason-Dixon Line looked more like the Iron Curtain during three decades running from his home in Washington, D.C., to places like Florida and Texas. The only way an outsider like him could survive was with help from friends. "There was Ruby in Fort Worth, and, in Tampa, Julia and Tiny, a big woman," Davis said of the ladies who offered food and a place to stay. "If it not be for those black women, we would have starved to death, all the women who catered to us Pullman porters from out of town. They were our refuge, you might say."[51]

The Pullman Company had its own renderings of racism. Along with their special blue blankets porters got blue pillows, just to make sure a conductor never had to rest his white head on a pillow used by a black porter. Fare receipts were color-coded, too, with a *P* on those handed out by porters. And Pullman offices in Miami and other districts maintained two sign-in windows: an indoor one for conductors while the porters' was out in the elements.[52]* That obsession with keeping things separate was even more apparent in the early days of the dining cars. A curtain was drawn around porters while they ate, creating a small coloreds-only space like the one used for the rare Negro passenger.† And the Pullman Company preferred light-skinned Negroes on its dining cars, in contrast to its dark-skinned porters. A hiring directive on porters clearly stated, "Do not employ a light complexioned man"; it did not explain why.[53] Hiring light-skinned waiters probably was a throwback to slave days, when softer-toned Negroes got favored jobs in the Big House, while the directive on porters seemed aimed at accentuating the wall of demarcation between served and servant.

Their different hues may have played a role in perennial tensions between porters and dining car workers. Although they shared backgrounds and often traded jobs, each had a list of grievances against the other. Waiters resented porters' supposed uppitiness, especially after they had their own union and higher wages. They were jealous that porters were potentates of the sleepers, while in the dining car the chef lorded it over the second cook, who bossed the third or fry cook, who took it out on the fourth cook-dishwasher. Waiters had it rough, too—taking orders from the steward and head waiter, even as other waiters poached their orders and high-tipping customers—and after

---

*A Pullman Company memorandum, prepared in response to a 1966 lawsuit brought by porters, took issue with the sworn testimony of porters. The company insisted that porters' use of separate blankets, pillows, and sheets ended after World War II. Dining restrictions, it added, were a "railroad problem, ended in the 1940s." The *P* marking was "a bookkeeping requirement for benefit of porter." As for porters' repeated complaints about having to report to an outdoor window rather than the indoor office, the memo said there was "no such rule." Martin J. Rock to David C. Miller, October 6, 1975, "1966 Suit 1523—*Earl A. Love v. Pullman Company,*" Pullman Company Collection, Newberry Library.

†Other railroads took the obsession over coloration a step farther, coordinating crews by skin shade as well as height. "Down at headquarters they try and put the same kinds of niggers in a squad. Medium mulattos go in one car, tall blacks in another. It sort of helps dress the car in a uniform fashion," a steward for the New York Central told a magazine writer in 1914. Edward Hungerford, "Eating on the Train," *Harper's Weekly,* March 21, 1914, 13.

an evening serving three hundred passengers they had no patience when porters came in looking for discounted food and mannerly service. Such strains became more pronounced during stopovers: dining car crews who worked cheek by jowl on the train hung together off, at bars, pool halls, and cathouses. Porters were more independent, often heading to dinner, then bed, which added to their image as snobbish and unsociable.

"There wasn't a whole lot of warmth between a Pullman porter and waiters; there wasn't a whole lot of brotherhood," recalled Dean Denniston, a Boston-based waiter. "They had to try and make people feel comfortable; our job was to appeal to the inner man. Absolutely we had the better job. As the French would say, *sans doute.*"[54]

Porters saw things differently. They tipped waiters more than many passengers did, and felt entitled to first-class service. They were in charge of an entire car and believed that trumped anything the kitchen crew did. And if porters sometimes worried that making beds was less than manly, what did that say about chopping vegetables and washing dishes? The best way to calibrate those tensions, as always, was with language. A piqued porter would call his dining car colleague a "raggedy-ass waiter." The server shot back with "sheet shaker" or, if he really was het up, "fart shaker."

Antagonisms between Negro porters and Caucasian conductors were even deeper-seated and more understandable. Porters resented being barred from rising to conductor. They disliked having to accept a conductor's edict as final the same way a private in the army did with his sergeant. (The Pullman rulebook mandated that militarylike discipline as early as 1888, warning porters that if a conductor's "requirements are thought to be unnecessary, that fact must not prevent obedience to his orders.")[55] Most of all, they hated that conductors earned almost twice the salary for considerably less heavy lifting.

That was how porters felt about conductors as a class. But for the flesh-and-blood men they worked next to, porters realized that conductors worked long hours, spent too much time away from their families, and, like all Pullman workers, were subject to endless rules and iron discipline. The consensus among porters was that while some conductors were impossible, most were okay. That was partly humanity winning out over group identity, partly self-preservation. It was a "fallacy that in order to be a proper conductor it was necessary to bully and soundly berate the porter," Herbert O. Holderness observed in his 1901 monograph *Reminiscences of a Pullman Conductor.* A smart conductor, he went on, learned to make an ally of the porter, who "is in reality the *deus ex machina,* whose word is law and by whose frown or favor the passenger is either very comfortable or supremely unhappy."[56] Most porters were equally practical.

There was one more incentive for porters and conductors to get along: stealing. Insiders called it *knocking down.* Conductors pocketed the berth fee, then gave half to the porter in return for turning a blind eye. Just how common such pilfering was is unclear. Most porters and conductors insist it was rare, but in 1913 Micheaux, the Negro filmmaker and former porter, wrote in his autobiographical novel that *knocking down* had become "a veritable disease among the colored employees who, without exception, received and kept the company's money without a single qualm of conscience."[57] Micheaux said the practice was winding down, but two years later an ex-conductor told a congressional commission that it still was widespread.[58] Another Pullman conductor, Marshall Keiley, said that everyone knew about *knocking down* but "I never figured my job was worth the couple dollars you were able to get that way."[59]

That was not the only scam concocted on the sleepers. Dining car crews loaded their own oranges alongside the company's, selling theirs first and keeping the dollar each glass of juice fetched. They would slice a precut breakfast steak in half, serving two riders (generally women, presumed to have smaller appetites) rather than the intended one, and pocketing the second payment. Some even tossed whole chickens, hams, and legs of lamb to relatives or friends waiting along the rails. Bartenders mixed drinks behind the bar rather than in front of the passenger, stretching one miniature into two drinks or using their own stash of cheap liquor, then billing full price and retaining the difference. And for the right price porters would sell their own berth when no others were available, or look the other way while riders shot craps, drank after hours, or hooked up with a whore. The Pullman Company was wise to most tricks, inventorying every orange and lemon, insisting that servers break the seal on liquor in full view of the passenger, and perpetually tightening other regulations. Which simply meant the game was on, as crews searched for new ways to loosen the rules.

Most porters rationalized their flimflams by saying the Pullman Company stole their labor by paying so little and covering so few expenses. George Smock was more honest, estimating that his rackets netted him more than fifteen dollars on long trips and saying, "It's another form of stealing, but then that's another way of making life pleasant for yourself."[60]

Other rackets were aimed at helping out family members or train colleagues. Every cook knew how to trim the edges off steaks, potatoes, and all the other ingredients needed for a mulligan stew he could serve the crew for free. Porters, grateful for that food, found the chef an open berth or shuttled a waiter's wife among empty seats to ride cross-country gratis. And entire crews conspired during Prohibition to sneak whiskey across the border from Canada, for their personal use or, more often, to sell to liquor-starved passengers. It generally came off smoothly, defying bids by government and company to find their hiding places or penetrate their network. But in 1922 prosecutors charged forty-four Pullman porters and conductors with smuggling whiskey from New Orleans to Chicago aboard sleeping and dining cars. The whiskey, the government said, was distilled in Cuba, ferried to New Orleans aboard a submarine chaser, and ended up in Chicago's swank speakeasies.[61]

WHEN THE PULLMAN Company made news in its early years, the story generally was about luxury rather than larceny, and trust-building rather than bootlegging.

George Pullman spent the late 1800s tightening his vise on America's sleeping car trade. He launched his car-building business in

Detroit in 1870 and added to it with manufacturing or repair shops in Elmira, New York; St. Louis; Wilmington; Buffalo; Atlanta; Italy; England; and the town he founded and lent his name to on the banks of Lake Calumet just south of Chicago. *Revolutionary* is a word journalists and historians use too cavalierly in characterizing the early stages of industrial activities in the United States, but in the instance of the first Pullman plants it understates the case. They used a standardized design and prototype assembly line that anticipated Henry Ford and his Model T by thirty years. They also foreshadowed today's recycling mania by melting down iron scraps for axles and wheels and reusing everything else that other industrialists of the age tossed in the junk heap. The motivations were the same ones that drove George to regularize the training of his porters: minimize costs, maximize efficiency, and ensure that a product produced at one end of the Pullman empire was identical to that turned out at the other end.[62]

As busy as he was with manufacturing, George was even more intrepid persuading railways to lease his sleepers. He landed all lines out of Chicago even before he incorporated in 1867. Then he reached across the country, driving out or buying up archrivals, winning over railroads that tried running their own night trains, and aggressively signing on new routes. His fleet ballooned from 50 sleepers in 1868 to 300 by 1870, and 700 by 1880. In 1895, two years before he died, George had 2,556 sleeping cars coasting over 126,660 miles of American track. The last holdout, the Wagner Palace-Car Company, came aboard four years later, making good the cartel George had labored for since the launch of the *Pioneer*.

The more he controlled, the easier it became to pen sweet deals with the railroads. Early on George supplied the sleeping cars, porters, and other staff to run them, along with supplies ranging from blankets to soap. The railroads reciprocated by hauling the cars, heating and lighting them, and repairing anything below the body. The Pullman Company kept the two-dollar berth fee, with railroads paying more if the sleepers failed to generate sufficient revenues by year's end. Over time other arrangements evolved, with railroads sharing maintenance costs and revenues in return for marginally more attractive rates. The common denominators were that George made any concessions he had to, yet never yielded a penny more than necessary.

What seems most extraordinary looking back is less the deals he struck than how George could justify his monopoly. It was, after all, an era when the public was vilifying Jay Gould and his fellow robber barons, and Congress was passing the landmark Sherman Anti-Trust Act. George prevailed by arguing that it would be too expensive for any single railroad to stock enough sleepers to meet its needs during winter or summer peaks, or to carry huge groups to a football game or Elks convention. A nationwide carrier like Pullman balanced one region's peaks with another's valleys. The same rationale applied to maintaining consistent service over tracks owned by a multiplicity of lines, and fielding an army of porters and conductors. It was so convincing that even a railway like the Milwaukee Road, which kept the capacity to operate its own sleepers, eventually signed up with Pullman. One last reason it all worked: George made things just problem-free and profitable enough to keep the railroads contented, and to enlist their help in fending off trust-busting legislators and regulators.

The sleeping cars George leased to carriers at the dawn of the twentieth century had little resemblance to the *Pioneer* and even less to his first cars, the Chicago, Alton & St. Louis Railroad's refurbished day coaches 9 and 19. Rich coffee-colored exteriors were yielding to dark olive greens. Candles had given way to oil lamps, then acetylene, Pintsch gas burners, and electric lights, and cars were stretching out, the better to accommodate full kitchens and private rooms. As hot-water, hot-air, and live-steam heaters came aboard, Baker Heaters went from being a source of warmth to a quaint name for a porter gossip circle. Steel became the metal of choice for wheels, then underframes, and eventually the entire carriage. Horsehair toilet seats were replaced by velour, leather, and finally synthetic substances. And the company could throw away its placards imploring riders to "Please Take Off Your Boots Before Retiring."

Pullman's most improbable innovation was running his forty-five-thousand-pound cars on wheels of paper. The pulp technique was developed in 1869 and used widely from 1880 to 1915. Hydraulic pressure made the paper hard as ivory; then it was encased in steel. The result: an end to the deafening grinding of wheels and a ride as cushioned as sponge.

Names underwent their own evolution. Gone were the vanilla letters and numbers, replaced first by the appellations of women (*Victoria*), then preferred places (*Springfield*), statesmen (*Richard Henry Lee*), and Greek mythology (*Archimedes*). Myth had it that George's favored child Florence, Proust in hand, dreamed up the names; the truth was more prosaic and Pullmanlike, with a committee of administrators solemnly shaping the monikers. As demand grew, themes crept in: sleepers bound for Washington were named after signers of the Declaration of Independence, while those traveling a fixed route took titles of landmarks along the way.

But it was safety where the change was most dramatic and sorely needed. In 1888, 315 passengers died in accidents and other mishaps on America's railroads. The men who at one time were George's fiercest competitors, Theodore T. Woodruff and Webster T. Wagner, perished that way, the former in 1892 while riding an express train, the latter in 1882 while trying to cross the tracks near a station in New Jersey. George's sleeping cars always were stronger, heavier, and safer than standard coaches and were the first to standardize state-of-the-art air brakes, safety couplers, and air-exchange systems. Vapor heating eliminated the risk of scalding. Antipinch shields kept fingers from catching between doors and frames, while rounded corners took the sting out of traversing narrow corridors. In 1887 the Pullman Company patented an even more transforming safety device: an elastic-covered passageway called the Sessions Vestibule. It ended death-defying leaps from car to car. Ventilation was enhanced, oscillation diminished. And in the event of a collision, there was less chance the train would telescope or coaches split apart. Those improvements help explain why just 114 passengers were killed aboard U.S. trains in 1929, nearly a threefold drop from the 1880s. Of the 114, just 8 were riding Pullmans, even though the sleeping cars accounted for half of all rail miles that year.

Like most passengers, the poet William Rose Benét was less attracted by a Pullman sleeper's safety than by its aesthetics. "Green aisles of Pullman cars / Soothe me like trees / Woven in old tapestries," he wrote.[63] E. B. White recognized all that could go wrong in the closed quarters of a Pullman berth, but he concluded, "In my eyes it is a perfect thing, perfect in conception and execution, this small green hole in the dark moving night, this soft warren in a hard world."[64]

At their peak, Pullman sleepers accommodated 100,000 people a night, which was more than all the nation's top-notch hotels combined. That meant stocking 4,195,873 towels, 466,362 blankets, and 145,315 jackets for porters. All of which made Conrad Hilton look like a country innkeeper and made the Pullman sleeper, in the words of its most lyrical chroniclers, "an American institution comparable to baseball and Congress."[65] George had achieved his dream: he was, as his company boasted in its ads, the World's Greatest Housekeeper. And it was not just America that reveled in his accomplishments: in twenty languages, Pullman defined luxury, comfort, and safety in travel.[66]

Back home, however, the name Pullman was beginning to spell trouble, at least when it was preceded by George M.

His problems came into clearest focus in his namesake community, which was at least as much of a passion for him as the *Pioneer* had been. George began building the town in 1880, partly for reasons of engineering. Demand was soaring for sleepers, and he resolved to build the biggest railroad factory on Earth to mass-produce them. At least as critical was his fascination with social engineering. George and his fellow fat cats were bullish about their age's economic opportunities, but they knew that the social ills infecting America could spell an end to their enterprises. Population was exploding; Chicago alone nearly doubled in size, to 503,185, during the decade ending in 1890. European immigrants were packed into flimsy tenements, creating breeding grounds for tuberculosis and other fast-spreading diseases. Crime was on the rise, along with prostitution and drunkenness. And the problems did not stay in the ghetto. The Irish maid or Swedish nanny who visited her family over the weekend could carry the seeds of cholera back to the mansion Monday morning, even as her father and brothers, faced with a desperate situation at home and too little pay from the factory, grew bolder in pressing demands and staging strikes.[67]

George was savvier than most in recognizing the threat and responding. He believed that if he created a properly healthy living space for his European craftsmen and local laborers—one without beer gardens or Democrats, grime or labor agitators—his workers would never lose a day to drunkenness or discontent. What he got was the largest model community ever, 3,400 acres that were, in the words of a British visitor, "another of the wonders of the West."[68] A library and theater anchored the Venetian Arcade. Nearby were a grand hotel named after George's beloved Florence, a park with full bandstand, and brick homes laid out on a grid for nine thousand workers at his car-building complex. The architect Solon Beman wanted to name the community after himself, to which George is said to have replied, "We'll take the last half of your name and the first half of mine."[69] And so it was: Pullman, Illinois.

It was a brilliant vision, but like the Tower of Babel, it was built on so many contradictions it had to crumble. Rooting out social ills of the city was a princely goal, except when it required rooting out democracy. George's leases were reminiscent of his rulebook for porters, with tenants required to ask permission for everything from driving a nail into the wall to planting sweet peas in the front yard. The library and theater could have been places for residents to exercise their minds, but the former charged a fee that kept many away and the latter was purged of productions even remotely controversial. Alcohol may well have been a pernicious influence, yet workers wondered why it was okay for George's trains and his lavish Florence Hotel, but not for them. And while he hoped the town would be a safe haven, he owned all the housing and insisted rents be steep enough to guarantee a 6 percent profit. George, whose hair and goatee now were the color of ivory, could not see those conflicts because he never lived in the town, and, with his company so enormous, he no longer had candid conversations with workers.

Things began to fall apart in the depression of 1893, which was precipitated by the overexpansion of the railroad industry. George slashed workers' wages by nearly a third and pared back thousands of jobs, but rents went untouched, as did salaries of managers and dividends to stockholders. Workers were outraged, and in May of 1894 they declared a strike. It started locally but spread across the country as members of the American Railway Union refused to haul Pullman cars. It also started peacefully but ended with brick-throwing mobs overturning freight trains and turning Chicago into a flaming inferno. Calm was eventually restored, but not until twelve people were killed and two thousand federal troops called up, along with four thousand Illinois militia, five thousand deputy marshals, and the entire Chicago police force.

The strike paid big dividends for several of its major actors—helping lift Eugene Debs from obscure railway union leader to Socialist Party boss, Clarence Darrow from Debs's neophyte lawyer to America's most ardent advocate, and Jane Addams from strike investigator to the nation's best-known poverty worker.[70] It made the strike-busting president, Grover Cleveland, a hero, if only for an interlude. But the strikers themselves were big losers. They had to call off the work stoppage without any concessions and were left without jobs. For many, starvation seemed so imminent that the governor of Illinois had to step in.

The walkout did unmask one area of common ground between George M. Pullman and his striking employees: racial bias. In George's case, his town admitted just a handful of Negroes and no Pullman porters. Negroes were hired as waiters at the Florence Hotel, but few if any back then could land a prized job at his Calumet manufacturing or repair facilities. The American Railway Union's record was even worse. It may have been more radical ideologically than the old-line railway brotherhoods from which it broke, but it, too, had a constitution requiring that members be "born of white parents." When it came time to strike, Pullman porters were not enlisted and other Negro workers felt sufficiently spurned that they enthusiastically stepped in as strikebreakers. Debs, who had tried and failed to lower the color bar and wanted to polish his image as a racial healer, later speculated that integrating the ARU would have put Negro railroaders on the side of strikers and upped their odds of prevailing.[71]

George emerged from the strike the apparent victor, but it had damaged him beyond repair. Already alienated from much of his family, he now was isolated from his employees and many of his fellow plutocrats. He suffered a bout of nerves and depression that left him bedridden in September 1894, and the next year survived two would-be murders.*

Worse still was how his handling of the work stoppage smeared his legacy. He had heralded the assembly line and inaugurated mass production that would define American industry for half a century. His model town helped inspire the garden city movement that moved men and industry out of rotting urban centers. Most of all, he was the man who had revolutionized overnight travel. None of that mattered after the strike. He was called a pompous autocrat, industrial tyrant, and modern-day King Lear. Antediluvian, not avant-garde, was how reporters described him now, zeroing in on his passion for profit and ignoring his penchant for paternalism. The very success of his sleeping car enterprise and model town made him higher profile than the rest of the robber barons and an easier target for reformers. Had he lived longer, he might have polished his persona by becoming a benefactor the way John D. Rockefeller did. Instead, he responded to his critics with a blend of disdain and self-righteousness that merely fueled the insults. The master of spin, who

---

*The first incident involved a threat to shoot him by an assistant janitor in the Pullman building, who was apprehended and committed to an insane asylum. In the second, pipe bombs were sent to George and one of his wealthy neighbors. A man who appeared at both homes with a warning about the devices was believed to be the sender and was thought to be looking for a reward. Liston E. Leyendecker, *Palace Car Prince: A Biography of George Mortimer Pullman* (Boulder: University of Colorado Press, 1992), 243–244.

had so carefully crafted the image of his Pullman sleeper, proved totally incapable of salvaging his own image.

On the evening of October 18, 1897, George Mortimer Pullman hosted a dinner at the Chicago Club for the heads of the Pennsylvania Railroad, toasting them with fine wines and Pearl de Montana cigars. It was his last hurrah. The next morning he died of a massive heart attack. At the end the sixty-six-year-old tycoon was not merely confused and embittered but paranoid, perhaps rightfully so. Fearing that disgruntled ex-employees might snatch his corpse, he left instructions to be entombed in a wall of steel and stone. The funeral party waited until the safety of darkness to set off from the Pullman mansion on Prairie Avenue. George's mahogany casket had been lined with lead, and he was lowered into a grave wrapped with tar paper and covered with quick-drying asphalt. Another layer of concrete was added, along with heavy rails laid at right angles. The process took two days, leaving him more secure than the pharaohs of ancient Egypt.[72]

3

"My Name's Not George"

∷

BEING THE MIDDLE anything never is easy, as Garrard David Smock found out during his thirty-five years with the Pullman Company. His father, George Anderson Smock, was the first in the family to enlist as a porter. He jumped in just before George M. Pullman died, at a time when porters had too few job options and too many insecurities to question their life on the sleeping cars. Garrard David's three sons, George Henry, Virgil Orite, and Garrard Wilson, would follow him onto the Pullman rolls. They signed up at a moment when porters felt confident enough not just to raise doubts but to launch the sort of trade union George Pullman had vowed to crush.

Garrard David dove in at half tide, in 1917, when the current was pulling both ways. Porters had been working for the Pullman Company for precisely fifty years and would continue for another half century. Garrard David and his fellow porters were fully aware they had one of the best jobs in the Negro community, putting them on a social par with teachers, funeral directors, and even doctors and lawyers, many of whom worked their way through school as porters and a surprising number of whom came back after graduation for the easy money. Porters owned their own homes and were thought to be catches as husbands. They were racial diplomats, mediating between their all-Negro, mainly poor world and their riders' all-white, mainly middle-class one. That is why Garrard David started schooling his sons young in how to cook in jumbo quantities, count sheets and pillowcases, and perform the hundreds of other domestic duties needed to land a post on a Pullman sleeper. Years later he and his three boys worked together on the *Lark,* Southern Pacific's overnighter between San Francisco and Los Angeles, which made for a family affair singular enough to land them in Ripley's *Believe It or Not.*

But the best of jobs came at a hefty price, even if Garrard David did not share that with his sons until much later. There was the grueling workload of four hundred hours a month, sleeping three hours a night, and spending a month at a time on the road. He earned more than twice what his dad did, but less than half what his boys would. Even more bitter to swallow was the daily humiliation of being called "George." And while he was proud of his father, Garrard David did not want to die like him: keeling over while making down a berth, on a sleeper bound for Albuquerque. The elder Smock remained where his heart had failed him until a passenger, frustrated that his bed still was unmade, tapped George Anderson on the shoulder and realized his body was limp.

Discontent simmered within Garrard David for years but was slow to reach a boil. Porters in the early 1900s were angry but still scared. The Pullman Company was not quite the autocracy it had been under George Pullman. Abraham Lincoln's son Robert Todd was in charge now, and porters were nearly two generations removed from the specter of the plantation that had kept in line old porters like George Anderson Smock. But it would be another generation before they had a brotherhood that let them speak out without fearing for their job, getting them money and benefits in line with their middle-class values and their value to the company.

So Garrard David and his fellow porters learned to live in limbo. They celebrated their standing in the community and accepted their limits on the train. It was okay to oversee a sleeping car when there was no conductor on board, so long as they understood they would not earn a conductor's wages and could not aspire to his job. They could challenge accusations by conductors and inspectors; winning was the hard part. Contradictions became a part of their constitution. Garrard David chafed under the constraints, to the point where he joined embryonic efforts to organize a porters' union. He was fired or suspended more than once. But he always yielded, agreeing to comply with company rules. And he always got back his job.

Given the pulls and tugs he lived with, it is not surprising that Garrard David's dealings with his own children were at times uneven. "My father was strict to a certain extent but yet lenient in another way," recalled his youngest son, Garrard Wilson, known as "Babe." "Now if he'd tell you to do something, you'd do it. Now if he scolds you, he'll give you a whipping. He may give you a whipping, but five minutes later he's down on the floor wrestling with you. Playing with you. See, he's forgotten all about it. He never harbored anything. What is done is done. It's over with."[1]

Babe's brother George remembered how his father tried to shield the three boys from the worst his generation had to endure, especially when they crossed below the Mason-Dixon Line. After George ran into trouble on a trip to El Paso, Garrard David took up the matter with George's supervisor at Pullman. "'I told you never to send one of my kids down South,'" George recalled his father saying. "'He has never had to go through that foolishness, and with that he's gonna fight, and with that he will get put in jail or he'll have something happen to him. So don't ever send one of 'em down there.' Needless to say, the Pullman Company was about to get rid of me, but through the actions of my dad, why, they kept me working."[2]

THE ONLY CHILDREN of Pullman porters who understood what life on a sleeping car was like were those who, like the Smock boys, themselves worked on the sleepers. The rest knew their fathers the way they were at home and in the neighborhood, which was something else entirely. The kids were curious, but it was an unstated pact among porter-dads not to tell, especially early in the new century when things still were rough on the road. It was not wanting to worry the children. It also was being embarrassed by indignities they bore and preferring that their kids see them through the same rose-colored glasses as the rest of the community.

The porter mystique began with how coveted the job was. Simply wearing a starched uniform looked good to workers used to blue jeans and to getting them dirty. Who wouldn't prefer a valise to a lunch bucket? Shining shoes and making beds was not easy, but it looked cushy next to a backbreaking day sweating in the fields or laboring at the factory. And compared to tidying up in hotels, offices, and wealthy homes, which is what a full 50 percent of Negro males did in Chicago in 1910, getting to ride the rails along with their domestic's duties seemed irresistible. Add it up, and porters could rightfully claim theirs was the best blue-collar job open to Negroes.

Runner-up was the U.S. Post Office. "Pullman and Postal" was the standard reply then to queries about the most sought-after jobs for colored men, and that often was the choice facing enterprising Negroes without special skills or a college degree. Arguing for the post office was its government status, which meant civil service protection and insulation from the economic ups and downs that plagued a private firm like Pullman. It also meant being near family and community, and no heavy lifting. It was no panacea for Negroes, however, at least not before World War II. The post office was resegregated under President Woodrow Wilson, who served from 1913 to 1921, with Negroes relegated to separate and lesser facilities for everything from break rooms to restrooms. Virtually no front-office or other desirable jobs were open to them, which left sorting and delivering mail. As for money, postal workers "made more on salary but didn't make as much in tips," recalled Ollis Fellows of Chicago, who worked Postal and Pullman. "And the post office wasn't as glamorous as the railroad was." [3]

Another way to judge a job is by where it leads. Ex-porters had their choice of the best jobs at America's finest hotels and restaurants, which saw their years with Pullman as the equivalent of a Ph.D. in servitorship. Some made it all the way to 1600 Pennsylvania Avenue. The porter J. W. Mays went from serving President William McKinley on his sleeping car to serving him in the White House, where he spent more than four decades opening doors and cutting hair for Presidents McKinley, Theodore Roosevelt, William

Howard Taft, Woodrow Wilson, Warren Harding, Calvin Coolidge, Herbert Hoover, Franklin D. Roosevelt, and Harry S. Truman. The Baltimore & Ohio waiter William Brown ended up a butler in Franklin Roosevelt's White House. After riding on 397 of FDR's 399 Pullman trips, the porter Samuel Mitchell accepted a job as the president's messenger, although he still took charge of the president's car whenever Franklin, Eleanor, or a presidential guest was aboard. Mitchell was grateful for the job Roosevelt gave him but not for his five-dollar tips on weekend trips to and from Hyde Park; he eventually got himself transferred from the president's car to the one carrying reporters, who passed the hat each trip for forty to fifty dollars in tips.[4]

Pullman porters also climbed near the top of the Negro social ladder, to the same rung as head waiters in restaurants and barbers. Porters had dipped their toes in the Pacific and Atlantic, walked the promenades in New York City and Chicago, and traveled to fifty states with Wall Street barons and baseball gods. They were men with stories to tell, and everyone listened. No matter that the Pullman Company sold their services on the basis of their old South obsequiousness. What mattered back home was that many porters owned homes and cars, while most stayed groomed and sober, voted Republican, and were beacons of the church. Their skin remained black, but their tastes grew increasingly white and bourgeois, which in pre–World War I America was a measure of success. They were the aristocrats of Negro labor. Paragons of the community. Paradigms of sophistication. And at a moment when their competitors for those crowns, head waiters and barbers, were being challenged for their jobs by whites, more posts were opening for porters.

"The railroad waiter and Pullman porter tried to live like our passengers. We carried a suit or sports coat with us on the road; some even carried a briefcase with a *Wall Street Journal*," remembered Robert McGoings, a veteran of the B&O dining cars. "I worked in a private dining car once and found out the big boss of the car wore solid-color socks. To today, I wear solid-colored socks, while most men wear ones with some pattern. I used to go to the ball game in a suit; I didn't have any sports clothes. I was a suit-and-necktie man. . . . In the street they would call me an Oreo. I have more white values than the average black man. My likes are more white than they are black."[5]

Samuel Turner worked the dining cars during most of his forty-one years with the railroads, but since he was a teenager he "always wanted to be a sleeping car porter. They had those pretty uniforms on, they made tips, and they had those high-class people riding those sleeping cars, people who had money. All those porters had nice houses, beautiful homes. You were almost considered a doctor."[6]

Doctors and porters joined forces in New Orleans at the turn of the century to form the Illinois Club. The founder was Wally Knight, a Pullman porter from Chicago who was discouraged by how few opportunities there were in New Orleans for young Negroes to learn social etiquette. In 1894 Knight formed a dance school that presented a ball each year during Mardi Gras. The school evolved into a club, and the club became the toast of Negro New Orleans, enlisting physicians, railroad men, and others of stature in the community. While there are no Pullman porters as members today, they remain enshrined in the history of America's oldest African-American carnival club.

It was not just at social events that Pullman porters rubbed elbows with doctors, professors, and other Negro intellectuals and professionals. Thousands of Negroes in college, law and medical school, and other academic programs spent summers working as sleeping car porters and waiters. The salary and tips helped cover tuition and expenses, and they could hit the books while passengers slept. Negro schoolteachers, off for the summer and anxious for extra income, also signed up. The Pullman Company got plenty in return: workers it needed for peak summer travel, who were willing to accept any pay offered and expected the job to end at the end of the season. Although the occasional college kid let the company know that he resented shining and smiling, that was more than offset by being able to offer summer travelers an army of servants appropriately dark-skinned, eloquent in elocution, and lettered. The new recruits could memorize the rulebook in a tick, had no trouble counting linen or money, and let the company claim credit for helping young Negroes pay for college. The list of those who benefited from such temporary work with Pullman or the railroads is long and august, and includes Thurgood Marshall, the first Negro Supreme Court justice; Roy Wilkins, who ran the National Association for the Advancement of Colored People (NAACP) for more than two decades; and Benjamin Elijah Mays, the president of historically Negro Morehouse College in Atlanta.

Marshall, who worked as a dining car waiter on the B&O just after he got married in 1930, earned what he called "the munificent salary of fifty-five dollars a month." Wilkins said his work as a waiter was "grueling," but he added that "it offered me my first sense of the sweep and expanse of the country. For the first time I began to look beyond the comfort and safety of St. Paul to the larger, harder world beyond."[7] Mays, meanwhile, wrote in his autobiography: "Luckily for me, the Pullman Company was coming South each spring to recruit students for summer jobs. If a student was tall enough, strong enough, and had seventeen dollars to buy his cap and uniform, he had work for the summer. The Pullman Company paid the fare to New York and deducted it from the first money the student earned. I jumped at the opportunity to earn my way and to go North for the first time. . . . I spent the summer of 1915 and several more as a Pullman porter, working out of Grand Central Station in New York and South Station in Boston. I did fairly well. Indeed, I felt that I had done extremely well for I was able to return to school in the fall of 1915 all dressed up. I had two suits. Never before had I owned two good suits—or even one!"[8]

Most, like Mays, Wilkins, and Marshall, came and went without regret. Why would anyone on the way to becoming a doctor, lawyer, or teacher even consider a porter's life? Certainly no one would return to the rails *after* earning a diploma, would he? Difficult to fathom, but it happened, often enough to constitute a trend even if no one tracked the numbers.

The evidence came in snippets. In the April 1946 issue of the company newsletter, for example, there was an item about the porter J. H. Costin of Buffalo who doubled as an attorney. And a union official in the early 1940s reported that in his Chicago railway station seventy-two of ninety red-capped black-skinned porters had college degrees. Then there was the Pullman porter Theodore Seldon, who died in a train crash in 1923, and whose body was identified by tracking his Phi Beta Kappa key from Dartmouth's Class of 1922.[9]

"I see a lot of young fellows in there got BA degrees, PhDs, BSs, and glad to be shaking them sheets," said the dining car man Turner.[10] John Baptist Ford, a Pullman porter who delivered three lectures at Dartmouth in 1924, said that of the thousands of medical, law, and other students brought on each summer as porters, "most of the boys go back to school in the Fall, but some stick for a year or so, and some never go back. I know a couple of doctors—brothers—who stayed ten years in the service after they'd taken their degrees. They were saving money all the time. When they'd got enough they set up in practice." Ford himself had been studying to be a minister, although "I'm past that now,"[11] as he told his Dartmouth audience. "The Pullman Company gets the best men of my race. Thirty percent of colored doctors are ex-porters."[12]

Rather than moving him away from the ministry, Jimmy Kearse's time on the train convinced him to study at the seminary on the way to receiving his doctor of divinity degree. And after eighteen years as a dining car waiter, the Reverend Kearse was less willing than Ford to pronounce the professionals who worked alongside him the best of the breed. "We were on the train that goes from Washington to Pittsburgh, overnight train," he said. "This man was a lawyer already admitted to the bar but he made more money as a waiter because he couldn't get cases. So he would wait table[s] and he was standing between the two tables with his tray like this [arm held at ninety degrees and to the side with his tray overhead]. He'd do a little dance, a little shuffle. I went to him and I said, 'Len, why do you get out there and do a little shuffle like that?' He said, 'Well, if I do a little shuffle and act like old man Moz, they're going to give me a fifty-cent tip.' I said, 'I could give less than a damn about a fifty-cent tip. Your integrity means more to me than a fifty-cent tip. Be a man.'"[13]

That unlikely career path from barrister to railroad man was mainly a by-product of the size and structure of the community of Negro professionals in the early 1900s. There were half as many doctors, lawyers, and judges combined as there were Pullman porters, and those few were concentrated in Chicago, New York, and a handful of other urban centers. That meant distressingly little support for physicians and attorneys trying to bend the racial bars of their professions. Worse, with whites hesitant to hire them and most Negroes too poor to pay, wages were meager, especially at the beginning. All of which made their old job on the sleeping car look appealing, at least financially and temporarily. The trade-off was starker for those still in school: going back meant scraping by and running up debt, assuming they could get a loan; staying ensured a stream of paychecks and tips, and the rationalization that they were deferring, not deflecting, career dreams.

To young Negroes looking on, the message was double-edged. They might wonder about the point of getting a professional degree, or even a baccalaureate, if the result would be an unskilled job like Pullman porter. Or they might conclude that portering promised full pockets and fast adventures, a life so alluring that it won over even doctors and lawyers.

Either way, porters drew fellow Negroes into the railroad life and, with more sweeping consequences, helped fuel the Great Migration in which nearly 500,000 southern Negroes moved to the North between 1915 and 1919. Another million followed over the next decade. Those floods recast the agrarian economy in the South, which in 1915 was still home to 85 percent of America's Negroes. It reshaped cities like New York, Detroit, and, most of all, Chicago, which saw its Negro population swell by nearly 70,000 from 1916 to 1919. If the migration was, as historians say, the Flight from Egypt, then the Pullman porter was Moses. Most porters came from the South, knew firsthand the opportunities in places like Chicago, and wrote letters home hailing the higher wages and improved circumstances. Even better, they carried stories back. They talked about the Windy City as God's Country. They described homes purchased in swank neighborhoods like Morgan Park. Their very vestments, diction, and polish suggested a world of opportunities unimaginable to a Negro sharecropper near Montgomery or a mill worker in Atlanta.[14]

The porter's potency as proselytizer was magnified by the *Chicago Defender*. By World War I it was the largest-selling Negro newspaper in the United States, and the most effective champion for Chicago and the North generally. In the *Defender*'s pages Negroes were transformed into "race men." Lynchings were splayed across page one with all the bloody particulars, and southern whites became princes of darkness. In case anyone missed its signal to leave, the paper carried ads for jobs up North and stories on "migration fever." But its founder and editor, Robert Abbott, knew that for his message to reach a southern audience he needed the right messengers. He found them in Pullman porters. They were emblems of the "New Negro" Abbott was trumpeting, so who better to deliver his papers across the South? He offered porters money and courted them. Porter gossip appeared in a regular *Defender* column called "Sparks from the Rail." Their struggles for higher wages were documented in news stories. They were enlisted as news gatherers and converts to the cause.

The wooing worked. Porters gathered bundles of *Defenders* before each trip, stored them in their lockers, then left them with contacts along the route. From there they made their way to barbershops, churches, and individual subscribers in cities and hamlets across the South. White businessmen and farmers tried to disrupt the network, recognizing the threat it posed to their supply of cheap colored labor; Negroes responded by folding newspapers into groceries and other wares as copies were stealthily passed from reader to reader. By 1920 the *Defender* had a paid circulation of about 230,000, two-thirds of it outside of Chicago.[15]

The *Defender* was not the only journal that porters read or distributed. They picked up the *New York Times* and *New York Herald Tribune,* the *Wall Street Journal, Saturday Evening Post,* and dozens of other newspapers and magazines. Not off the newsstand but from seats and beds in sleeping, parlor, and dining cars. Passengers left the publications, thinking porters would collect them as trash. They were right about collecting, but not for the ash can. Porters read the papers at night, during stopovers, and at home. Their jobs and lives meant endless time waiting; many used it to peruse periodicals. And books, which riders also left. It was easy and electrifying for those who already were proficient readers, good training for ones still learning.

Staying informed like that was one more habit picked up from well-heeled, well-read passengers, along with following the stock market and learning to dress conservatively. It all happened beyond the gaze and the interest of those riders, and it changed porters' outlook on the world. "When you travel and come in contact with people, you just broaden yourself," Harold Reddick, an eighty-seven-year-old ex-porter and son of a porter, said as he bent back in a maroon easy chair, stroking his hairless pate and thinking about his thirty-seven years on the sleepers. "I used to bring those papers home off the train out of New York, and it'd be a couple days before that news would be in our Tampa papers. You never can tell what influence and experience you have reading different newspapers. You travel on that train and pick up a *Boston Globe, New York Times, Jacksonville Journal.* Put all that together, and it makes you know more than the average person who has been nowhere. Some of us porters had sense enough to do that.

"His teacher used to ask my son, 'How did you know so much?' My son could identify things because as a Pullman porter, I came into the passenger's refuse."[16]

Oftentimes there was no one at home to bring the publications to, or the porter had been out so long the news would have been stale. So he collected the newspapers, ones catering to whites and Negroes, and left them at coloreds-only cafés and boardinghouses. Or rolled

them up, bound them with string, and tossed them to people standing along the track. They were generally Negroes in remote areas
with no access to newspapers or books. The drops happened often
enough that they knew when and where to wait. Their very anticipation added to the mystique of the Pullman men.

"Sometimes the brakeman would tell you he's got family down
here, and you'd give them the papers. People were living close to the
tracks. They'd pick them up later or get them right away," recalled
Virgil Smock, the middle of the three brothers. "One time I had my
papers all wrapped up. We'd just left Tucson and were having
breakfast, and I got up to throw my papers off to a friend. All the
guys were laughing at me. There was a scarecrow in that field, and I
thought I'd been throwing them to someone."[17] Babe, Virgil's white-
haired younger brother, liked to toss his to hobos. "I'd have a bunch
of papers all wrapped up. I'd thrown them out the window, and
they'd wave at you. It was a hobo spot. Those guys ran freight
trains, and when they stopped at a junction a bunch would get off.
They'd have dinner there, wait for the next freight train to come by,
and hop it to go to the next town."[18]

As much as they influenced the wider world, porters' most lasting
impact was on the wives and kids waiting for them after every trip.
It never is easy to have your father away, but even the most itinerant
salesman was home more often than the typical Pullman porter. For
his wife, that meant dealing solo with the children's homework and
discipline. She stretched household budgets to conform to the modest income most porters received back then, and when that was not
enough, she found work as a housecleaner or babysitter. To be a
porter's daughter or son meant having a single parent much of the
time and getting used to Dad spending much of his time at home
catching up on sleep. When they were not sleeping, many porters
had a second job to attend to—from driving a taxi to selling auto-
mobiles at night, the only time many dealerships opened to Negroes.
Or they escaped to the local pool hall or Pullman's club. That meant
even less time with the family, and sometimes created big problems.

"As long as I brought money home, it didn't affect us at all. Not my family. I know it had an adverse affect on many families," said Jimmy Kearse, the minister and former dining car waiter. "Some husbands found that their wives were a little less than true to them. One man who had just started on the railroad got on in Washington. He'd been working, maybe, two months. Got on the train in Washington on his way to Chicago. The waiters would kid him. We'd kid each other. One of the things, if your apron would fall off, we would say that some man is with your wife. So this time this guy was a third cook and his apron fell off before he got to Martinsburg. We teased him. Just teasing, that's all; just talking. That boy got off the train in Cumberland, went back home, and sure enough, he found his wife in the embrace of another man.

"But they used to tease me a lot. When my children were born, [my fellow waiter] William Wilson said, 'Jimmy, I understand Louise is pregnant.' I said, 'Yeah, she's pregnant.' He said, 'Now, Jimmy, let me tell you what the first thing you got to do. You got to find out who the daddy is.' They said things like that. If I had gotten mad and said, 'Well, let's fight,' what would that have done? Not a thing. So I laughed with them and they stopped teasing me."[19]

Whatever the reality, porters kept their reputation as ideal catches as husbands. They learned on the train to whip up everything from an Illinois sandwich (brisket and smoked liver sausage on rye, with mayo and Gravy Master seasoning) to "the prettiest French toast in the world" (fried in grease, then baked), and brought home the recipes along with a willingness to use them. They knew how to make beds quicker and firmer than anyone else, keep dust at bay, and do other domestic duties that made them appreciate their wives' work and sometimes lend a hand. Their credit was topflight even when salaries were not, and over time wages went up. As for their children, the best affirmation of their esteem for their fathers was how many followed them into the sleeping car business. And the most precious inheritance those fathers could pass on was a job with the Pullman Company.

The job of Pullman porter "was handed down from generation to generation," said Babe Smock, whose own family made his point.

"The father worked for it, the grandfather was working for it, the children all worked for it. It was like on the plantations."[20]

CONDITIONS ON THE sleeper also had a lot in common with the plantation, and in some ways were worse.

Start with the endless hours. A porter's work month ran as long as four hundred hours during the first half century of the Pullman Company, when schedules were relentless, monthly wages were independent of hours or miles accrued, and few porters dared complain. While all work on the road involves long hours, a porter's four hundred translated into thirteen hours a day, every day of the week. There were breaks when he was home, and an occasional unpaid vacation, but most of his life was spent working at a pace his chattel grandparents would have found exhausting.

Things began getting better during World War I, when the U.S. government temporarily took over the trains. But although a conductor's work month was reduced to 240 hours, no comparable limit was set for the porter. In 1926 porters were still working an average of 343 hours a month; as late as 1934 their work month was 317 hours, twice that of the average manufacturing worker, according to studies commissioned by the porters' union and conducted by respected economists. It was not until 1937 that porters secured the 240-hour ceiling that conductors had won eighteen years earlier.[21]

To a spiritual man like the former porter Charles Frederick Anderson, a schedule like that seemed an affront to his Lord. He often worked forty-eight straight hours and sometimes sixty, Anderson wrote in 1904, doing without the slumbering that "an all-wise Creator intended that man, as well as the rest of His creatures, should do."[22] Robert E. Turner recalled how his family was affected by a trip in 1920 that kept him on the road for three months and nine days. When he finally got home, his wife was delighted to see him, if only because "neighbors had begun to think that I had deserted her. . . . My appearance on the scene stopped all further gossip."[23] For Happy Davis, such grueling itineraries ruled out any carousing during stopovers: "At the end of my route I was so damn tired I just went to bed."[24]

Sleep, or lack of it, became a fixation for Pullman porters. As early as 1888, the Pullman Company rulebook provided assurance that porters would "be off duty, for the purpose of sleeping, from 10 p.m. until 3 a.m." Nice idea, but later in the same paragraph the rules made clear that the porter had to be available at each food stop, as well as at "important stations."[25] He also had to keep the heater stoked all night, shine the shoes of passengers and the conductor, and answer the bell anytime a rider rang. He had to hope the smoking room was quiet enough to let him sleep, and that the porter on the adjoining car had time to cover for him while he tried to get some shut-eye.

Several subsequent editions of the rulebook dropped any reference to specific hours, or even total time, that porters could sleep. In 1929, at the urging of porters and maids, the company again set a goal, albeit a more modest one: "approximately" three hours a night. And those came with a caveat: that porters sleep only "where the train schedule at station stops and other operating conditions will, in the judgment of management, permit." A 1937 Pullman Company memo reviewing historic policies on porters and sleeping conveniently forgot the 1888 five-hour rule, concluding that the 1929 version "is the only rule we have ever had concerning sleep or rest for porters while enroute."[26]

Whatever the rules said, in the early years porters seldom got even three uninterrupted hours of sleep. The results were a bit better later, as suggested by a 1927 survey of 777 porters: 57 percent said they slept three hours a night, 23 percent got more, 4 percent less, while 16 percent generally did not sleep at all on the sleeper.[27] Many retired porters say they slept every other night and catnapped when and where they could. If they were lucky enough to get a berth, it was over the wheels or watercooler, where the ride was rough. Sometimes two porters had to use the same berth, which they dubbed a *hot bed;* each set his bell cord so that while he was dozing the other porter could respond to his passengers.

"That's the way I still sleep now, for just four hours. I don't get back to sleep after three or four o'clock," said Lester Arnold of Atlanta, whose thick biceps would have been a big help during thirty-seven years pulling down Pullman berths. "But I found you could nap all during the day between stops. I could sit up and nap. I'd wake up every ten to fifteen minutes and check my watch."[28] Leroy Parchman recalled a fellow porter who "would get down on his knees in the smoking room and sleep. This conductor, who was very religious, would come by and say, 'Oh well, he's saying his prayers,' and leave him alone."[29]

Long hours and short sleep might have been bearable if the pay were ample or even adequate. It was miserly. The salary for a Pullman porter in 1879 was $10 a month. It rose over the years, first gradually, then more steeply—with the average monthly wage reaching $30 by 1897, $40 in 1916, and $81.75 by 1924. In the first years everyone was paid the same, but gradations crept in, with more money going to porters on parlor, tourist, and private cars. Government takeover of the railroads during World War I helped boost wages, and in 1920 the company added a second set of steps, paying more to porters with more seniority.

One way to measure those salaries is comparing them to other Pullman workers, the way the U.S. Railroad Administration did. It found that the average monthly pay for all porters was $34.09 in 1915. That made them the lowest-paid of the operating staff. Conductors' average of $94.09 a month was nearly three times as much. Barbers got almost double. Car cleaners earned $49.70. Even messengers made more, at $36.46. As for senior officers, they averaged $819.82 per month, twenty-four times more than the porter they said was critical to the success of their sleeping cars.[30]

It was conductors with whom porters compared themselves most often, since they worked shoulder to shoulder. A conductor deserved more, the company explained, because he had all the responsibilities that came with overseeing a car and supervising a staff of porters. That explanation fell flat when the porter was put in control. Even though he seldom supervised anyone, a *porter-in-charge* was the ultimate authority in that car, collecting tickets and assigning berths the way a conductor would have, as well as doing his own dirty work as porter. His pay for that extra duty: ten to fifteen dollars a month more than a normal porter's salary, and barely half a conductor's. The Pullman Company regularly assigned porters to such in-charge duties on a single car, although it resisted giving them the two or more cars a conductor would oversee, because in that case the conductors' union required they be paid the minimum conductor's wage. As for getting the title along with the duties of a conductor, a porter's ebony skin ruled that out.

That is one in a series of contrivances George Pullman and his successors created to steal from porters. Another was not to pay for time getting ready for and receiving passengers, or for counting linen and other tasks once they arrived, which together accounted for more than 10 percent of a porter's hours at work. Time lost due to late departures and arrivals was the porter's problem, not the company's. Same for time spent at the office, answering an inspector's charges or checking schedules. As for *doubling out,* when a porter was ordered out on another sleeper just after arriving, the rate of pay was lower and opportunity for rest rare. Some rules began to be loosened during the federal takeover of the railroads during World War I. A monthly mileage limit was established and overtime paid for longer trips, but those bars were set so high that it was unusual for a porter to earn even the modest extra pay the company offered.

Pity the porter injured during one of the seemingly incessant crashes in the early years of train travel. The Pullman Company required him to sign a contract waiving any claim to damages. Joshua Diffendaffer, a porter permanently crippled during a collision in 1900 near East Buffalo, New York, sued to overturn that contract and was promised five thousand dollars by a lower court. But in 1903 the U.S. Court of Appeals held the contract valid and sent Diffendaffer home empty-handed.[31]

Porters did get some things for free, like lodging, but only in certain cities and in the Pullman Company's questionable quarters. They could earn bonuses, but that took a near-perfect record. Meals were half price, but at dining car rates that still could eat up a day's wages, which is why most porters ate just twice a day and, when they could, brought food from home. The company paid for a porter's white jackets, but he had to put in ten years before it would spring for the two required dress uniforms of blue jacket and pants.

That was just the beginning of the tally of what a porter had to pay. Shoe polish was his responsibility, along with brushes and rags to apply it. He needed pencils, indelible preferred. Uniforms must be dry-cleaned, on his tab. And they must be bought from Marshall Field, the Chicago department store whose founder was a large Pullman stockholder and whose price, in 1915 dollars, was $17.75 for a summer uniform and a dollar more for the heavier winter variety, the equivalent of two weeks' pay. A porter's biggest expense was a by-product of sticky-fingered passengers. They stole towels, blankets and pillows, combs and brushes, ashtrays, and, most of all, linen. Hundreds of thousands of dollars of linen went missing each year, and the porter was held responsible. Pullman officials insisted they were passing on only a portion of charges, but many men saw one dollar a week deducted from paychecks that averaged less than eight dollars a week.

"I remember one time I was a penny short in fares collected. They called me downtown," said Leroy Parchman, who had to pay for the trolley to Pullman offices and go on his own time. Virgil Smock recalled: "[My passengers] would take a coffee creamer, and they would take silverware. You'd tell the conductor and point the fella out. We had to pay for that stuff if we didn't account for it."[32]

The only way porters could hope to pay those expenses and have anything left was by soliciting tips. The company counted on that, which is why it paid its highest wages to porters on cars like parlors and tourists, where it knew tips were stingiest, and paid least on lucrative sleepers between cities like Chicago and New York. Tips saved the company an estimated $2.5 million a year in the early 1900s.[33] Those savings continued after retirement, as did losses to porters, because low wages translated into one of the most miserly pensions awarded any railroader.

An even more compelling motivation for the Pullman Company to build tipping into its pay structure was to ensure that porters were attentive to passengers' every whim. The California Railroad Commission found that approach—and the company's denial of it—unconscionable. "The Pullman Company deliberately attempts to pay the employees which it hires from the gratuities given by the public," the watchdog agency wrote in a 1914 decision. "It is hard for us to determine which should be criticized the more, the attitude of this company in its action in this regard, or its supposition that it could make this Commission believe a thing which every one knows is not true, and which any man with ordinary common sense knows is not true." The panel ordered the company "at once to see to it that a condition is brought about whereby its employees are not required to live off the public."[34] The company said nothing and did nothing.

Were the tips that incensed the commission sufficient, together with a porter's meager wages, to live? Not according to the Labor Bureau, a New York research group that in 1926 surveyed hundreds of porters who said they had earned an average of $698 a year in tips. Add in wages, subtract unreimbursed work expenses like uniforms and hotels, and they were left with $1,230—$298 less than the minimum the U.S. Bureau of Labor Statistics said a family of five needed.[35] Seven years later Professor Edward Berman, chairman of the Economics Department at the University of Illinois, did another survey. Tips, he found, had tumbled to $237, or almost exactly what a porter faced in work-related expenses. That meant living just off wages, which averaged $880—$309 less than the Bureau of Labor Statistics minimum for that year. Berman's conclusion: "The Pullman porter is one of the worst-exploited workers in the country."[36]

Berman and the Labor Bureau were both hired by an interested party, the nascent porters' union, but few contested their evidence. No one could accuse Robert Todd Lincoln of sharing any such predisposition in favor of the Pullman porter. Lincoln succeeded George M. Pullman as president of the Pullman Company and served in that role until 1911. Four years later, as chairman of the Pullman board of directors, Lincoln testified before a congressional commission looking into the conditions of workers at Pullman and other industrial firms. Asked by the commission chairman whether $27.50 a month was enough for a porter to support his family "in comfort and decency," Lincoln did not hesitate: "Absolutely not. I want to say that situation annoys me very much indeed." A short time later the former president's son hedged: "If you increase their wages without in some way stopping their tips, you simply make a larger income for them, and the question is whether that is desirable to do." Finally, asked directly whether porters deserve higher wages, Lincoln said, "I think there ought to be a change in our system." "In that direction?" a commissioner persisted. "Yes, sir," Lincoln answered.[37]

In 1938, a dozen years after Lincoln's death, company officials were preparing material for the media on salaries paid porters during the period Lincoln referred to his testimony. In a cover memo, a senior official warned: "Citation of actual rates paid porters would of necessity show a rather low rate existing in 1913, which unquestionably would not make good publicity for the Company. I suggest in considering broadcasting material we avoid mention of any specific rates." Duly noted, and done. The rest of the document was bereft of potentially embarrassing figures but filled with the sort of self-justification and congratulation that would have made George Pullman proud.[38]

How, then, could so many Pullman porters have owned their homes and cars, and seemed like men of wealth if not leisure? Some had choice routes, with tips considerably higher than average and salaries pumped up by their years on the job. Others lived beyond their means or looked wealthier than they were in those preunion years. The rest relied for extra income on extra jobs, theirs or their wives'. A porter's salary also has to be seen in the context not of the general society back then but of the Negro community, where wages were universally low and it was easy to look rich by comparison. As for the perception that porters were as solidly middle class as anyone with black skin, that was true even when their modest wages seemed to belie it. Porters believed in higher education before they had the money to procure it for their children, and embraced the gospel of economic mobility in an era when it seemed forever beyond their grasp. The American dream was as palpable to them as to the passengers they saw living it every day, which made having to defer it all the more tormenting.

Low wages were just one of the humiliations porters silently suffered, although they were the easiest to quantify. Another was being asked to bark like a dog or let a young boy ride him like a horse. Customers wanted porters to entertain them or their children, which is not surprising given that they already played roles ranging from doctor to nursemaid. The company unveiled its own vision of porter as showman in 1922 when it hired Major N. Clark Smith, the old music director of the Tuskegee Institute, to launch eight porter choruses across the country. Each would have at least fifty singers, would entertain on and off the train, and would capitalize, as one Pullman official noted, on Negroes being "a singing race."[39] The head of their union would later characterize those porter-crooners as "the monkeys of the service."[40]

Harold Reddick found the idea of porters doubling as entertainers ludicrous: "Passengers asked you to tell jokes or act like a fool to entertain them. I said I can't sing, neither can I dance."[41] In Eugene E. Bowser's case they went farther. "Sometimes I'd be cleaning my club car and they'd say, 'Hey boy, why don't you tell us some nigger jokes,'" he remembered. "'Come up here and let us rub your head.'"[42]

Even more annoying was repeatedly being addressed as "boy." Reddick would shoot back, "Don't call me 'boy.' My mommy and daddy named me Harold."[43] "Nigger" was used so often on Pullman cars that porters were convinced passengers must not have known or cared how much it wounded. Jimmy Kearse recalled waiting on a drunk passenger during a run from Chicago to Washington: "He said to me, 'You know, you look just like that nigger that I met in Cincinnati.' He said, 'Are you that nigger?' I said, 'No sir, I'm not that nigger.' Then when I finished serving and he got ready to go, he said, 'You're a nice nigger.' And I said, 'Thank you.' He said, 'I want to give you ten dollars.' I said, 'I'm happy to wait on you, sir, but I will not take your ten dollars until you get a better attitude.' That man apologized, with tears really. He was serious, and said, 'Please take it.' I did, but only after he apologized."[44]

"Uncle" was another favorite indignity, especially among older riders. Then there were "Sam" and "Joe" for porters named neither. While they learned to absorb the insults, porters delighted when circumstances let them strike back. "One night a man in the whiskey car got so high that the bartender told me he needed to go back to his room," said the retired porter John Thomas Harrison, who grew up on a farm in Mississippi with parents who had been slaves. "The man said to me, 'Don't tell me what to do, peckerwood. Ain't no nigger putting me to bed.' I didn't fly off. I got him back to his bed, put him in bed, took his clothes off, and put him to sleep. He had a lot of sour whiskey on his breath, and he spit up a whole lot. I landed him one in the face. I beat up his lip and hit him all in the face and mouth. The next morning he got up and said, 'What happened last night? I feel like a truck ran over me.' I made a good customer out of him, and he never did know what hit him."[45]

Names had always been a preoccupation for porters, probably because passengers seldom knew or used theirs. Porters had their own expression for indignities like "boy" and "nigger": being *called out of one's name.* They had their own pet names for one another (from "Sweet Lips" to "Sandwich Red"), for passengers ("Mr. and Mrs. Home," "Mr. Eddie and Miss Ann"), and for conductors ("Mitchell the Czar" and "Mussolini of the Pullman Company"). And they had a way of deflecting the brickbats: only tell passengers and even other porters your initials, never a first name. Being called by your Christian name seemed childlike and far too familiar; safer not to have a first name. For some, it was another way of mimicking wealthy white passengers. "J. P." was good enough for Mr. Morgan the financier, why not for Mr. Morgan the Pullman porter? Most of all, initials were a backlash to being addressed by that most defamatory and habitual forename: "George."

"George" was used so often that naive riders thought it was a preferred nickname. It inspired endless commentary in newspapers, including a 1918 column in the *New York Tribune* by Opie Read suggesting that, with Uncle Sam's wartime takeover of the railroads, porters henceforth "be addressed not as George, but as Sam."[46] A 1949 story in Iowa's *Clinton Herald* chronicled George W. Dulany Jr.'s founding of the Society for the Prevention of Calling Sleeping Car Porters George, and his recent recruitment of a duo of remarkable Rumanians: Prince George Brancoveanu and Minister of Agriculture George Jonescu Sisesti. "We are glad to welcome these distinguished Rumanians to our fold," said Dulany, a lumber executive. "George Washington, our patron saint, always warned against entangling alliances, but our lofty ideals transcend internationalism."[47]

Being called "George" was no laughing matter for George Mortimer Pullman, whose first name had been borrowed, in the manner of the plantation, as moniker for his Negro porters. He was too solemn to permit workers to address him directly at all, or to encourage even his managers to call him by his given name. That, as his biographer writes, "was a privilege he accorded only to members of his family."[48]

As for his porters and waiters, most winced when they heard "George." Not responding was grounds for dismissal. Answering meant admitting they had no name of their own, no identity as an individual. It was like drip torture, it happened so unrelentingly, and each porter developed his own way to cope. "I just plain ignored it," said Babe Smock.[49] His brother Virgil joked, "They can call me anything they want to call me just so long as they call me to dinner."[50] Robert McGoings had turned the other cheek one time too many. "I got a one-man car and I'm behind the booth and a crowd of soldiers got on at Cambridge, Ohio, on Christmas Eve in 1943," he remembered. "They're noisy; they were going home. I had on the counter my display of candy, and when I came back one said, 'George, God all mighty, where have you been?' I said, 'If you want somebody called "George," you make the baby and call it "George."' He said, 'You don't like it?' I said, 'No, I don't like it.' He grabbed a plate from my display and threw it at me. He left a gash that I still have and broke my eyeglasses. I had a knife for making sandwiches, and I threw it at him. It didn't hit him, but it got him away from the empty bottle he was reaching for.

"Later the railroad held a hearing, and the manager wanted to know what was so bad about being called 'George.' I said, 'It's synonymous with "nigger,"' and he said, 'Oh.'"[51]

The slur of "nigger" vanished from Pullman cars quicker than "George." The former was more clearly recognized as an affront, as McGoings found with his bosses, and was attacked by Negroes in all occupations along with fair-minded whites. The latter, by contrast, was making its way off the sleeper and was used to address Negroes in restaurants, on shoe shine stands, and in other service professions. On the train, "George" stuck even after 1926, when the Pullman Company tried to root it out by inserting cards with the porter's name on each car. Why not call porters "George" when the entire backdrop of their profession, from shining shoes to playing for tips, seemed built on a foundation of slavery? When George Pullman himself had plucked his first porters from the cotton patches and fed them the social cake of servitude? When, as the NAACP chief Wilkins recalled of his days on a Pullman diner, "we worked like house slaves on roller skates"?[52]

William Howard Brown, a porter for fifteen years, attributed the persistence of name-calling and other affronts to the fact that "there were no shortage of racists working for the Pullman Company. They wanted to keep your mind in a derogatory state all the time; they were demeaning all the time. You never were addressed by the Pullman Company as a 100-percent man. You never were addressed as mister. The company wasn't built that way."[53]

THE YEAR WAS 1917, and something momentous was happening to Pullman porters and the nation they traversed. The United States was about to jump into the Great War, and the Pullman Company was helping muster the troops. Its ambassadors of hospitality by then were more than two generations removed from slavery, long enough to feel freer from its psychic echoes. A country going to war was so desperate for men to serve, and to man factories at home, that it was bending old rules on race. The result was that Negroes had options, at work and beyond, not there a generation before, or even a year. Porters like Garrard David Smock, who joined the Pullman ranks that very year as a part-timer out of Los Angeles, were beginning to believe they were 100 percent men. And for the first time they asked to be treated as such.

Porters also had a new take on their employer. Most still were grateful for their jobs and as obliging as ever. But every time they boarded the train they could savor just how good times were for the Pullman Company. More and more railroads were running "all-Pullmans," engines pulling just sleeping, parlor, dining, lounge, and observation cars, all built and run by Pullman. The finest of the breed were name trains like the *Twentieth Century Limited,* launched in 1902 and featuring, along with its berths and meals, a barber, valet, stenographer, ladies' maid, and train secretary who had memorized the name of every passenger. A three-hundred-foot crimson carpet embossed with the train's name was laid out for each boarding at Grand Central Station, and newly installed hundred-pound rails made it possible to reach Chicago in the then-remarkable time of twenty hours. While the *Century* set the standard, other name trains measured up, from the *Broadway Limited* to the *Royal Blue* and *Black Diamond.*

"Where trains were composed of both coaches and Pullmans the occupants of the former were strictly interdicted from intruding upon the diners and club cars of the preferred patrons," explained Lucius Beebe, whose writing celebrated that golden age of steam transport. "To go Pullman was a way of American life. Even the socially elect hoboes and drifters bragged that they rode the brake gear and unguarded open platforms of nineteenth-century Pullman equipment, while more humble and less dexterous stiffs rode the slower freights, which they in turn designated side-door Pullmans."[54]

For those who wanted still more, and could afford purchase prices up to $500,000, there were private Pullman carriages. Railroads bought them for their top executives. Henry Ford had his own and named it *Fair Lane,* after his country estate. Jay Gould had one, too, as did Charles M. Schwab, Mrs. Henry Flagler, John and Mary

Ringling, and the legendary racehorse Seabiscuit, who stretched out in a specially modified eighty-foot car cushioned with the finest straw. Marble bathtubs were a staple on private coaches, as were gold-filled plumbing, cedar wardrobes, and jewel safes. "Swimming pools," Beebe wrote, "were for successful greengrocers and electrical contractors. Palm Beach and charge accounts at Cartier were for well-placed stockbrokers. The private Pullman, its dark green varnish and brass-railed observation platform headed for Florida or Del Monte or the Adirondacks, was for grand seigneurs and the feudal overlords of the American economy. Each lent a dimension of magnificence to the other."[55]

Its dominance of the market for such magnificence, as well as for more mundane sleeping car services, translated into unprecedented profits for the Pullman Company. Investigations by the Interstate Commerce Commission and the press laid bare the facts. The $100,000 in cash that George Pullman used to launch his first sleeping cars in the 1860s had, forty years later, mushroomed to 4,700 cars worth $80 million. The company was earning 500 percent a year on its investments. It exercised a virtual monopoly: only four railroads still ran their own sleepers, with the rest renting from Pullman. Its reach extended not just across the United States but across Canada and Mexico, and profits came not just from operating sleepers but from building them.[56]

Those successes meant a bonanza for stockholders. They earned $187,880,000 in cash dividends and stock value from 1898 to 1910—enough for the *Chicago Daily Tribune* to dub Pullman "the richest of corporate melon patches." Even during the strike of 1894, when George cut wages without reducing rents, not a single dividend was delayed and the company continued to sit on $25 million in undivided profits. Not surprising, perhaps, since stockholder interests were shepherded by a board that included America's first families of pelf: the Morgans and Vanderbilts, Mellons, Fields, and Sloans.[57]

The implication of such fantastic profits, the Interstate Commerce Commission said in 1910, was that the Pullman Company had to be bilking the public and should lower its berth fees. Journalists and historians have offered up more poetic ways of seeing how plethoric Pullman's profits were, and how tightly it held on to them. Parlor cars on the popular New York–to–Philadelphia route were 200 percent more remunerative than a suite of equal size at the Ritz-Carlton. Pullman conductors got one hundred dollars a month less than those on the railroads, while its office workers were among the lowest-salaried in America. Yet of all its workers, porters were squeezed hardest. They comprised 44 percent of the Pullman operating division's workforce yet received only 27 percent of its payroll. In the end, the labor historian Greg LeRoy concluded, they were the "largest, cheapest, most profitable craft group, by far the most important contributing group to Pullman's monopolistic triumph."[58]

Porters did not know all those details, but they read newspapers left on train seats and tracked the Pullman Company's finances enough to know it was flourishing while they were struggling. They remembered repeatedly standing alongside management during labor strife, most recently when car cleaners went on strike in 1916. They watched as conductors prepared to launch a union, and as their brother porters in Canada did the same. Now it was their turn.

The first hint of their impatience had turned up a generation earlier. In 1890 there was a threat to strike by porters calling themselves the Charles Sumner Association. Drawing inspiration from the deceased archabolitionist senator from Massachusetts, they asked for higher wages, then backed down in the face of a threat to hire white replacements. In 1897 porters rallied again, this time against a rule ordering conductors rather than porters to collect payments for food, which imperiled a time-tested route to tips. Porters in eastern cities came up with their own scheme for increasing earnings: draw up a list of passengers who decline to tip, then decline to serve them. Though short-lived, those movements suggested porters were on a shorter fuse than their bosses and riders realized.[59]

There was more ferment in 1901, this time in St. Louis, which had more porters than anywhere but Chicago and New York. A group claiming to represent Pullman porters nationwide, identified only as the "Committee," got its appeal for higher salaries and reduced hours published on page one of the *St. Louis Post-Dispatch*. Current pay, the porters wrote, "is not enough to support a boy." Current job insecurity is such that "the average porter goes out thinking every trip may be his last." Even as it printed the pitch, the Pulitzer family's newspaper suggested its contempt by running on page one its own ode to porters. "But now with humble looks and meek, Commisera-tion doth he seek," the poem read in part. "From those who, lately in his care, He spurned with autocratic stare, And begs them wait a bit, till he, Can get a raise of salaree."[60]

Perhaps wary of how a newspaper might twist his words, or add its own, the former porter Charles Frederick Anderson self-published his call to action in 1904. The Pullman Company was forcing porters to work double the hours of other train staff for half the pay, he wrote, and the fastest route to redress was to join his Pullman Car Porter's Brotherhood. Anderson's book cost twenty-five cents and covered forty-six pages, although the title told it all: *Freemen Yet Slaves Under "Abe" Lincoln's Son*. "If you do not lend a helping hand by co-operating with those already interested in your personal welfare, and at least try to help yourselves, you certainly will not deserve the sympathy or support of either the press or traveling pub-lic in any attempt you may make hereafter," intoned this porter-turned-agitator. "So, DON'T BE A DRONE, but come along and help us."[61]

A national spotlight on their cities was the common denominator in two other bids for change during that first decade of the new cen-tury. The first came in 1904 back in St. Louis, which at the time was hosting the Olympics along with the World's Fair. The Pullman Company was so busy, it sent one porter on three back-to-back runs with no rest. He nodded off, a conductor reported him, and he was fired. Eleven of the porter's colleagues met with the Pullman super-intendent to talk things over, but the talking did not last long: all eleven were sacked.[62] Five years later, porters in Seattle spoke out when their city was the site of the Yukon Exposition. Twenty or so secretly drew up bylaws for an organization, but it dissolved when the exposition closed and Pullman discontinued the Seattle service that had brought the men together.

Each new gambit showed how determined porters were, and how many obstacles they faced. That they were on their own was clear from the start. Few all-white unions wielded as much power, or were as antagonistic to Negroes, as the railroad brotherhoods, which were waging a violent campaign to force Negro firemen off the trains. Thanks in part to such racism, porters did not trust unions and were skeptical about any attempts to unionize them. And lest there be any doubt about how the Pullman Company felt, the calamitous strike of 1894 made clear there was nothing George and his successors hated more than workers demanding anything.

So porters tread softly, and avoided the dreaded *u* word. "We don't mean to have an organization of that nature, but rather, an organization to create business and positions among ourselves, which will lessen the percentage of humiliation and brutality on the part of our boys," the porter Frederick E. Edmunds wrote to Booker T. Washington in 1914, as he explained his dream of an industrial association of Pullman porters. "Two or three good men and myself got together and suggested this proposition, if carried through, to be one of the direct met[h]ods in the solution to the great problem which confronts seven thousand men today." Washington, who preached a don't-rock-the-boat doctrine of Negro advancement, applauded the idea, saying it "would greatly help in maintaining a higher standard of efficiency, not only as employees but as men." It ended up going nowhere and helping nobody.[63]

The broadest-based bid to stand up to the Pullman Company was launched by Robert L. Mays, a dining car waiter who chaired the Railway Men's International Benevolent Industrial Association. It was founded in 1915 as a fraternal group and cast a wide net to take in brakemen, firemen, waiters, shopmen, porters, and other Negroes working for the railroads and the Pullman Company. As conditions changed, it became more combative—first battling exclusionary policies of the whites-only railway brotherhoods, then fighting for higher wages and an end to segregated carriages.

World War I turned upside down those organizing efforts the same as it did everything else on the railroad and in the United States. Tips fell. Less-traveled routes were temporarily abandoned in favor of handling the main lines and shuttling soldiers. Tensions with conductors rose as porters were put in charge of entire trains of troops, and many porters resigned. But the federal takeover of the Pullman Company in 1918 gave porters more than the war took away: a 25 percent hike in wages, four full days off a month, as well as seniority rules, overtime provisions, and a system for hearing grievances. All were big steps forward, even though none were guaranteed to last once Uncle Sam turned control back to Pullman. The government also had spurred porters to think about unionizing—although labor peace, not progress, was its intent—by saying that on matters of wages and working conditions, it wanted to hear from groups, not individual workers.

Mays's industrial association capitalized on the wartime ferment, on a newfound labor militancy that saw the unionized share of the U.S. workforce quadruple from 1900 to 1920, and especially on federal officials' willingness to listen. He testified, lobbied, and sued. He courted the Negro press and white labor unions. By 1920, his association claimed 180 locals and a membership of fifteen thousand. In the mid-1920s, however, Mays fell victim to a postwar reconstruction of racial barriers in unions and society generally, as well as his own inability to deliver on promises to unite competing crafts of Negro railroaders. Still, his efforts stand as a critical bridge between the ad hoc, unfocused efforts of porters at the turn of the century and the irrepressible drive by the Brotherhood of Sleeping Car Porters in the 1920s and 1930s. Although it had taken more than a half century to get there, the Pullman porters now were committed not just to organizing themselves but to demanding their full rights as workers and men.[64]

UNIONS WERE ALSO topic number one among Pullman executives over the first two decades of the twentieth century. And while

George Pullman deserved his epitaph as his era's most hell-bent labor baiter, his successors went him several better.

Their first weapon was spies. Porters called them "spotters," since they were there to spot porters breaking rules. The company preferred a title pilfered from law enforcement: "special agent." Whatever they were called, they were everywhere. Or so it seemed to porters and conductors who were always on edge, which is where the company wanted them. Special agents' mission was to unearth newspapers draped across empty seats and bathrooms with dirty floors, cuspidors, or towels. Dust on the sill was enough for a red-tapist to file a report, although most were after bigger infractions: call bells unanswered, bedlam at bedtime, or porters caught drinking, smoking, or fornicating on the job. Even worse were *knocking down* fares, failing to write up food orders, or any other scheme to steal the company's money. Breaches became demerits on a porter's record and often meant the loss of an annual bonus; serious ones resulted in suspension or firing.

Undercover agents were there almost from the start of Pullman operations. It was reasonable for the company to police its rules and root out theft of property and money. There was plenty of both that went on, which is not surprising given all the money and expensive supplies that changed hands, and the reality that conductors and porters were out there on their own, hundreds of miles from the watchful eyes of Pullman managers. But if porters and conductors are to believed, the spies sent out as management's eyes and ears had quotas to fill and invented transgressions when they could not find them. "These 'spotters' come on board and pretend that they have not quite money enough to pay the regular fare, and want us to carry them for a little less, saying to us, 'Put that in your pocket,'" the porter Nadd Rillar wrote in an 1887 letter to the *Chicago Tribune*. "Failing in this they try to get us to drink or smoke with them. Finally failing in everything they concoct a lie to report. Within the last six months the great sleeping-car company has discharged over 100 conductors and porters on the false reports of these mercenary liars." In a second letter ten days later Rillar added that "the only difference between the porters and the slaves of twenty-five years ago is that the porters are not bought and sold. Twenty-five years ago the slaves were hunted with four-legged bloodhounds, which, when they barked, barked the truth; but today the porters are hunted by two-legged curs, which bark nothing except lies."[65]

Others painted the spotter as more buffoon than bloodhound. "Notwithstanding all the precautions used by the secret service agency who sends him out, he is generally *known wherever he goes,*" Herbert O. Holderness wrote in 1901 in his *Reminiscences of a Pullman Conductor.* "The subject of our sketch is usually a man of from 30 to 45 years of age (in rare cases 50 or over), without any peculiarity of dress to distinguish him, but *trade marked* with a furtive, secretive look, that is doubtless born of his own knowledge *that he is what he is.* It is a hard matter for the public executioner to conceal his identity, and equally so for a spy, whose life is passed in a disgusting espionage of the acts of others, and who only holds his position by virtue of his ability to find a flaw in the character or methods of the man he is sent out to watch. . . . When he enters the car he always (if he can do so) takes a seat in the *second section* on either side of the rear end of the sleeper, from which vantage he can see all that goes on, watching the porter make up the berths at night or that he uses his duster in the daytime, and that the conductor issues checks to every passenger. . . . He (the spotter) is usually silent and very rarely talks to any one, apparently being deeply absorbed in a book or newspaper, over the top of which he can observe how affairs are going on."[66]

A survey of files left behind by the Pullman Company makes clear that Holderness and Rillar were right about one thing: there was hardly a porter without some breach on his record. Most had many. Garrard David Smock's personnel records show he was suspected of bootlegging, reprimanded for letting his car become overheated, and issued warnings for everything from sleeping on duty to "failure to tender pillows." Likewise for his sons, Babe, Virgil, and George, who worked as Pullman busboys, then attendants, and who were cautioned for infractions like "loss of salt and pepper caster" and "failure [to] properly serve beer."[67]

Porters fought back by becoming adept at spotting the spotters. When they unmasked one, they had their own prearranged systems for tipping off compatriots. One was to hold a hotel guidebook in the window for other porters to see as their trains whizzed by, indicating that a spy was aboard and might get off and be waiting for them on their return trip. Other times a blue dust cloth was displayed—or even a ketchup bottle. If the secret agent happened to have black skin, the signal was a black skillet. A more subtle approach was to make a mark on the inspector's shoe or suitcase, something so tiny he would not notice but distinctive enough that it would read like a scarlet letter to a savvy porter down the line.[68] Add up all the warnings, and the result was "it was never a surprise; we always knew when an inspector was going to get on," said William Howard Brown.[69]

Picking out Pullman inspectors working off the train was dicier. Sometimes it was "welfare workers" checking up on a man applying for a porter's job, or ensuring that a working porter was not spending too much time in bars or gambling dens. As dissatisfaction among porters grew in the early 1900s, welfare workers began gathering information on how many Model Ts or Victrolas a porter owned, the better to argue against a pay hike. And spies on the streets began focusing on signs of a stewing union, recruiting perfidious porters to help with the snooping.

Porters were not the only ones the Pullman Company recruited to keep tabs on and try to contain union activities. The Negro press was the most efficient way to reach large numbers of porters, and several leading Negro journalists, including the head of the Associated Negro Press, were anxious to oblige. So were YMCAs, colored churches, the Chicago Urban League, and key Negro politicians. They would play mainly supporting roles until the battle heated up in 1925, but like generals preparing for war, Pullman managers began enlisting troops and dispensing largesse more than a decade in advance.

Recognizing the inevitability of porters banding together in some way, the company tried to set the form, control the function, and guarantee that the organization stayed friendly. The Pullman Porters Benefit Association got things started. It was supposed to be independent, but its first chairman was Arthur A. Wells, George Pullman's longtime private car attendant and personal assistant, and its expenses came from company coffers. It began in 1915 with the mission of providing death benefits, but by 1921 it was dispensing sickness insurance, too, and overseeing an array of promotional and ceremonial affairs. Its most festive was the annual convention. At one such gathering the former porter Jesse Binga, who founded and ran South Chicago's high-profile Binga Bank, proudly recounted how "George M. Pullman was the first man to enter the Negroes of this country into the industrial life of the world" and "the Pullman Porters are the only group who can show sixty years of service without a strike." The benefit association's most formal and somber ceremony was "Thanksgiving and Memorial Day," staged in each Pullman district on the third Sunday of May, with up to twenty-five hundred porters and family members attending. Roses were cast. Candles were quenched. And the roll was solemnly read in memory of porters who had died the previous year. Then there were speeches by a minister, a Pullman Company executive, and a benefit association official. "Imagine," wrote the historian LeRoy, "such an awesome triumvirate—your pastor, your paycheck, and your policy—telling you not to bite the hand that feeds you and prepare for the next life for you may be next."[70]

To ensure porters nationwide knew about such pageantry and rituals, the company underwrote a magazine supposedly by and for porters, the *Pullman Porters' Review,* and an in-house journal, the *Pullman News.* There were baseball games and concerts, barbecues, and an annual picnic in Jersey City that attracted porters from as far as Denver and was dubbed by the *New York Times* the "Newport of the colored social world." All were aimed at breeding good feelings between porters and their employer—and keeping out a real union.[71]

A company union, however, was just fine, and porters got theirs in 1920. It was called the Employee Representation Plan. It handled porter complaints and grievances and had the authority to advise although not consent on wages. The company did dispense occasional wage increases—8 percent in 1924, another 8 in 1926—but as part of a strategy to deflate pressure for an independent union rather than empower the representation plan. Even with grievances the company kept a tight grip, as its own master sleuth—the Associated Negro Press founder Claude A. Barnett—made clear in a secret memo to the Pullman Company president in 1925. "In nearly every district the men elected [to the Employee Representation Plan] are usually what we call 'office' or 'company' men," Barnett wrote, repeating what he had been told by a porter he thought was characteristic of the craft. "Even when we get some of the rank and file or when the group elected seems fearless, it's not long before they lose their back-bone. Ask one to go to the office for a favor and four times out of five he'll come back, shrug his shoulders, and say, 'I can't see the "old man" today; he's sore. Come in next trip.' The fact is the fellows we elected are thinking about their own jobs."

As for filing a grievance, Barnett's source said, that meant "submitting our grievance before-hand to the man whose administration it may be criticising. . . . Suppose you get the blank and file a grievance, and it is turned down. Under the law, you can go farther, but you dare not for fear of getting in bad. They have a thousand ways of harrassing us, change or loss of run, ten, twenty, thirty days in the [suspension] book, getting the reputation of being a 'smart nigger.' . . . It's the result of a system and habit, and since the war things have steadily grown worse. Always there hangs over our heads the almost despotic power of the superintendent, plus the fact that a black man's word against anyone else means nothing. We are not all liars, you know, but that's the general attitude which greets us."[72]

That general attitude went well beyond the Employee Representation Plan, and it upset more porters than him. Pullman exercised control partly through its use of *extras,* the thousands of part-time porters who showed up every day at company offices nationwide hoping a regular porter was sick or otherwise unavailable. Some were old porters who had lost their regular runs and were willing to *mooch,* which meant helping young porters make down beds for a fifty-cent tip. Most were young, able-bodied, and desperate for work. They would take any trip offered—the men called it *running wild*—and many days they had neither job nor money to show for all the time waiting. Their presence ensured the company enough staff to operate no matter the circumstances. It also gave management leverage over full-time porters, who knew that dozens of men were eager to step in if they stepped out of line.

Corruption was preordained in the *extra* setup. With so many porters to select from, the sign-out men who chose often developed favorites and sometimes took bribes. "I'd learned that those porters that kept making those trips always brought this old sign-out man liquor," recalled Cottrell Lawrence Dellums, an extra when he went to work for Pullman in 1924 and later the president of the Brotherhood of Sleeping Car Porters. "Oftentimes they gave him money, a kickback, to show appreciation for the good trip that he gave them. As a matter of fact, when I went on the road there was a common expression that originated in the dining cars among the railroad men: 'there is a good story on page one hundred.' Now passengers would leave magazines on the train after they'd finished reading them. So traditionally the porters would go through the train when the passengers had gotten off and pick up a magazine. If it was one of these kickback trips, they'd clip some money to page one hundred. They'd get in and take it to the dispatcher and say, 'Mr. So-and-so, I picked up a *Newsweek* (to use a name) on the train for you because I'm pretty sure you'll like the *Newsweek*. There's a good story on page one hundred.'"[73]

Porters were also kept in line the old-fashioned way: a stick wielded by an ornery boss. The Pullman Company was modeled after the military, with the porter as buck private. He took orders from the conductor, the ultimate authority on the sleeping car, and from district superintendents, vice presidents, the general manager, and other high-level Pullman officers. And porters were "subordinate" to officers of the railroads that pulled their sleeping cars, as the very first words of the porter rulebook made clear. "Everyone on the train was the porters' boss," said the ex-porter Jewel Brown.[74]

Leroy Parchman remembered a conductor who insisted that "any time a porter sleeps in a roomette it has got to be fumigated before a passenger uses it."[75] Harold Reddick said it all goes back to the beginning: "I didn't know George Pullman, but he hired some bastards to run the company."[76]

Reddick was right. Most techniques the Pullman Company used to keep workers in line in the 1900s had been pioneered by George the previous century, including hiring managers who could be tyrants. George had used spies to keep tabs on workers in Pullman, his namesake town, as well as on his sleepers. He knew that cutting wages one craft at a time undermined bids by workers to form a united front, and that bringing in the police made sense if workers resisted. He blacklisted agitators, fired men who remained out of work, banned union meetings in his town, and publicly denied doing any of that. He also schooled his lieutenants, including the one destined to succeed him, to be as antiunion as he was.

Robert Todd was Abe and Mary Lincoln's sole child to survive to maturity. Just twenty-one when his father was assassinated, he gave the president little inkling of his success to come. He failed his entrance exams at Harvard University, although after a year boning up at Phillips Exeter Academy he reapplied and got in. He was accepted to Harvard Law but dropped out to join the army in time to catch the end of the Civil War. Even though he was on General Grant's staff far from the front lines, he managed to be at Appomattox when General Robert E. Lee surrendered. Things went more smoothly after his father's death, when Robert Todd became a lawyer, served as minister to Great Britain, and was secretary of war under President James A. Garfield. He also became famous for his superstitions about assassinations, well-founded though they seemed. As a young man he was rescued while falling from a train by Edwin Booth, older brother of John Wilkes Booth, who would murder Robert Todd's father. Later this president's son was nearby when President Garfield was shot at Washington's Union Station, and at the Buffalo Pan-American Exposition when President William McKinley was shot there. From then on he declined invitations from presidents, noting,

"There is a certain fatality about presidential functions when I am present." His sense of apprehension might have been piqued had he known that John F. Kennedy, the fourth president to be assassinated, would be buried near him at Arlington National Cemetery.[77]

Robert Todd showed no such reticence when it came to affairs of the sleeping car monopoly. In George's day, the young Lincoln was friend, confidant, and special counsel. He stood by the founder's side during the infamous strike of 1894, although he never made public his feelings. Pullman may have played a parentlike role for Lincoln, who had lost his father and ten years later had his troubled mother briefly committed to a mental asylum. George's will named Robert Todd as one of two executors of his estate, for which he shared a $425,000 fee, which was considerably more than George left his twin sons. And Robert Todd was so impressed by the way George had his casket secured in concrete that he paid $700 to rebury his own father in Springfield, Illinois, putting the president's remains a full ten feet underground and fortifying them with steel and cement.[78]

Robert Todd Lincoln was named president pro tem of the Pullman Company shortly after George's death in 1897, and in 1901 the board dropped the temporary from his title. His ten-year reign was characterized by decisions at least as hardheaded as his predecessor's, but without George's penchant for publicity. He said no to a newspaper editor seeking renewal of his traveling pass and to a U.S. senator seeking a job for a friend. Company ties to the town of Pullman were severed. Pullman workers seeking his intervention in matters of discipline were sorely disappointed. He presided over the greatest period of growth in Pullman history and proved his devotion to the firm not just by staying on as chairman until 1922 but, only ten days before his death, agreeing to travel to a company meeting in New York to ensure a quorum.

There was one more service Robert Todd rendered the Pullman Company: lending it the ideal family name to draw on in its bid to keep out unions and keep under control its Pullman porters. Just how conscious he was of that exploitation is unclear. There is no record, for instance, whether he approved a company pamphlet titled *The Pullman Porter, the Benefits of His Racial Monopoly*, which read in part, "It is a fitting coincidence that Robert T. Lincoln, the son of the great emancipator, should have been associated with the Pullman Company as general counsel, President and Chairman of the Board, and even now, despite his advanced years, as a director."[79]

It was after Robert Todd's tenure that Pullman launched its full-fledged campaign to beat back the Brotherhood of Sleeping Car Porters, although he certainly laid the groundwork for that bare-knuckled initiative. The *Racial Monopoly* pamphlet itself became a skirmish in that war, drawing the following response from A. Philip Randolph, the Brotherhood's leader: "It is unfitting though interesting to note how the Pullman Company is desperately trying to make a case for the wages and treatment it now gives the porters and maids by sentimentally appealing to the name of Abraham Lincoln through his son. It is a most unhappy and pathetic gesture; for Abraham Lincoln freed Negroes from economic exploitation as *chattel slaves*; whereas his son, Robert T. Lincoln, has lent his influence and name to the notorious exploitation of Negroes as *Pullman slaves*."[80]

What did Robert Todd think of repeated early bids by porters to unionize? He denied ever hearing of any, "not the slightest," when he testified in 1915 before a congressional commission investigating industrial relations. Would he block such a bid? "I do not think any administration likes to deal with unions," he said. "They would prefer to deal with their employees as we deal with ours in the Pullman Co. We have never opposed, as far as I know, the formation of a union among our employees, but our company insists on the right to hire and discharge its employees." Was it true, the commission chair asked, that the Pullman Company hired spotters and spies to root out, then fire, union activists? "I never heard of such a thing," the Pullman boss replied. "I fully recognize, Mr. Chairman, the right of the employees to organize."[81]

A harsh judge could conclude that Lincoln perjured himself during his testimony. His own general manager, L. S. Hungerford, appearing earlier before the same commission, had been asked whether the Pullman Company ever fired a porter or conductor for union activities. "There is one or two of these so-called federated men that were so active in condemning the company's methods, seemed to be so busy forming this union," Hungerford acknowledged, "I thought it was well to let them devote their entire time to it."[82] The Smock boys, meanwhile, insist that their father, Garrard David, was fired for his union work and rehired because the Pullman Company needed more porters. Company records say he was "dropped" in 1919 because of "failure [to] report [for] several months," and he was brought back in 1920 "providing he comply with rules and regulations."*

Robert Todd surely was sheltered from such details, and he was probably willing to shade what he knew. He had already proven himself as steel-willed and unsentimental as his mentor, George Pullman, although to him entrepreneurship was duty more than joy. While Robert Todd left behind few clues as to his state of mind regarding unions and none on how he felt about Pullman porters, three generations of Smocks along with other Pullman workers offered their own verdict on his reign. Abe Lincoln, they agreed, freed Negroes like them only to have his son exploit them. They revere the father as the slayer of chattel slavery but revile the son for personifying industrial slavery.

---

*That firing and rehiring, outlined in Smock's official service record, occurred years after Lincoln testified before the commission but while he still was chairman of the company and presumably influenced its strategy on matters as important as labor policy.

4

Saint Philip and the Battle
for Brotherhood

⠶

AT LONG LAST, porters gathered in the sweltering heart of Harlem threw the first stone at the great giant who had controlled their lives for so many decades. It was an August night in 1925, and the steamy auditorium of the Imperial Lodge of Elks was packed with somber-faced porters who cast anxious eyes about the cavernous room. As Pullman spies filtered through the crowd, union organizers, who had resolved this time for sure to crack the nerve center of the most antiunion company in the nation, felt the sweat stream down their faces. So anxious were porters about losing their jobs just for attending the meeting, organizers of this new Brotherhood of Sleeping Car Porters did them a favor and refused to let them speak. In their hearts, everyone had something to say.

At the podium stood a most unlikely man to speak on their behalf. His name was A. Philip Randolph, and he talked in the arch cadence of William Shakespeare. His listeners were lifetime Pullman men. He had never worked as a porter nor even ridden a sleeping car. He was an atheist preaching to true-believing Christians. His list of union activities was long—working with steamboat workers, elevator and switchboard operators, dining car waiters—but it included not a single success. His *Messenger* magazine crowned itself "The World's Greatest Negro Monthly," but its circulation had plummeted to five thousand and it was surviving issue to issue. A self-proclaimed provocateur and socialist, Randolph had so riled the government with his pacifist jeremiads during World War I that

President Woodrow Wilson's administration branded him the "most dangerous Negro in America."[1]

Brotherhood strategists believed the most dangerous Negro in America was just the man to lead them into battle against the nation's largest employer of Negroes. The five veteran porters who had met secretly to launch the union two months earlier knew it would take daring strokes, even dangerous ones, to keep their bid from flaming out like all the others over the last twenty-five years. They put a nonporter like Randolph in charge to insulate him from Pullman Company intimidation. A recent speech before the New York Pullman Athletic Association confirmed he was Harlem's most impassioned orator. A barrage of articles in the *Messenger* showed he understood how porters' jet-black skin and economic precariousness were used to exploit them. He was enough of an optimist to see porters not as the sum of their fears or self-interests, the way the Pullman Company did, but as the most sophisticated of Negro blue-collar workers. Even his Brahmin accent and aloof air became assets, as generations of porters saw their leader as the equal of his adversaries in bearing and nobility. He was a warrior, but a gentle one.

And so Randolph took the Elks stage that August evening, with the temperature nearing ninety and the room filling with smoke from a hundred cigars and cigarettes, to unveil the union he was tapped to lead. Aware that many porters were distressed by his street-corner evangelizing against the church, he opened the meeting with a prayer and a tribute to his preacher-father. Knowing how timid previous union-building bids had been, he was direct. "What this is about is making you master of your economic fate," Randolph intoned, explaining that he would demand a minimum monthly wage of $150, a limit of 240 hours, and, in a statement sure to waken anyone snoozing in the heat, an end to the sacred practice of tipping. He acknowledged never having ridden a Pullman car but called that a testament to his poverty and a sign that "the price is too high."[2]

"I ran the whole meeting myself," he recalled decades later, saying he muzzled porters to protect them. "I told them I would now give the invocation, and I gave it. I told them I was going to sing the

Brotherhood's song, 'Hold the Fort,' and I sang it. I told them I was going to make the announcements and introduce guest speakers, and I did. I told them now I was going to make the main speech, and then I did. At the end of the meeting, I moved the vote of thanks, said the benediction, and told everyone to go home and not hold any discussions on the street corners."[3]

That was too much to ask. What they had heard was too exhilarating and unnerving. It was a call to action that promised a new dignity and affluence—provided they did not lose their jobs in the process. As he finished speaking, "you could hear a pin fall," Randolph remembered. "Nothing like that had ever occurred before, because it was looked upon as simply hopeless to try to organize a group of men who were under the grip, the moral and intellectual and economic grip of a mighty corporation such as the Pullman Company was, and so I told them how grateful and proud I was to see them come to this meeting in good numbers."[4]

The press had not been invited, for fear of getting porters in trouble by having their names printed, but word circulated and the meeting made the papers. The *New York Times* said two hundred porters had signed up on the spot, with the Brotherhood hoping to enlist two thousand in New York and twelve thousand nationwide. Randolph, the newspaper said, had "urged a quiet organization of the men until they became strong enough to deal with the company openly." The *New York Herald Tribune* ran a similar story with the same numbers, which could only have come from the Brotherhood. This time, however, A. Philip appeared as "J. Philip," suggesting just how obscure the one-day labor and civil rights leader was.[5]

New York's Negro press was more triumphal. James H. Hogans, who authored a regular column in the conservative *New York Age* on "things seen, heard and done among Pullman employees," wrote after the Elks meeting that the Pullman porter was "the most conspicuous, as well as the most picturesque worker in America today." Randolph, realizing the "sad plight" of the porter, "has essayed to become his Moses to lead him out of his industrial wilderness by unionizing him so that he may better the conditions which at present surround him." Hogans called the bid for a union "really and truly a laudable effort," but he wondered how many of Pullman's traditionally loyal porters would go along. The *Amsterdam News,* New York's leading Negro paper, expressed no such reservations. It called the session "the greatest labor mass meeting ever held of, for and by Negro working men." It put the number of porters in attendance at five hundred, two and a half times what the white papers estimated, and said they loudly cheered the proposed union of their Pullman brethren. "Veteran laborites," the *News* added, "claimed the meeting was one of the most enthusiastic ever held in the big city. A few of the company's spies and several old hat-in-hand porters were there, waiting to get information to carry back to the Pullman offices."[6]

A. PHILIP RANDOLPH'S story and that of the Brotherhood of Sleeping Car Porters are as interwoven as those of George Mortimer Pullman and the Pullman Company. Not only did Randolph lead the union for almost all its life; he became synonymous with it in the minds of members and the public. And much the way Pullman's upbringing in the tiny town of Albion planted values that would define his career as sleeping car monopolist, so Randolph's roots in Jacksonville, Florida, set him on his course of confrontation with the mighty Pullman Company.

Poverty was a defining feature in the early life of Asa, as he was called then. James and Elizabeth Randolph moved to the all-Negro Oakland neighborhood of Jacksonville in 1901, when Asa was two and his brother James four. The Randolphs lived in a rented home—two rooms upstairs, two down—with a fence missing so many pickets that chickens, cats, and dogs wandered in and out of their yard. James was minister at a nearby African Methodist Episcopal church that met in rented rooms. His congregation of several dozen sharecroppers paid him so sparely and sporadically that he had to supplement his income by preaching at three country churches. Even then his salary often came as a side of pork or sack of sweet potatoes, forcing him to set up a series of side businesses. He and Elizabeth repaired, dyed, and cleaned clothes, ran a meat market, and bought wood wholesale, reselling it to neighbors for cooking and heating. All were done with gusto but little business acumen, and they yielded more debt than income.

As modest as the Randolphs' surroundings were, they seemed plush next to those of Asa's maternal grandparents, whose rotting cabin he visited often. In the winter he helped fill holes in the walls with newspapers and rags. During the summer he relished lying in bed and gazing at the stars through gaps in the roof. The message that you could get by without much money would prove instructive over the long years he went with barely any salary while battling for his Brotherhood.

Another reality of Asa's young world was that café-au-lait skin like his closed doors and created hazards. Jacksonville began the twentieth century as one of the Deep South's most racially welcoming cities, with the NAACP leader and native son James Weldon Johnson calling it a "good town for Negroes." Five Negroes were elected as aldermen and one a municipal judge; thirteen of thirty policemen were Negro, as was the commissioner. While that was reassuring to the city's sixteen thousand Negro residents, it was disconcerting to enough of its twelve thousand whites that they went on the offensive with poll taxes, all-white primaries, and gerrymandering of Negro council districts. Not long after the Randolphs moved in, Negroes were dislodged politically and given their own, second-rate sections at schools and hospitals, in theaters, jails, and saloons, on streetcars, and in government itself. Sometimes the venom turned violent, as in 1910 when Negroes celebrating the victory of the colored heavyweight Jack Johnson were beaten by gangs of whites. Nine years later, two Negroes charged with killing a young white were taken from their jail cells and shot, with one dragged through the streets and dumped in front of the elegant Windsor Hotel.[7]

Asa saw that antagonism up close each time he and his brother James were pushed to the back of the line by white delivery boys when they picked up their *Times-Union* papers. He heard about it when parishioners lined up at the Randolph home with tales of racism at work, and pleas to help brothers or sons unfairly arrested. And he watched it sting his father, which was when it hurt most. Asa regularly accompanied his dad as he returned tailored clothes to the white foreman of a local sawmill. "Get the hell out of here," the manager yelled one day at Reverend Randolph and his small son. "Take the clothes to my house, or I'll throw you off the property."[8]

Religion helped Asa untangle his racist surroundings. Not the "superreligious" sort practiced by his mother and grandmother, who held prayer meetings each morning with sermons laying out the surest route to heaven, ended Sunday services in a flood of tears, and limited their social circle to affairs of the parish. His father's gospel was far more alluring, focusing not on Scripture but on social justice and racial redress. The AME church itself grew out of the battles against slavery and racism and became a voice for Negro self-reliance. On the Randolph pulpit, Jesus and Moses had dark skin, and revelation was a call to political action. At home, the divine word was that racial identity was what you made it. Asa's mulatto mother, whom he described as "almost white," and his maternal grandfather, who often was mistaken for Caucasian, had at least as much racial pride as his father, whose skin was the color of coal. From their time as toddlers Asa and James were fed a diet of Negro men who had made a difference, from Hannibal to Nat Turner, from the Boston Massacre hero Crispus Attucks to the Haitian rebel Toussaint-Louverture.

It was their parents' actions that the boys remembered more than their utterances, and that added James and Elizabeth to their list of race heroes. The incident that stuck with Asa longest was the afternoon in 1909 when a group of neighbors stopped by the Randolph home to warn that a white mob was planning to string up a Negro jailed on charges of molesting a white woman. James set Elizabeth up in a chair on the front porch, her long arms cradling a shotgun, to watch over the boys. Then he rounded up friends to form an armed guard around the jail, standing down the lynch mob. "This was a demonstration on the value of unity on the part of a people who are victims of racial hatred and persecution," Asa, who was ten at the time, recalled seventy years later. "If you stand firm and hold your ground, in the long run you'll win."[9]

James and Elizabeth showed the boys that even as youngsters, they had the power to fight back. Asa and James were forbidden from going to the coloreds-only reading room in the Jacksonville Public Library. Jim Crow streetcars were out, too; better to walk anywhere they wanted to go, as their parents did. While they were as firm as the Puritans on what not to do, the Randolphs also instilled in the boys what to be *for*. Reading topped the list. James Randolph had on hand the sonnets of Shakespeare, novels of Walter Scott and Jane Austen, poetry of Keats and Shelley, social theory from Charles Darwin and John Calvin, and memoirs by Frederick Douglass and bishops in the AME church. It was a collection surprising in reach and refinement for an impoverished, self-educated preacher.

How his boys read mattered almost as much as what. They were taught to articulate deliberately and precisely, the way James had heard troupes of Oxford actors do it, with the broad *a* of *Hahvahd* and the endless *e* as in *bean*. At first the New England baritone sounded postured from Asa, a son of the South, but listen longer and it took on rhythm as well as resonance, reflecting the precision and passion with which he pleaded his causes. He and his brother turned it all into a contest, testing each other on the meaning and pronunciation of words. "We played quiz games at home," he wrote years later, "the way others played catch." The point to Reverend Randolph was to take control of language as life. To make each word and action count. To matter. "He had a great future in his mind for my brother and myself," Asa said. "We were told constantly and continuously that 'you are as able, you are as competent, you have as much intellectuality as any individual, any white boy of your age and even older than you are, and you are not supposed to bow and take a back seat for anybody.'"[10]

That message was reinforced at the Cookman Institute, Florida's first high school for Negroes, founded in 1872 with money from white Methodists up North. Cookman was an extraordinary enterprise, with elderly ex-slaves sitting alongside boys and girls in classes that ran day and night. For the Randolph brothers, it meant a pot-pourri of courses in Greek and Latin, ethics, drama, and music that were inconceivable during their seven years at Oakland public schools. There were practical programs, too, in sewing, shoemaking, farming, and printing. Negro teachers came from across the South and white teacher-missionaries from as far away as New Hampshire. While tuition was free at Cookman, the Randolph boys had to pay for books and clothes. Asa had been working since he was a child, fetching a white grocer's lunch from his home. Later, he clerked in a market, delivered newspapers, and, during a summer vacation in New York that would ignite a lifelong passion for that city, helped his janitor-cousin clean apartment buildings on the Upper West Side. In school, Asa loved English as well as public speaking and drama, all of which were instrumental in his later career. He was a standout singing bari-tone in the choir, with classmates saying he could have had a career in music, and on the baseball diamond, where his performance behind the plate and at first base might have qualified him for the Negro League.

Classmates tagged him "Old Asa," a sign of how brooding he was even in his teens, but they liked him enough to pick him as grad-uation orator. "He was always over-earnest. Dogged diligence— that's Randolph. If he has any gaiety in his nature or any sense of humor, he never shows it either in private conversation or before the public," said one long-ago friend. Another, James Parker, recalled that at Cookman Asa "spoke impeccable English, but wouldn't open his mouth unless asked. He and his brother never raised hell like some of us, who would cut class sometimes and run off with the girls. They were two of the most handsome boys at Cookman, but they weren't the kind of fellows girls would pick to go out and have a good time with. Morally, they were beyond reproach."[11]

Parker was not the only one to lump Asa and James together as if they were of the same skin. James was Asa's closest friend, then and forever. Although James was two years older, they began Cookman at the same time and graduated together. They spent endless evenings together on the porch, reading. "We were brought up together, you know," Asa recalled. "As a matter of fact, there were many things that he taught me."[12] Among them were how to do better in mathematics and languages, in which James was gifted. He also taught his younger brother never to back away from fistfights, no matter that the stakes were a purloined marble and the aggressor was twice his height and weight. Elizabeth, who despite her hell-and-brimstone religiosity "hated nothing so much as a coward," gladly attended to their cuts and bruises even as the Reverend Randolph argued for pacifism.

The brothers conspired as well on ways to foil their father's plan to have one or both follow him into the ministry. "My father and bishops of his church brought great pressure to bear on me to become a preacher, but I was not greatly impressed," said Asa. "My brother and I dreamed of doing many things, of leading the fight for human rights as congressmen, or working as educators, scientists, doctors and writers because we were exposed to constant parental discussion on the race question."[13]

Upon graduation the more affluent of his Cookman classmates were off to college, and Asa, too, pored over catalogs from the likes of Harvard and Princeton. But those were out of the Randolphs' financial reach, and Asa instead bounced from a job collecting premiums for Union Life Insurance to delivering drugs for a chemical company, stacking lumber, and laying rails and cross ties for the railroad. His passion, however, was reserved for his readings of Shakespeare or the Scriptures at Negro churches and theaters, singing in a barbershop quartet, and, best of all, playing the lead in an acting company that performed such works as *Way Down East*. "When I passed him in the streets, he bowed and lifted his hat," recalled Ruth Lofton, who often shared the stage with Asa and worked in the Negroes-only section of the Jacksonville Public Library. "Of course, he was a star actor. He had a wonderful voice, a fine physique, and a Christian military bearing that few men had, and he was the more handsome because of it."[14]

Asa also had an urge to test the possibilities beyond the confines of Jacksonville and Florida, inspired in part by a fascination with

W. E. B. DuBois's monumental treatise *The Souls of Black Folk*. DuBois was preaching the same spirit of Negro achievement that James Randolph had drilled into his sons, and Asa imagined himself a part of "the Talented Tenth" that DuBois saw as saving the race. Asa had been captivated by Manhattan since the summer he spent there mopping floors for his cousin the janitor. So in April of 1911, just as he was turning twenty-two, he set off for New York on the steamboat *Arapahoe* with his neighbor and friend Beaman Hearn. He told his mother he would be back by the fall, but, like George Pullman when he abandoned Albion in his twenties, Asa had no intention of returning for anything but a visit.

The New York that greeted him was precisely the cauldron of ideas and opportunities that Asa hoped for. Negroes were moving in by the tens of thousands. Like him, most were from the South and drawn to an expanding Harlem bordered by 128th and 145th streets, between Fifth and Seventh avenues. He and Hearn shared a room on 132nd Street, for $1.50 a week. They landed their first job by a fusion of shrewdness and wile that would prove useful in Asa's wars with the Pullman Company. Answering an ad for attendants at an all-white apartment building on West 148th Street, they found a line of Negro men ahead of them. So Asa spread the word that, unless they knew how to type, there was no point applying. Typing had nothing to do with the job at hand, but the ruse worked. Hearn was hired to operate the elevator, Randolph to run the switchboard.[15]

That job, like others he would land and lose over the next six years, meant little to Asa. All his work was menial and a means to pay the rent and support his true passions, acting and ideas. He performed in Shakespeare productions by a Methodist church in Harlem and claimed to have memorized every line from *Othello, Hamlet,* and *The Merchant of Venice*. He caught the eye of Harlem's leading bards and seemed on the verge of realizing his dream of a career on stage. To his father, that was a nightmare. He had to accept Asa's decision not to enter the ministry, James explained, but the theater— particularly in the City That Never Sleeps—was out of the question.

Adoring his father, Asa accepted the edict and turned his attention to his second love: politics. He already had begun studying at City College, which was ideal because it was free and at the center of radical student politics. Now he dropped courses like public speaking in favor of history, philosophy, and political science. His studies ignited an interest in socialism. Negroes, he came to believe, were exploited economically as well as racially. His list of heroes expanded to include union stalwarts like Eugene Debs, who had been catapulted to head of the Socialist Party through his leadership of the strike against the Pullman Company. "[I] began reading Marx as children read *Alice in Wonderland*," he later told his biographer. It was "like finally running into an idea which gives you your outlook on life."[16]

Like many young people in their twenties, Asa was testing his capabilities and playing out his passions. He attacked college with a thirsty mind, impressionable yet inquisitive. Carrying his ideas outside their ivory tower incubators, he launched a leftist current events forum and backed an insurgent Negro campaigning for Board of Aldermen on the slogan "the black man first, the black man last, the black man all the time." He adopted mentors: Morris Raphael Cohen, a professor of philosophy and politics who pushed students to critically question every assumption, and Hubert Henry Harrison, the "black Socrates" who blended socialism with black nationalism. He even picked different names for the new life he was building, joining the avant garde who had begun using *black* interchangeably with *Negro,* and having friends use his middle name, Philip, instead of Asa. Whatever he was called, the young Randolph was sufficiently audacious, and gifted, to prosper despite the handicaps of his Deep South roots and perpetual impoverishment.

To pay his way, he took any work he could find: waiter on the steamboat line between Boston and New York, porter at the Consolidated Gas Company, counterman at a restaurant in New Jersey. At each he tested his new precepts on economics and politics, rallying fellow workers, generally blacks, to rail against their shabby conditions, generally without success. On the steamer he lasted one trip. His diners ordered littlenecks along with their steaks, and Philip, never having heard of the clams, delivered the beef entrée before the seafood appetizer. That was all the large black head-waiter needed to know of his new recruit to banish him from the dining room. Philip, however, was soaking in damning details on how waiters and cooks were forced to sleep in the cramped quarters of the "glory hole," wagering away their meager salaries during all-night poker games. He tried to stir fellow workers to protest, but his ineptness as a waiter ensured he was not around long enough to make changes. The result was the same at Consolidated Gas, where, he recalled, his coworkers "had no ear for that kind of talk," and in the end he "gave up and left."[17]

With so much time in school, out speaking, and at work, there was little left for socializing, which was okay with the habitually shy Philip. He may not have been looking, but he did respond to an opportunity for romance that presented itself when he went to work for an employment agency targeting new black arrivals to New York. While the work was not absorbing, his attention was drawn to a beauty salon just down the hall owned and run by Lucille Green, a thirty-one-year-old widow with light skin, short-cropped silver hair, and a keen intellect. Trained as a schoolteacher, Green opted for the more lucrative hair-straightening business when her lawyer-husband died. She learned her technique from the majestic Madame C. J. Walker, a black millionaire who boasted a chauffeur-driven limousine to shuttle her between her Edgecombe Avenue townhouse and Irvington-on-Hudson estate. Walker saw Green as a protégée and ushered her into Harlem's worlds of affluence and ideas.

Philip and Lucille shared an April 15 birthday (she was six years older), along with interests ranging from theater to politics. They also had the same nickname for one another: "Buddy." He took her to lectures and an occasional stage show; she invited him to Madame Walker's soirees, although he seldom went. After just a few months they married. She got to choose the church, the highbrow, all-black St. Philip's Episcopal. He picked the "honeymoon": a round-trip ride on a city streetcar from their apartment in Harlem to the southern tip of Manhattan.

Lucille made life considerably easier for Philip. She earned enough money unkinking the hair of affluent black women, and even wealthier whites, to liberate him financially. (Madame Walker also helped out.) He no longer had to fight off unwelcome advances from women or worry about uncomfortable social settings. He now had a confidante and friend the equal of his brother, which would become even more valuable in his isolated days as a union pioneer and after James died at the young age of forty-one. Lucille helped him write speeches and organize meetings. And she introduced him to the man who would become his closest collaborator from 1915 to 1925.

Chandler Owen was Philip's alter ego, his Trotsky to Randolph's Lenin. Philip was straight-backed, tan-skinned, and, no matter his destitution, dressed as if every item was tailored to his lean physique. Owen was shorter, rounder, lighter, and less polished. Their personalities, too, were polarized: Randolph was cerebral, soft-edged, and reserved to the point of seeming impermeable; Owen was drawn to riches and fast times, trenchant and facile enough that he would be dubbed the Negro Mencken, and sufficiently spirited to puncture his colleague's formidable reticence. The contrasts proved complementary, with Randolph fine-tuning his powerful oratory and Owen concentrating on his gifts as writer and publicist for the cause. The two spent endless hours together, bringing back to Philip and Lucille's apartment an assortment of political bedfellows for discussions that lasted into the morning, then taking to the streets for tub-thumping sermons on upheaval and reform. Generally, the focus was economic inequality and racism, but like southern preachers they were agile in advancing the tempo or switching keys. "I remember being on the soapbox, presenting my position on the origin of racial discrimination, and there came two Irish cops trailing their billies," Philip said. "I knew they were coming to make us come in, you know, run us from the corner. So I began talking about the oppression of the Irish people by British imperialism. And these Irish cops came until they got round the edge of the meeting, then turned around and began to move away. . . . To find somebody of the darker races presenting their position and criticizing Great Britain—this was something that they not only would not stop but would help."[18]

In a world where every close friend warranted a nickname, Chandler and Randolph, with self-conscious irony, called one another "boy." Both also were willing to let Lucille underwrite their lifestyle as gadflies. "We were on an uncharted sea. Chandler and I had no job and no plan for the next meal," Philip recalled years after Lucille died. "But I had a good wife. She carried us."[19] In 1917, Philip and Owen finally landed their first job: editing a monthly magazine for the Headwaiters and Sidewaiters Society of Greater New York.

Launch of the *Hotel Messenger* offered yet another opportunity for Randolph to reinvent himself namewise, this time for the sake of a byline. With the knowledge that writers seldom alter a signature once selected, he opted for the stately if somewhat stiff "A. Philip," which is how the world came to know him. The new appellation lasted considerably longer than the new journal. Eight months into the job, Owen and Randolph published an exposé showing how headwaiters were inflating the price of uniforms they peddled to sidewaiters. The stories delighted the low-level waiters who were being exploited, but infuriated powerful headwaiters who controlled the society and summarily fired the two editors.

Randolph and Owen responded by dropping *Hotel* from the title and relaunching the *Messenger* with a masthead proclaiming it "The Only Radical Negro Magazine in America." *Only* might have been an overstatement, but not *radical*. The magazine, a central part of Harlem's New Crowd Negro movement, condemned the U.S. government for waging war abroad in the name of democracy when it deprived American blacks of their democratic rights. It was equally opposed to postwar restoration of the status quo, racial or economic. There were stinging attacks against Republicans as well as Democrats, and against old-style black leaders of the Booker T. Washington school along with ones who modeled themselves after

DuBois, who had once been an inspiration to Randolph. He and Chandler showed little sentimentality, defaming foes as "mental mannikins" and "intellectual Lilliputians" and publishing writers too revolutionary for more mainstream magazines like the NAACP's *Crisis*. Their offices consisted of two cluttered rooms on the third floor of a brownstone on Seventh Avenue, while furnishings were a battered old Underwood typewriter and files scattered across tables and floors. Still, the duo managed to reach a circulation of twenty-six thousand, making it the most widely read of left-wing black journals. No matter that a third of its readers were white.

The *Messenger*'s most potent venom was directed at the black nationalist Marcus Garvey and his back-to-Africa movement. At the start Randolph, like millions of American Negroes, was enchanted by the upstart from Jamaica who promised to unite the world's black-skinned peoples into a single proud nation. But much the way DuBois and other more conventional black leaders came to see Garvey as a corrupt demagogue, so, too, did Randolph and the *Messenger*. Their animus derived partly from jealousy: Garvey had built the biggest mass movement ever in the black community, claiming more than 4 million members, and his Black Star Line shipping company was one of the largest all-black businesses. There also were ideological and ethical schisms. Garvey's trust in capitalism collided with Randolph and Owen's creed of socialism. His back-to-Africa mantra and call for an all-black political party diverted attention from the integrationist, American-oriented agenda Randolph, the NAACP, and others were pushing. The last straws for Garvey's critics came early in 1922, when he was indicted on twelve counts of mail fraud and, even worse, held a secret meeting with Edward Young Clarke, imperial wizard of the Ku Klux Klan.

The *Messenger* already had put itself at the forefront of the "Garvey Must Go" campaign, having branded Garveyism "sinister viciousness" and vowed to drive him "from the American soil." In the fall of 1922, with those battles in full throttle, Randolph received a package at his office marked "from a friend." Inside was the severed hand of a white man, along with a note saying, "We have sent you a sample of our good work." Randolph could be the next victim, the writer implied, unless he joined Garvey's "nigger improvement association." The letter was signed by the KKK, which no doubt liked Garvey's idea of shipping America's blacks off to Africa, but Randolph suspected the package came directly from Garvey's people. The self-anointed provisional president of Africa responded by charging that the *Messenger* had staged the mailing as a publicity stunt. Garvey was convicted the next year of mail fraud, eventually was deported to Jamaica, and died in London in 1940. Years later his widow accused Randolph and Garvey's other critics of "mouthing the white man's thoughts to keep the race apart, and destroy them more easily. Yes, they made Garvey's life a living hell in America."[20]

The *Messenger* and its editors also had a list of people and causes it regularly toasted. At the top was the Bolshevik Revolution, which they dubbed "the people's form of rule" and applauded as "it bids fair to sweep over the whole world. The sooner the better. On with the dance!" They vowed to "lift [their] pens above the cringing demagogy of the times, and above the cheap peanut politics of the old reactionary Negro leaders." They were cheerleaders for Debs's Industrial Workers of the World and radical trade unionism generally, as well as for the American Civil Liberties Union and its leader, Roger Baldwin. As for Negro America's growing impatience with racism, they proclaimed "the rights of blacks to arm themselves in their own defense."[21]

If its goal was to get attention, the *Messenger* was a stunning success. Federal agents arrested the two editors in 1918 in Cleveland, one stop on a national speaking tour inveighing against the war. J. Edgar Hoover, head of the Justice Department's new General Intelligence Division, worried in a letter in September 1919 that the *Messenger* and *Crisis* were "exciting the negro elements in this country to riot and to the committing of outrages of all sorts." Two months later the Justice Department filed a report with the Senate on radicalism in the black press, concluding that the *Messenger* was "by long odds the most able and the most dangerous of all the

Negro publications. . . . No amount of mere quotation could serve as a full estimate of the evil scope attained by the Messenger." A task force appointed by the New York Legislature to investigate sedition was only slightly less damning in labeling the journal "distinctly revolutionary in tone. It is committed to the principles of the Soviet government of Russia and to the proposition of organizing the negroes for the class struggle." Congressman James F. Byrnes of South Carolina, who later became a U.S. senator, Supreme Court justice, and secretary of state, blamed the race riots of 1919 on the black press, and especially the Messenger, which he said "deliberately planned a campaign of violence." The postmaster general was alarmed enough that he pulled the journal's second-class mailing permit between 1918 and 1921, forcing it to pay first-class rates it could ill afford.[22]

Randolph and Owen were defiant, at least at first. When the judge in Cleveland let them go, thinking he was sending them home to their parents and local draft boards, they went straight to the next antiwar rally. When they and their journal were branded "most dangerous," they took it as a badge of honor and reprinted the label in issue after issue. And they did not let Byrnes have the last word, lashing back: "If the demand for political and social equality is Bolshevism, label us once more with that little barrack behind which your mental impotency hides when it cannot answer argument." Over time, however, their rhetoric died down, their passion for the Reds flamed out, and their relationship with groups like the American Federation of Labor (AFL) went from foe to friend. One way to measure that evolution was by watching the masthead: "The Only Radical Negro Magazine" yielded by 1920 to "A Journal of Scientific Radicalism," then to "The World's Greatest Negro Monthly," and finally to "The New Opinion of the New Negro." A more apt banner, given its editors' increased courting of black business and publication of pictures of "prominent colored ladies and their nice homes," would have been the poet Langston Hughes's surmise that it was "God knows what."[23]

The decline of the Messenger was partly a function of the times.

The Harlem Renaissance was in full bloom, and arts—not politics—were now the preoccupation. Still, Randolph and his friend Owen were determined to push ahead with an agenda of politics and reform. If their journal was less read than earlier, they would try other formats. There was the Friends of Negro Freedom, founded in 1920 to carry the word to the masses but seldom reaching beyond a closed circle of believers and totally fizzling within two years. Their Independent Political Council already had died, as did their Socialist Club. The National Association for the Promotion of Labor Unionism never really got off the ground, nor did the Tenants and Consumers League. Their United Brotherhood of Elevator and Switchboard Operators, founded just after they were fired by the headwaiters union, was taken over by the Elevator and Starters Union. Randolph also entered the political fray, in 1920 running as the Socialist candidate for state comptroller at the same time Owen and Lucille ran for the legislature, and a year later bidding for secretary of state. All failed to win or even come close.

In 1923 Owen abandoned politics and New York. Randolph suffered an even bigger loss the next year when his father, at age sixty, died of heart and kidney ailments. The *Messenger* always had been financially precarious, although Randolph was famous for staying even-keeled in the face of rent he did not have and printers' bills he could not pay. Actor that he was, he soothed his creditors and staff. His theater critic's only compensation was free theater tickets, his book reviewer's, free books. Other writers agreed to work without a salary. He took readers wherever he could find them, including residents of the federal penitentiary at Leavenworth, and took ads and even stories from whoever would pay, including Negro nabobs in Chicago and peddlers of products to straighten black women's hair and whiten their skin.[24] By the early 1920s even he became concerned as already-meager ad revenues were plummeting, support from the socialists had dried up, and circulation was down to five thousand, less than a fifth of its peak. Randolph was watching his political base crumble and his mouthpiece lose its echo. Even Lucille's dependable beauty salon was in decline. And they now had as permanent houseguests his mother, Elizabeth Randolph, who had moved to New York after his father died, and James Jr., who came two years earlier after giving up work in Jacksonville as a Pullman porter.

In 1925, at the young age of thirty-six, A. Philip Randolph's time appeared to have passed.

JUST WHO BAILED out whom is debatable. Randolph needed a job, a salary, and a new focus for his crusade to unionize Negro workers. The five lonely Pullman porters plotting to launch a union in 1925 needed a crusader capable of waging holy war, for that is what it would take to defy porters' twenty-five-year history of organizing fiascoes. Both were desperate. Both found what they were looking for.

Randolph and his recruiters were aware how careful they had to be each step of their early campaign. Three of the five who comprised the International Brotherhood of Sleeping Car Porters' organizing committee—Ashley Totten, Roy Lancaster, and William H. Des Verney—had played central roles in Pullman's in-house union and knew firsthand how tough the company could be. They had fought for shorter hours and higher wages but were outvoted by management, which had an equal number of proxies in what was supposed to be a union of porters. They had watched Pullman executives tempt other porter delegates with fine wine and cigars, banquets, a band, and even hookers, and seen how well the strategy worked. So they were particular about everything they did in those early days, even about choosing a name for their organization.

"We used the word Brotherhood for its psychological organization effect," Randolph explained later. "The purpose was to get the men convinced of the fact that they were brothers and have a common interest, each one, in helping make it possible for all porters to have a better life."[25] Likewise, they called themselves a union of *sleeping car porters* rather than *Pullman porters* more for psychological than practical reasons. The former suggested that porters were a profession and their union's reach was industrywide even though the industry and profession were dominated by George Pullman's company. As for *international,* it made clear the union wanted to represent porters in Canada and Mexico as well as the United States, although the focus always was on the latter, and even union officers generally dropped the "international" when referring to their brotherhood.

Words mattered even more in setting the terms of engagement. Where they slept, what they earned, and how many hours they were made to work would be what counted in the end to porters and Pullman management, but those were not grand themes to rally men to war. As every president who has called a nation to arms knows, there must be a greater purpose, a nobler cause. Abraham Lincoln took the nation to war to Preserve the Union. Woodrow Wilson wanted to Make the World Safe for Democracy. George W. Bush made his war against Iraq a War on Terror. So it was with the porters. They were battling for black manhood and Negro pride. They had the power, their union said, to transform the porter from a symbol of obsequiousness to one of empowerment. Brotherhood slogans captured those high stakes: Fight or Be Slaves. Service Without Servility. Independence Without Insolence. Courtesy Without Fawning. Opportunity Not Alms.

Who better to hatch such shibboleths than a professional wordsmith and rabble-rouser like A. Philip Randolph? He was a master strategist and tactician, a propagandist and publicist to rival George Pullman. He even had a magazine of his own, the *Messenger,* which in 1925 became the official organ of the Brotherhood. And he had hundreds of union members willing to carry the *Messenger* across America to porters and anyone willing to read about their plight. "A new Pullman porter is born. He breathes a new spirit. He has caught a new vision," Randolph heralded in a 1926 issue of the journal. "The new Pullman porter is a rebel against all that the 'Uncle Tom' idea suggests. The [Uncle Tom porter] possesses the psychology of let well enough alone. The [new porter] that of progressive improvement. The [Uncle Tom porter] relies upon charity and pity; the [new porter] upon his intelligence, initiative and thrift. . . . The new porter thinks hard but says little."[26]

One reason porters said so little during the Brotherhood's infancy was a fear of Pullman stool pigeons overhearing. Delivering the *Messenger* was enough to arouse suspicions. So was carrying a union card, attending a Brotherhood meeting, or talking about attending. Randolph and his union brothers had anticipated that, which is why they forbade porters from publicly airing grievances beginning with that inaugural meeting in the Harlem Elks hall. Porters got used to creeping into the *Messenger* office after dusk, and to recognizing the secret union organizer in each district as well as the public one. They surreptitiously slipped dues to Brotherhood representatives in barber shops, pool halls, or passing in the street. When they sighted Randolph coming their way, they walked to the other side of the street so company operatives would not catch them talking to the man everyone called "Chief."[27]

Stealth became such an obsession that there was a secret password, *solidarity*, which Randolph explained was "the *Key* to freedom of all oppressed and exploited races and classes." There was a secret signal, too—a clenched left fist with that arm extended downward—which "denotes that the Brotherhood realizes that only through a fight can justice and freedom be achieved." Porters joined the Brotherhood at a secret initiation ceremony, where they were sworn in with a secret oath. Wives were critical in sustaining the subterfuge: they collected dues at coffee klatches, visited other wives to disseminate union literature, and stood in for their husbands anywhere there might be a company spy. "It was almost impossible to discuss the organization's program because you never knew whom you could trust," said Benjamin McLaurin, the Brotherhood's top organizer in the East. "We had to function through the women at that time because they could attend meetings, they could pick up the literature. But we had couriers who did a great job in taking literature from one section of the country to the other, making contact with the officers, that sort of thing."[28]

The case the Brotherhood was trying to make in its literature and meetings focused on a finite number of grievances. It insisted on an end to doubling out, where porters were ordered on consecutive runs with no rest between and at a lower rate of pay. It demanded at least some pay for porters who reported to work but were not sent out, and a conductor's pay when a porter did the work of a conductor by running-in-charge. Wages must be more than doubled, time-and-a-half instituted after 240 hours a month, and porters must be compensated for time preparing for and discharging passengers, the union said. As for sleeping, there must be a prescribed place and time.

The sons of George Pullman and Robert Todd Lincoln understood how popular those demands were, though they pretended not to. They knew a showdown with the union was inevitable, and had spent twenty-five years fine-tuning their union-busting strategies. They probably even recognized that someday porters would get their own union the way conductors had. But they would not give way until they had to. And these paragons of capitalism certainly would not negotiate with A. Philip Randolph, whom they saw at best as an archetypal socialist and more likely a menacing Bolshevik determined to reimpose the federal control of the railroads that had prevailed during World War I.

The company was prepared to strike back with every implement it could muster, starting with the subtle slice of a butter knife. That meant, for starters, convening a meeting of the in-house union and agreeing to boost wages—although by just 7 percent, not the 130 percent the union wanted. It offered free legal advice to the *Chicago Whip,* a black newspaper that was suing the *Messenger* for libel. There was a tilt back to hiring southern porters, presumed to be more compliant, and away from strong-willed northern college students, even as summer fill-ins. And it called in every chit it had handed out over the years to individuals as well as organizations.

Nowhere was that debt collection easier to decipher than in Pullman's base of Chicago, home to the most militant Brotherhood local, and with that most cherished of institutions, the black church. The Pullman Company had turned to preachers over the years for job referrals, giving them enormous cachet with congregants anxious to land a cherished post on the sleeper or at its car-building plant on Lake Calumet. The company-backed Pullman Porters Benefit Association had provided much-needed cash to black churches by renting them for its meetings, and if more was needed, the company itself contributed to everything from staffing the nursery to sprucing up the chapel. Most black ministers already were politically conservative when it came to labor matters. They resented the white racist unions that packed such clout in Chicago, and had heard rumors of Randolph's sermonizing against the black clergy. So the Pullman Company had only to ask, and the ministers rallied to its cause against the upstart Brotherhood, banishing Randolph and other organizers from their pulpits and reminding parishioners every Sunday, "Don't rock the boat, don't bite the hand that feeds you."[29]

The pattern was the same at the Wabash Avenue YMCA on Chicago's black South Side. It got a ten-thousand-dollar donation from the Pullman Company, porters were encouraged to join, and its facilities were rented as a dormitory for out-of-town porters and a meeting place for the benefit association. The Y staff returned the favors by perpetually reminding porters and other black workers that the way to protect their jobs was to reject unions. Civil rights leaders were successfully wooed, too, including the Chicago chapter of the National Urban League, which liked the contributions it got from Pullman and declined to back the union even when its national organization did. Politicians were the easiest of all to influence, as the Perry Howard case suggests. The ex-porter and lawyer had become a Republican National Committee member and special assistant to the U.S. attorney general, and now he was offering himself as a mouthpiece for the company. In 1925 he attacked Randolph and his cronies as "visionaries, recalcitrants and discharged employees" who were "indirectly representing Russia." The charge might have stuck had its author been less of a buffoon and not been on Pullman's payroll.[30]

The company was making its case, but not fast enough. A more efficient way to shape the opinion of porters was through the media, and especially black newspapers, the way Randolph had been doing via the *Messenger.* Pullman sought to gin up favorable coverage by putting out press releases like one on the modest wage hike it gave porters in 1926, which carried the screaming headline "Grant Porters Million Raise." It worked, generating stories in the *Chicago Defender,* America's biggest black paper, as well as the *New York Times.* Not only did the *Times* use a headline almost identical to the company's— "Pullman Porters Win a Million More Pay"—it noted that "Pullman porters and maids have suffered no reduction in wages, as have other railroad employees, since the wartime peak."[31] It also left out several critical facts: their higher salaries still left porters substantially below the government poverty line, the five-dollar-a-month wage increase was eighty-two and a half dollars less than what the Brotherhood had requested, and wages were hiked mainly as a tactic in the ongoing battle between the company union and the Brotherhood. The story, in fact, made no mention at all of the struggle over unionizing and carried no comment from the Brotherhood.

When it could not spin its way into the press, the company tried buying it. That generally meant purchasing big ads in, and handing out free to porters thousands of copies of, black papers like the *St. Louis Argus, Denver Star, Seattle Enterprise,* and *Chicago Whip.* Such advertising and circulation revenue meant a lot to papers whose finances were tight, and it continued so long as the papers continued publishing stories flattering to the Pullman Company. Pullman certainly was not the first corporation to flex its financial muscle to sway a newspaper's editorial judgment, but it may have been the most brazen. It advertised Pullman's elegant sleeper service to black readers, most of whom could not afford it; those who could were often banished to second-class carriages by Jim Crow laws. When ads were not enough, Pullman used heavier-handed tactics. In Chicago, a Pullman lawyer is said to have quietly bought a controlling interest in the *Chicago Whip* about the time it switched from urging porters to organize to attacking the Brotherhood. Brotherhood officials say Pullman similarly strong-armed the two most influential black papers of the day, the *Chicago Defender* and *Pitts-*

burgh Courier, both of which vacillated between backing the union and bashing it.[32]

It is not necessary to rely on critics in making the case that Pullman massaged and manipulated the news for porters and other black readers. The company's own records make it even more compellingly. In the 1920s Pullman hired Claude A. Barnett, the founder of the Associated Negro Press, to publish a supposedly apolitical journal called *Heebie Jeebies.* It included a compendium of news, social listings, and features that were intended, as its logo announced, "so the man who runs may read." It also was intended to poison porters' sentiments toward the Brotherhood, although that only became clear in secret memos from Barnett. "The fight begins," he pronounced in a 1925 note to James Keeley, an assistant to the Pullman president. His plan for attacking the Brotherhood, he explained in a follow-up memo, was to "get under the skins of some of the disturbers by mentioning their organization, thus seeming impartial, but handling the news in such a way as to discount it and cast doubts as to its influence and intentions." Another note in 1926 revealed that it was not just *Heebie Jeebies* doing the bidding of Pullman president Edward F. Carry, but Barnett's Negro press service, which served 112 newspapers across America. "Please call Mr. Carry's attention to the fact that I have gone along and served during this entire period of unrest," Barnett wrote, "and that I have placed at your disposal the service of the Associated Negro Press."[33]

Just how well-spent the Pullman Company's money was is open to question. *Heebie Jeebies* did coin catchy epithets for Randolph as "Philip the Fooler" and the "Great Pretender," but the journal did not survive long or seem to sway many porters. The *Defender* and the *Whip* were more convincing and persistent. The former argued that the Brotherhood was setting a dangerous precedent by trying to preserve the job of the Pullman porter as a black "monopoly," saying, "We believe there should be black and white porters, and that there should be black and white conductors, all employed according to their abilities and not according to their race." Whatever its intent, its logic was compelling. The *Whip* based its attacks on the

Brotherhood's alliance with the allegedly racist and leftist American Federation of Labor, which struck a chord with blacks who knew firsthand the long antiblack record of white labor.[34] But neither Chicago paper succeeded in quelling enthusiasm in that city for the Brotherhood. At the same time a host of other black papers—from the *Amsterdam News* in New York to the *Boston Chronicle, Kansas City Call,* and *Philadelphia Tribune*—played it straight in their reporting of the struggle between Pullman and the Brotherhood. So did influential white-oriented newspapers and magazines, which realized that the powerful Pullman Company's battle with its black porters made for compelling copy, and saw the precedent-setting effort to dislodge a company union as an important business story.

Behind-the-scenes efforts to influence public opinion and indirect approaches to winning over porters were great when they worked. But for the butter knife to truly do its job, it had to be backed up with a meat cleaver. Pullman managers wielded their hatchets most efficiently and frequently in a ceremony dubbed "the Sack." Exactly how many porters were fired for their affiliation with the Brotherhood is unclear. McLaurin, the union organizer, said six hundred were dismissed nationwide over the years, including him, and one hundred were sacked in a single day in St. Louis.[35] Others put the number nationwide as high as eight hundred or as low as one hundred.

The company denied firing anyone for Brotherhood-related activities. It generally could come up with another justification, from insubordination to violating any of its 217 rules. Among union leaders, it became a badge of honor to have been sacked. Milton P. Webster, the firebrand head of the Chicago local, said he was "canned" for his pre-Brotherhood union efforts; the company said he "resigned to avoid dismissal" for pocketing passenger fares. The situation was similar with Cottrell Lawrence Dellums, known as "C. L.," who ran the Brotherhood's Oakland division and eventually succeeded Randolph as international president. The official reason for his firing was "sleeping on duty, car unguarded." But a Pullman memo confides that "no Company would retain a man in their service who was so disloyal as to go around distributing propaganda. . . . The sooner we rid our ranks of this disloyal type of employe[e] the better it will be for our service and interest, as he is the kind of fellow who will have bad influence over our loyal porters, and poison the minds of the traveling public against us."[36]

Sometimes outright firing was unnecessary. Just the threat could keep porters in line and out of the union. The best way to convey that warning, the company learned, was by prying open ever so slightly the vise blacks held on the job of Pullman porter. Filipino immigrants were the best wedge. The first were hired in 1925, just two months after the Brotherhood was unveiled, and were used on private sleepers taking fans from Chicago to University of Illinois football games in Urbana. The Filipinos "not only made a natty appearance but scored a decided hit," the company's *Pullman News* announced.[37] It might have added that these young, single Asian men shared many of the attributes that initially made Negroes so attractive to Pullman: a reputation for service, few job choices, and a willingness to do whatever the company asked.

At first porters and the men trying to unionize them brushed off the Filipino menace. The company had threatened but not carried out a similar campaign back in 1905, when it raised the specter of bringing in a squad of Japanese porters. Orientals, black porters told themselves, were too short to reach the upper berths, too weak to handle all the other lifting and lugging, too foreign to catch on in the United States. "Don't worry; the Company has too much brains to exchange workers, efficient and able, whom it knows," Randolph wrote, "for a foreigner who neither knows the language or the customs and manners of the American people."[38] That argument was believable when there was just a trickle of Filipino workers, along with Japanese, Chinese, and Mexicans. But the number from the Philippines slowly swelled, eventually reaching four hundred. Filipinos started as porters but eventually were put on a separate seniority list for busboys, cooks, and, most of all, attendants. Club car attendant was the best job available to a nonwhite on a Pullman train, with a starting salary of eighty-five dollars a month, twelve and a half dollars more than for a sleeping car porter, along with more responsibility and more opportunity for tips. The Pullman Company's message was unmistakable: you can be replaced and will be if you put your faith in the Brotherhood.[39]

That warning would be reinforced in other ways. Ashley Totten, one of the gang of five who founded the Brotherhood, was beaten badly enough to fracture his skull by an assailant who later testified that one of the men who hired him was a police captain formerly employed by the Pullman Company.[40] Morris "Dad" Moore, a retired porter in his seventies who ran the Brotherhood's Oakland branch before Dellums, lost his fifteen-dollar-a-month Pullman pension and his company job as caretaker of two old sleepers used as dormitories by out-of-town porters. And Randolph was lambasted for his alleged advocacy of everything from free love to class warfare, miscegenation to atheism.

The Pullman Company was understandably obsessed with Randolph and compiled detailed reports on everything he had ever said, done, or written. And he had said, done, and written enough in his younger, more radical days to prove embarrassing. The company also put together reports suggesting how flush porters were, noting in 1926 that 3,811 of 11,278 owned homes and 1,401 had cars. And it compiled lists of "colored employe[e]s who are entitled to special consideration on account of their earnest efforts to promote loyalty to the Company among their fellow employe[e]s and their commendable attitude in the face of severe criticism by the radical element and outside disturbers." Porter Alonzo Fields of Pennsylvania was listed as "a loyal missionary for our cooperative plan," while A. J. Brown of Fort Worth was "100% Pullman at all times."[41]

But Randolph and his colleagues were learning how to bite back. They took money and endorsements from anyone willing to give it, which in those early days was the Chicago Federation of Labor, the socialists, and the largely Jewish needle trades unions. They hired economists to support their call for higher wages and brought in high-powered lawyers, including the former chairman of a congressional commission that in 1915 had grilled Robert Todd Lincoln and other Pullman executives on their labor relations. White churches— Methodists and Congregationalists, Lutherans and Catholics—were successfully courted to embarrass black ones into extending a hand. Civil rights groups like the NAACP were enlisted to take on company propagandists like Perry Howard, shrugging him off as a "silly black lawyer." And while the Pullman Company was adept at branding Randolph a Red and provocateur, he was at least as quick to denounce anyone who got in his way as an Uncle Tom or handkerchief head.

He also was press savvy, an outgrowth of years publishing the *Messenger* as well as growing up in a house of avid readers. Sometimes he used the *Messenger* to strike back, as he did with the *Chicago Whip* and its editor, Joseph D. Bibb. "You are not opposing the Brotherhood of Sleeping-Car Porters because you think it is connected with the American Federation of Labor. That's merely *a* reason, not *the* reason. You had to hunt for a convenient excuse to justify your unreasonable and foolish attack on the most vitally constructive, economic movement ever begun by Negroes in America," he wrote in a 1925 article titled "A Reply to Joe D. 'Blibb,' 'Idiot-or' of the Chicago 'Flip,' Mis-Named the 'Whip.'" "The real reason is the advertising you are getting from the Pullman Company to oppose the movement. . . . You are just like the little boy on the knee of the ventriloquist. You appear to be speaking, but you are not speaking. The voice comes from behind. It's your master's voice, the Pullman Company, which is waving the long green before your blinking eyes. Without the slightest compunctions or scruples, you are willing to betray and sell out your race for a miserable mess of pottage."[42]*

---

*Although he was not shy about directly attacking his adversaries, Randolph sometimes prevailed on others to do his bidding. His old friend Chandler Owen obliged early in 1926, writing a scathing exposé in the *Messenger* called "The Neglected Truth." It accused Bibb of using blackmail to draw in advertisers and called him "a man whose presumption is exceeded only by his ignorance."

Ironically, the *Messenger* itself apparently was involved in an equally unseemly arrangement with wealthy individuals willing to pay for favorable coverage. "There were a number of Negroes in Chicago and some businesses and

Randolph's most hell-bent media campaign was the one he waged against the *Chicago Defender,* which for twenty years had been the porters' most effective ally. It pushed for higher wages and fairer treatment, and even called for porters to organize themselves. But when the Brotherhood was launched in 1925, America's leading black paper had a change of heart. Randolph, stung by the *Defender*'s criticism, lashed back. The paper should really be called "Surrender" or maybe the "World's Greatest Weakly," Randolph argued in print and on the stump, adding that it had given in to "gold and power." Porters and their friends were urged not to buy the paper or deliver it. Circulation began to fall, and by November of 1927, the *Defender* had again reversed position on the porters and their union, this time even more dramatically. "After a careful survey and review of the determined and lawful struggle of the Pullman porters, led by the brilliant and fearless A. Philip Randolph over a period of two years, the *Defender* herewith announces its determination to fight with the porters, arm in arm, shoulder to shoulder, for a living wage and better working conditions," the paper proclaimed in an editorial almost certainly ghostwritten by Randolph himself. Even more extraordinary, the *Defender* published a front-page article under Randolph's byline in which he pilloried the paper and its editors for their previous stance. "Some prominent men of color hired their souls for Pullman gold to lie and deceive," Randolph wrote. "In one of America's most sinister, sinful and sordid chapters of industrial crime, debauchery and deviltry, black men, alleged leaders, conscienceless, crooked and corrupt, seeking to redden their hands in the blood of their brothers for greed and gain, clutched the pulsing throats of innocent black babes with their filthy, murderous

---

even Negroes who had no businesses who were prominent and wanted to have a—have the country, especially black people, to be aware of their life and work," Randolph admitted in an interview half a century later. "They would have Chandler write up stories about them. He'd send them to me and we would publish them. But that source of income finally ceased."

Chandler Owen, "The Neglected Truth," *Messenger,* January 1926, 5; A. Philip Randolph, "The Reminiscences of A. Philip Randolph" (New York: Oral History Research Office, Columbia University, 1973), 221–22.

fingers of graft, to stifle their piteous cry for more bread, for more life, vouchsafed by the labor of their fathers. In pulpit and press, like mad dervishes howling for the blood of their victims, they hunted, hounded and harassed, libeled and slandered those militant men who stood their ground for the right of porters to organize and be men."[43]

The *Defender* episode taught the Brotherhood how to push hard and, when it had the upper hand, go for the jugular. A group called the Black Klan, based in Omaha and operating secretly, tried to intimidate porters into signing up with the Brotherhood. W. R. Estelle, a porter who was part of the company union, got a typed letter warning, "Now listen old boy we are still here In Omaha and shell be here the rest Of our lives you had better join the Union and show your receipt in the next Meeting of our club; if not we will make you spend more than five Dollars by shelling your home if you dont spend The money for one thing you will spend It for another." Another handwritten letter cautioned that the Christmas holiday would bring danger to Estelle. It closed by warning, "Don't take this as a Joke. We mean Death."[44] The threats never were carried out. And there never was explicit proof of the existence of the Black Klan or of a link between it and the Brotherhood, any more than between the Pullman Company and the illegal or unsavory deeds attributed to it. But the message was clear: two could fight dirty.

The apostle of choice when it came to getting tough was Milton P. Webster. If Randolph was the Brotherhood's high priest, Webster was its hellfire evangelist. He was one of them, a porter for eighteen years and a man of common clay. Where Randolph sipped tea and spoke in the cadence of King James, Webster snarled like a bulldog, chomped on cigars, and guzzled bourbon. The two looked their roles, Randolph beanpolelike and frail, Webster thickset and imposing. They complemented each other more even than Owen had Randolph. A. Philip offered up theory and broad strokes; Milton made the trains run on time. Randolph reigned over the union; Webster ran it. They were called the most harmonious one-two team in American labor, the gold-dust twins. Reared in the roughhouse politics of

Chicago's South Side, Webster held jobs as a bailiff and manager of apartment buildings, which gave him the same freedom as Randolph from Pullman intimidation. He used it to do his own intimidating.[45]

When the Pullman Company tried to have Randolph arrested as he got off the train in Chicago, Webster pulled out his bailiff's badge, fended off arresting officers, and deprived the company of pictures of the Brotherhood boss behind bars. When a black minister tried to back out of a vow to let the union use his church, Webster told him, "If we don't meet in this church this Sunday, you're going to find all these stones in the middle of the street." Webster built his local into the Brotherhood's biggest and most loyal, right in the Pullman Company's backyard. He took on black churches and the black press, triumphantly. He reminded Randolph and the New York hierarchy that the verdict on their union would come not from the public or government but from porters on the sleepers. He vowed to fight "till Hell froze over, and then get a pair of skates and fight on the ice." Years later he recalled: "As soon as we started to organize, everybody started telling us what we ought not to do. But we didn't compromise, and we didn't moderate, but we fought. We're not here because anybody loves us. We are here because we pushed everybody out of our way, that's all."[46]

The Webster-Randolph tandem of bully-charmer offered a winning formula, or so it appeared. A quiet poll on and off the trains by union representatives found that just over half of Pullman's 10,875 porters wanted to be represented not by the entity set up by their long-standing employer but by this new and slightly dangerous Brotherhood. It was an extraordinary achievement barely one year after the inaugural meeting in the Elks hall.

THE PULLMAN COMPANY saw things differently. It had a different count on how many porters there were: 12,354. Its survey yielded a different answer on which organization those porters wanted to act on their behalf: 85 percent voted for the company's in-house union.

And it had a decidedly different verdict on the Brotherhood: that it did not then, or ever, reflect the best interests of Pullman porters. Such was the company's disdain for Randolph and his union brothers that when it filed its poll results with federal mediators, it refused even to acknowledge there was a Brotherhood of Sleeping Car Porters. It referred instead to "such persons mentioned."

The battle that had begun with daring parries and counter-thrusts, with each side testing the other's limits and ratcheting up its own, was entering a second critical phase that can only be described as trench warfare. The new theaters of conflict were the courts and arcane federal agencies, the White House and the halls of Congress. If the first year was high energy and promised speedy resolution, this stage made clear that nothing happened fast. Which is precisely what the Pullman Company counted on. It had the money to outlast the Brotherhood, the lawyers and lobbyists to outduel it, and the knowledge that the status quo meant no union. For the Brotherhood to prevail, members would need the forbearance of Job and leaders the wisdom of Solomon.

Neither virtue was visible in the battle against tipping. What Randolph wanted was a wage hike, but knowing there was no direct way to make the Pullman Company comply, he tried an indirect one: petitioning the Interstate Commerce Commission to ban tipping and order the company to pay a livable wage. Unions representing waiters, cabdrivers, and other workers who relied on gratuities had long argued that tips debased their members, lowered wages, and ensured second-class service for customers who would not or could not pay. None, however, had taken the daring step the Brotherhood did in the fall of 1927 by seeking government redress. Randolph understood the company's cynical strategy of using tips not just to save it from paying higher salaries but to ensure that porters attended to every passenger whim. He tried to make that case to the ICC. Three of seven commissioners bought it, but the majority said the Brotherhood's argument boiled down to whether or not the ICC could set salaries at a private firm like Pullman. The answer, they added, was no.

The verdict by porters themselves was more lopsided, with the union again the loser. The whole crusade against tipping seemed to them harebrained, threatening to ban tips without ensuring a rise in wages. Regardless of what the ICC said, the public now had the perfect excuse to cut back on gratuities. Brotherhood members would have told their leader all that if he had asked, and he would have known if he were one of them. Such misgivings percolated on their own but were given a second boil by the Pullman Company, which sensed that Randolph was out of sync with his membership on tipping and got its in-house union to send the ICC petitions of porters opposing the ban.

Another master at getting under Randolph's skin in those years was the *Pittsburgh Courier* and its owner-editor, Robert Vann. In the Brotherhood's early days, Vann was its most bullish supporter among the black press. He published sympathetic articles on porter grievances, ran a regular feature on "Brotherhood Progress," and explained in a letter to a friend that "the *Pittsburgh Courier* must fight the battle of the porters almost alone. In fact, the other colored papers seem to be afraid of the Pullman Company or too willing to accept its money." His battle was waged partly out of conviction, partly from self-interest. Readers seemed fully engaged, which helped circulation, and porters themselves subscribed to as well as delivered the *Courier,* carrying thousands of copies across the South, Midwest, and West. Randolph, who in 1921 had pilloried the *Courier* as "the journalistic spokesman of the petty black bourgeoisie," by 1927 considered Vann's publication "the most progressive, enlightened and militant of all race newspapers."[47]

A year later the détente dissolved. On April 7, 1928, Vann wrote to Randolph: "[The porters] are standing at the Red Sea under your leadership with no possible convenience in sight to get them across. The Pullman Company will not divide the waters so long as you stand as the Moses." Seven days later the *Courier* went public with its call for Randolph to resign. "Mr. Randolph has been informed that the company will not deal with him because of his history as a socialist," Vann wrote in a page-one appeal to porters and maids.

"He is now at the place where he can go no farther and it is time the porters realized it and worked out some other way to get some of the things they want." Randolph replied with characteristic bite and brimstone: "*Why did he support the Brotherhood for two years led by a Socialist, when, as he now says, American capital has refused to deal with such organizations?* There is a certain colored gentleman in the wood pile somewhere, and the Brotherhood will smoke him out before this fight is over." Vann had the last word. "The whole world is in the pay of the Pullman Company—except one man, and that man is Randolph," Vann penned. "He is the ONLY SIMON PURE man in all the world. All the others are 'crooks,' 'bribe-takers,' 'Niggers-in-the-woodpile' and enemies of the Porters."[48]

Vann's change of heart might have been sincere. He was a capitalist, wanted the porter-Pullman dispute resolved, and saw how wide the impasse had become between Randolph and the company. Or payola may have been the motivator. That was the prattle in Brotherhood circles, and Vann's biographer quotes an anonymous source saying that Pullman gave Vann fifty thousand dollars. The last and likeliest explanation for Vann's reversal involves that centermost of human sentiments, ego. Five months earlier the *Defender,* the *Courier*'s archrival for the mantle as America's leading black paper, had done a reverse about-face, from foe to friend. Vann felt betrayed that Randolph now leaked as many stories to the *Defender* as to the *Courier.* The *Courier* editor also dreamed of being crowned America's number one Negro and could have calculated that replacing Randolph as prince of the Pullman porters would be a shortcut to the throne.[49]

Vann had disparagingly dubbed Randolph the Brotherhood's Moses, but at that juncture the Brotherhood leader felt more like Pharaoh bearing the burden of God's ten plagues. Two years earlier the union, armed with survey results showing it was backed by a majority of porters, had decided to push for recognition as the porters' bargaining agent under the just-passed Railway Labor Act, which promised "prompt and orderly settlement" of labor disputes. The union wrote the Pullman Company asking to meet; the company ignored that letter and a follow-up, but it did launch its own polling of porters over the next two months, coming up with the 85 percent show of support for its in-house union. The Brotherhood, knowing Pullman never would go along on its own, in October 1926 petitioned a federal mediation board to intervene.

Randolph had right on his side, but that was all. The Brotherhood felt sure porters had been coerced into voting for the company union, and collected affidavits from nearly one thousand of them saying so, yet after six months the mediation board still had said not a word and union members were getting antsy. Rather than counseling patience, Randolph wrote the Pullman president a fifteen-page letter assuring him that "none of the leaders of the Union are either Atheists or Communists," and promising that the Brotherhood's goal "is not to dictate but to cooperate, with every honorable means in a sympathetic and harmonious spirit for the mutual good and benefit of Company and porter."[50] The tone he sought was reasonableness; to his union members and Pullman management, it sounded desperate. Worse still, Randolph and his colleagues did not seem to understand the Railway Labor Act. It gave the mediation board power to investigate complaints like Randolph's but not to order companies to comply or even force them into arbitration.

The result: the Brotherhood won the battle, with the mediation board ruling in June of 1927 that Randolph's union represented a majority of Pullman porters. But before the summer was over it had become clear that the war to force the company into negotiations was lost. The board announced in August that, after spending two months trying to get Pullman to sit down with the Brotherhood, it had failed. The defeat was compounded when two black papers already critical of the Brotherhood suggested it was time to surrender. "The proper thing now for those who have given him [Randolph] money is to demand so much of it back, dismiss him from their case, and try through some other means to get their cause before the proper parties," wrote the *St. Louis Argus*. The *Defender* called on porters to drop their bid for a union and asked the company to forgive them. "The affair," the editorial concluded, "now is ended. Let it be forgotten."[51]

The Railway Labor Act, toothless though it was, did offer another way out for the Brotherhood. It could threaten to strike, and if the mediation board believed the emergency was real, the board could ask the president to step in. Knowing how low morale had sunk and how few options they had, Randolph and his lieutenants decided to try the strike route. Slowly at first, then single-mindedly, they rallied support, and by the spring of 1928 they announced that 6,013 porters had voted for a strike, with fewer than 50 against. That was the easy part. Tougher by far was convincing the mediation board that the election meant anything, especially in the face of the Brotherhood's own written assurance to members that "a strike vote IS NOT A STRIKE."[52] The Pullman Company, meanwhile, made a compelling case that in the unlikely event the Brotherhood called a strike, the few porters who walked off could easily be replaced by thousands of retirees and young job applicants. The board believed the company, and, on June 6, it wrote the Brotherhood to say there was no emergency or need for presidential intervention. His bluff called, Randolph had to decide whether to go ahead with the strike that was due to begin in two days.

In Kansas City, Ashley Totten and his men were ready, having collected sawed-off shotguns, knives, clubs, and boxes of matches in anticipation of a long battle. In Oakland, Dad Moore and C. L. Dellums expected 90 percent of their men to honor the walkout. They had soup kitchens ready for stranded strikers, and leftist labor allies promising that no train would make it out of Oakland. Chicago was prepared, too, with Webster predicting 85 percent participation and having trouble convincing his men not to walk out on their own. The timing could not have been better for maximum disruption of the rails and the nation's peace of mind: the Republican National Convention was being staged four days later in Kansas City, the Democratic National Convention was set to go two weeks after that in Houston, and families across the country were heading off on summer vacations.[53]

Still, it is likely that more porters nationwide would have stayed than struck. Blacks historically had been strikebreakers, not strikers, and porters knew full well Pullman's history of crushing labor revolts and the workers who joined them. They knew, too, that the company already had called up new men, bivouacked loyal porters at railroad yards in case they were needed to replace strikers, and hired an army of Pinkerton police. And it was a dead certainty that only the most leftist white unions would back any work stoppage, which ruled out even the AFL chief, William Green, who—almost certainly at Randolph's urging—sent a telegram the morning of June 8 urging that the strike be postponed. Randolph never had wanted to go through with the strike, hoping to bluff the board into believing he would, and he used Green's telegram as a pretext for calling off the walkout.[54]

The Brotherhood boss called it a postponement. His critics called it a sellout. "Despite Pullman's traditional, hard-boiled stand against organized labor, its greatest asset in handcuffing organization of its porters at this time is the leader of the de facto 'Brotherhood of Sleeping Car Porters,' Mr. A. Piffle Randolph," Rienzi B. Lemus— the head of the Brotherhood of Dining Car Employees and a fierce Randolph rival—wrote the next month in the *New York Age*. "This milk-fed cornerlogist, Piffle Randolph, is a millstone about the necks of Pullman employees which, if not disengaged, will carry them into the depths of the sea of oblivion with it (him, All Piffle Randolph), generalissimo of the Afric huslerati." The Communists were even more incensed, holding a rally in Harlem to lambaste Randolph and charging that leaders of the Brotherhood "have forsaken the policy of militant struggle in the interest of the workers for the policy of class collaboration with the bosses and bluffing with the strike." Randolph, already livid over the way the Communists were trying to infiltrate his Brotherhood, fired back that the charges were the "sorriest nonsense and silliest tommyrot which could only emanate from crack-brained fanatics or low grade morons."[55]

His defense notwithstanding, a disturbing pattern was emerging in Brotherhood behavior. Power increasingly was concentrated in Randolph, but his exercise of it looked increasingly feckless. He understood the need for accommodation, but not when to stand and fight. Starting projects was his specialty, failing to finish them his Achilles' heel. He placed infinite trust in federal laws he did not fully understand, and his buoyancy in the face of repeated defeats made him seem blind to the truth. Critics groused that the porters themselves had never voted him into his all-powerful office, and that the Brotherhood that cost some of them their jobs had gotten him his. They called him *haughty, aloof,* even *dictatorial,* the very adjectives used thirty years before to describe George Mortimer Pullman.

Those tensions came to the fore in a rift between Randolph, the Brotherhood's philosopher, and Webster, its ward heeler. Webster remained the loyal lieutenant while Randolph petitioned the ICC and the mediation board, then bluffed a strike. But Webster worried that the union was losing touch with porters' core concerns of wages and working conditions, and with the porters themselves. He watched Randolph centralize power in New York, which meant taking it away from districts like Chicago, St. Louis, and Boston that provided the bulk of manpower and money. At least twice he threatened to quit. Finally, he challenged Randolph directly, convening a meeting of district directors during the summer of 1928 at which substantial authority over policy and funding was stripped from Randolph and New York, and given back to the locals. But rather than dethroning his king, Webster had saved him. The Chicago strongman used his new powers to provide even more effective nuts-and-bolts leadership of the union, leaving Randolph free to continue as orator and sage. "The feudal lord," the Brotherhood historian William H. Harris wrote, "was reminding the king where power now lay."[56]

Patching things up with the union's members was not so easy. Frustrated by hopes raised then dashed, a strike called then canceled, members left en bloc. From its peak of 4,632 in 1928, the Brotherhood roster fell to 2,368 in 1929, then to 1,091 in 1931. "I imagine 90 percent of the men joined up in the first six months of our campaign, but just as soon as the pressure was on, 90 percent of them went out again!" recalled McLaurin. In fact, fewer than half had ever joined, and of them, only one in three paid dues regularly.

Six years after its kickoff, the union looked less like a brotherhood than a ragtag band of brothers.[57]

The setbacks hit Randolph especially hard. It was not just the rebellion he faced from Webster and other deputies, and the abandonment by his members. His cherished *Messenger* was gone, too. White liberals and middle-class blacks stopped reading it because, as the official organ of the Brotherhood, it had become one-dimensional. Porters had given it up, too, in frustration with the Brotherhood and because just carrying a copy was grounds for firing by Pullman. With so few dues coming in, the union no longer could underwrite the publication, although beginning the next year it occasionally put out a new journal called the *Black Worker.* The last issue of the *Messenger,* published in June of 1928, had no acknowledgment of the fantastic forum it had been for radical politics, no obituary for its drive toward interracial unionism.

By then Randolph had no tears left. He still was mourning the death, five months before, of his brother, James. His mother and father already were gone, and James had been living with him in New York. A. Philip was proud of how close his older brother was to finishing at City College, and of his plans for graduate studies at the University of Berlin. Then diphtheria took over, eating away at his airways and poisoning his heart. "I cannot bear to live in a world without my brother," the union leader told a friend in Harlem. Facing James's death, he wrote another friend, was harder than to "fight a dozen Pullman Companies."[58]

DESPONDENT, EVEN DESPERATE. That was the state of mind among Brotherhood leaders in the late 1920s and early 1930s. It was not just their union that was disintegrating, but also the United States. The Roaring Twenties were a time of introspection and self-absorption, when the nation denied rather than dealt with social schisms like racism and economic inequality. Young people sat on flag-poles, swallowed goldfish, and bopped until they dropped at dance marathons. John T. Scopes underwent a trial for teaching evolution instead of creationism in his Tennessee classroom, while the Ku Klux Klan underwent a revival. The poor discovered jazz and credit. The rich got richer. You could track it all on George Pullman's sleepers, where personal rooms and private cars increasingly were the compartments of choice in this era of speed and opulence. There were barbershops and beauty parlors on wheels. A ticker tape let affluent men watch their stocks soar and, if they followed long enough, fall through the floor. The Great Depression hit farmers first, but by 1930 the hurt had spread to everyone who kept money in the bank or had bought the pitch to "buy now, pay later." A decade of troubles for labor unions got worse as unemployment rose, the courts grew less friendly still, and employers tried to take back wage increases agreed to when the economy was robust. None of this boded well for giving birth to a new union, especially one whose members were black.

Things were bad enough for the Brotherhood that two eminent labor historians, Sterling D. Spero and Abram L. Harris, penned its death notice. "The great pity of the virtual collapse of the porter's union lies not merely in its effect upon the porters who have grievances which sorely need correction but in its effect upon Negro labor generally," they wrote in 1931. "The hope that this movement would become the center and rallying point for Negro labor as a whole is now dead."[59]

The men who launched the Brotherhood might have been tempted to give up and go back, but most no longer had the option. The Pullman Company had made clear it would not take them back. The Brotherhood, meanwhile, had metamorphosed from a job to a mission. Its leaders had learned to dig deeper into their pockets and souls to sustain themselves, and to keep alive the union during four fractious years when most members had given up. If the first phase of their struggle had been the quick hit and the second trench warfare, this third phase was the last-man-standing approach the Soviet army would take during World War II: showing it could withstand a siege longer than the Germans dreamed, waiting for that uncertain moment when it could hit back. Brotherhood officers' recollections of those years sound like letters home from soldiers during wartime, with the same sense of sacrifice for higher purpose, bonding with comrades, and faith in prevailing.

"I am fiting not for myself but for 12,000 porters and maids, and there children," Oakland's Dad Moore, the oldest and least lettered of the leadership, wrote to Webster shortly before he died in 1930. "I has bin at Starvasian Door but it had not change my mind, for just as the night folows the Day we are gointer to win. Tell all the men in your Dist that they should folow Mr. Randolph as they would folow Jes Christ."[60]

In St. Louis, the Brotherhood director, E. J. Bradley, was evicted from his office, and his furniture was sold to cover back rent. He started working out of his car, but debt collectors confiscated it. He lost two homes when he could not meet the mortgages, and a wife when he could not support her. He lived with his daughter and friends, and often ate quail killed with his shotgun, one of his last possessions. Headquarters told him to disband the St. Louis division, but he refused, earning the title "noblest Roman of them all." In New York headquarters, too, the phones were shut off and lights turned out. The staff was forced to take up residence in the front rooms of McLaurin's apartment on 140th Street. "Saturday night, we used to have regular suppers. I used to cook chitterlings and pigs feet. Those were the big things. I used to cook a hundred pounds of chitterlings, a couple of hundred pigs feet, make plenty of slaw and potato salad," he said. "It was on this income, for two years at least, that we kept headquarters together."[61]

The stories about Randolph during the lean years were even more inspired, and were retold at Baker Heater Leagues until they became part of Brotherhood mythology. The Chief wore shoes with no soles. His blue serge suit was the same style favored by George Pullman, only Randolph had just one, and it was so worn "it began to shine like a looking glass." When he took a train to outlying districts, he had only enough money to get there; colleagues had to raise the return fare. "Brother Randolph, Brother Totten and myself, Brother O.W. Bynum, we worked for the organization for years and never knew what a payday was," remembered McLaurin. "It was not unusual for us—two of us—to share a bottle of milk and a loaf of bread, trying to keep body and soul together, in those days. I had no problem of weight at that time, because I was down to the core."[62]

Weight became a gauge of sacrifice for Brotherhood bosses, including Dellums, who took over for Dad Moore. He recalled that Randolph "was so tall and thin that once in a while he put his hand on his hip and it would gradually slide down. He was so thin, he didn't have a hip. . . . One thing that always impressed me about the real revolutionary leaders of struggles was that they were always *thin* men. Never saw a fat one yet! I just deduced then that the fat ones never stuck because they worried too much about their stomachs."[63]

Randolph had a chance to fatten his wallet and his stomach. A check for ten thousand dollars arrived one day with a letter urging him to take a vacation in Europe. It was signed by a man he suspected was connected to the Pullman Company. He was hungry, the rent was due, and it must have been tempting, but A. Philip Randolph sent it back by registered mail. So goes one version of this most famous of Saint Philip legends. Others have it that the check was for twenty-five thousand dollars, or that he could write in any amount up to $1 million. William Bowe, who succeeded Ashley Totten as the Brotherhood's secretary-treasurer, said he was hiding in the next room when a porter from Philadelphia known to be a Pullman stool pigeon offered Randolph a check and told him to fill in the amount. "Take this blank check back to where you got it," Bowe recalled Randolph saying, "and tell them I'm not for sale."[64] Roy Wilkins, the head of the NAACP and a colleague of Randolph's, passed down a variant of the story to his favorite nephew, Roger, in which the offer was made three times—all by George Pullman himself. First it was for ten thousand dollars, then twenty-five thousand dollars. "Maybe a year later, when it really looked like they were going to make it, Mr. Pullman called him in again and

said, 'Randolph, I want you to look at this check carefully,'"
recounted Roger Wilkins, a Pulitzer prize–winning journalist and
former assistant U.S. attorney general. "And Randolph looked at it
very carefully and didn't say anything. Pullman said, 'You'll notice
that it doesn't have any figures written in there. You can write in
your own figure.' Mr. Randolph handed back the check and said,
'This is not about me. This is about getting decent working conditions for the men. Thank you and good day.'"[65] It was the best version of all, except that at the time he was supposed to be offering the
bribe George Pullman was embedded in his fortresslike grave, where
he had been buried nearly forty years before.

Men always starred in such stories, but they could never have
held things together during those years without their leading ladies.
Porters' wives took in laundry and deferred dreams of kids attending college when their husbands were fired or furloughed. To raise
money, they ran fish fries, boat rides, bake sales, and contests to see
who had the best "bobbed" hair, the daring style of the day as black
women and white sheared their locks to look like flappers. Lifting
morale also was left to them. So, in the worst of times, was enlisting
members. They organized into Colored Women's Economic Coun-
cils and, later, into the Ladies' Auxiliary to the Brotherhood of
Sleeping Car Porters. "It was," as one of their leaders claimed, "the
women who made the union."[66]

Their union-bolstering job was made harder not just by the Pullman Company, which sent welfare workers into the home to spy,
but by their husbands, who were radical regarding unions and race
but unapologetically sexist. Modeled after women's divisions of the
white railroad unions, the Ladies' Auxiliary was expected to serve
tea and cake and take orders from the Brotherhood. The auxiliary
bylaws made that point. So did the head of their husbands' union.
The Ladies' Auxiliary, Randolph wrote, "[is] the Brotherhood's
assistant. It is its helpmeet. The Brotherhood in common parlance is
the boss."[67]

He and his porter-brothers were even harder on the black maids who for years had been working alongside them on Pullman's ritziest runs. They fed and babysat children and the aged, nursed the sick, and scrubbed bathrooms. Their main charges were ladies, rich ones, whose hair they set, hats they boxed, berths they tucked in, breakfast they brought to bed, and other up-close needs they met in ways that would have gotten porters lynched. Much the way porters' home on the train was the smoking room and their preoccupation shining shoes, maids lived in the ladies' lounge and spent their lives sewing, washing, and ironing. By 1926 there were two hundred Pullman maids, one for every fifty porters. All wore gray dresses with starched white collars, cuffs, and aprons. As taxing as a porter's life could be, maids had it tougher. Their wages and tips were lower, and they were prohibited from socializing with porters. The Pullman Company hired Chinese maids as a threat to its black ones the same way it used Filipino attendants to put the fear of God into black porters. But whereas those porters could count on the Brotherhood to stand up for them, maids were treated as second-class citizens by their aspiring union as well as their employer. The Brotherhood's new constitution, approved in 1929, did not refer to maids. Even more telling, the International Brotherhood of Sleeping Car Porters and Maids underwent a name change, lopping off the seldom-used "and Maids."[68]

"Some porters probably thought they were too few in number to matter, while others appear to have considered maids unequal to male union members," explained Melinda Chateauvert, a historian who documented the Brotherhood's sexism toward wives and women colleagues. As for precisely where maids fell under the 1929 constitution, "the place for females, the document implied, was the Women's Economic Council."[69]

Writing a constitution and holding its first national convention demonstrated that the Brotherhood still had a pulse. It also had a plan, albeit a more modest one than the campaigns Randolph launched during the union's early years. There were two main targets in the late 1920s and early 1930s: the mainly white American labor movement and the black community.

Trying to pry open the AFL was controversial in several ways, starting with its record of racism. The federation had long barred its unions from explicitly discriminating based on race. But it ignored its own edicts when unions like the Brotherhood Railway Carmen excluded blacks, and it looked the other way when other unions made enlistees promise to propose for membership only whites. The result: as of 1930, only fifty-six thousand of 1.3 million black workers were unionized, or 4.3 percent, as opposed to 21 percent for the workforce as a whole. Rather than opening up in the aftermath of World War I, the way it had promised in repeated resolutions, "the A.F. of L. has less positive power and influence among Negro workers than at any other time in the last thirty years," Ira De A. Reid, the chief researcher at the National Urban League, wrote in 1930. "When the American Federation of Labor condones practices similar to the above mentioned, and sugarcoats these practices with its palaver about all workers being organized despite race," he added, "the Negro worker may justifiably reply: 'Applesauce.'"[70]

Randolph knew firsthand about AFL exclusion, having been rebuffed as early as 1927 in his bid for an international charter. A decade earlier, as editor of the *Messenger*, he had led the charge against the federation, calling it a "machine for the propagation of race prejudice" and urging black workers instead to join Debs's Industrial Workers of the World. But in 1928 Randolph renewed his request for the House of Labor to make room for his Brotherhood. Economic progress was a precondition to racial progress for blacks generally and for his porters, Randolph believed, and the AFL, whatever its racism, could be a powerful ally against the Pullman Company. The federation partially relented early in 1929, admitting the Brotherhood not as a united union with full-fledged international membership—which would have further outraged existing AFL unions that hoped to sign up the porters—but as thirteen locals, each granted a "federal" charter. That was the strange designation the AFL used for all-black unions, limiting their jurisdiction and independence, forcing them to pay a thirty-five-cent-per-member monthly tax compared to a full-fledged union's one-cent fee, and making clear to everyone their second-class status.*

The Brotherhood's other big push during the interlude years was introspective. It rallied support within the black community, making the battle against Pullman about racial as well as economic justice, and casting itself as the black David against the Pullman Company's white Goliath. It drew on the know-how and dynamism of women flush from victory in their battle for suffrage and still pushing the campaign against lynching. Key black ministers were courted, along with the NAACP, Urban League, and other political and

*From the start, the setup posed problems for Randolph. It gave new stature to local Brotherhood leaders and further eroded his national standing. It embarrassed the Brotherhood when even its biggest locals were suspended for failure to pay the AFL's exorbitant dues. And it gave grist to critics who charged he was cozying up to powerful white interests. Still, the new arrangement gave more than it took from the Brotherhood and the AFL. The federation president, William Green, got an emissary to Negro labor, a hedge against charges he was a racist, and, best of all, a true-believing ally in his crusade against communist labor organizers. Randolph got prestige and, over time, a voice within the inner circle of America's most powerful league of labor. Both sides trumpeted their triumphs when Green came to Harlem's Abyssinian Baptist Church in June of 1929 to personally welcome the Brotherhood into his federation. The AFL boss's unprecedented appearance at the black church, alongside four Negro clergymen, "was heralded as presaging the passing of the traditional George of the Pullman car, sleepless and largely dependent on tips for his salary," the *New York Times* reported the next day. Randolph, the paper added, "enthusiastically introduced [Green] as a second Abraham Lincoln, come to relieve industrial bondage."

Oratory and puffery were two of many skills Randolph had been fine-tuning. He and his union colleagues developed techniques for extracting dues in days when members were more reluctant than normal to pay. One was to collect *before* the men took their modest paychecks home to wives who had budgeted every bit of them, and to pass the hat at mass meetings *before* Randolph spoke, since afterward the audience was fired up and headed off to talk things over. They also learned to tread softly when organizing below the Mason-Dixon Line. Jacksonville authorities underlined that lesson when they arrested the Brotherhood's man there, Bennie Smith, charging him with "preaching social equality" and, according to Smith, threatening to string him up. After that the union did its organizing in the South one-on-one, with little high-profile presence. It had southern locals, but the only ones with more than a handful of members were Richmond, Norfolk, Jacksonville, and New Orleans.

William H. Harris, *Keeping the Faith: A. Philip Randolph, Milton P. Webster, and the Brotherhood of Sleeping Car Porters* (Urbana, Ill.: University of Illinois Press, 1977), 153–61; "Green Is Heckled by Negro Radicals," *New York Times*, July 1, 1929; Jervis Anderson, *A. Philip Randolph: A Biographical Portrait* (Berkeley: University of California Press, 1972), 183.

professional leaders. To prove his common touch, Randolph even joined the Improved and Benevolent Order of Elks of the World, a popular black fraternity whose Grand Exalted Ruler was an exporter and whose initiation rituals, Randolph confided, "nearly killed me."* The Brotherhood's campaign for black support was most visible in Chicago, which now was ground zero for its organizing efforts with more than double the members of the next-largest local in New York.[71]

Returning to their black roots was a blend of passion, expediency, and desperation for Randolph, Webster, and their colleagues. They had not given up on white institutions. During those same years, Brotherhood leaders were justifying their new coziness with the AFL, an institution that embodied racial exclusiveness. And they had depended from the start on support from mainly white institutions like the Garland Fund, *Jewish Daily Forward,* and Amalgamated Clothing Workers Union of America. But the Brotherhood brain trust, Randolph especially, had always seen the battle for a union as bigger than just the porters. They saw themselves striking a blow for blacks generally and for social justice. What better time to plant those seeds and replant their roots than now, when nothing else seemed to be working? They could imagine no better way to keep morale up among those few porters who still were paying their dues and pledging their fealty.

RANDOLPH AND THE rest were doing one more thing during those lean years: praying. Not for anything specific; just a miracle. Their savior came in the unlikely form of the new Groton- and Harvard-trained president from Hyde Park, Franklin Delano Roosevelt. His election in

---

*The Elks' rituals, while secret, were said to range from having a barber scrape the faces of blindfolded initiates with a dull file they thought was a razor, to making them walk over eggshells they were told were broken glass. Arthur J. Riggs, a cofounder in 1898 of the black Elks, was an ex-slave and Pullman porter. When Riggs somehow obtained a copy of the white Elks' secret rituals, he was threatened with lynching. http://northbysouth.kenyon.edu/ and www.phoenixmasonry.org.

1932, and the new bankruptcy and transportation laws he pushed through, seemed to be precisely what the Brotherhood needed. Not only did this legislation outlaw company unions and "yellow dog" contracts that kept workers from unionizing, it changed the nation's mood toward organized labor. Roosevelt convinced America it could overcome its fears, made workers believe that government was back to being their friend, and, most important to the Pullman porters, told blacks they were part of the New Deal he was offering the nation.

So palpable was the anticipation that the Brotherhood built back its membership from a nadir of 658 in 1933 to 2,627 the following year. But when it petitioned the government to investigate porters' grievances, it was devastatingly rebuffed. The Pullman Company was not covered by the new Emergency Railroad Transportation Act, Roosevelt's railroad czar said, because in the eyes of the law it was not a railroad. Consequently, porters remained unprotected.

Randolph and his allies went to work on Capitol Hill, and by 1934 they had a law that went even farther than they had asked, requiring companies to negotiate with unions chosen by a majority of their workers. Although some black railroad workers were left out, Pullman porters were explicitly included. There were more obstacles ahead, but armed with the new law and renewed confidence in its mission, the Brotherhood surmounted each. When the Pullman Company substituted its handpicked Pullman Porters and Maids Protective Association for the in-house Employee Representation Plan, the Brotherhood demanded a secret ballot. Just as summer was starting in 1935, porters rendered an incontestable judgment, voting for the Brotherhood by a margin of 5,931 to 1,422. When the AFL tried to pry away the Brotherhood's right to organize porters and give it to the Order of Sleeping Car Conductors, Randolph screamed foul. Not only was that bid dropped, but a year later the Brotherhood got an international charter that finally made it a full-fledged member of the House of Labor. Best of all, on July 29, 1935, the Pullman Company for the first time sat down with Randolph, Webster, Dellums, and four other porters to begin bargaining.

Two more years of hard negotiating lay ahead. A federal mediation board had to be called in. The Brotherhood hired its own consultants to detail the economic privations facing porters, from low salaries and shrinking tips to high costs of living. Porters reflected their refound faith in the union by continuing to reenlist, swelling its ranks to 4,165 in 1935 and 5,938 in 1937. The company, however, refused to fully recognize the union even as it was bargaining with it, or to grant its requests for work changes or wage hikes. It balked at the idea of mediation and remained hopeful about a pending court challenge of the Amended Railway Labor Act.

But behind the scenes things were changing. Pullman managers had gotten used to Randolph the radical, and he had become less so, outdoing even the company in his tirades against the Communists. Company executives saw the political tide turning against them in Washington and suspected their court challenge would fail, which it did. Ridership on the sleeping cars was plummeting, and with it revenues. Most ominous, the five big railroad unions were stuck in contract disputes and, on August 25, 1937, announced plans for a nationwide strike of 250,000 railroad workers. Pullman porters said they might walk out with them.

Still, what happened that same morning in the Chicago conference room where the Brotherhood was negotiating with Pullman representatives shocked everyone on the union's side of the table. The Pullman Company vice president, Champ Carry, entered the session and announced, "Gentleman, the Pullman Company is ready to sign." He then circled the long bargaining table, shaking hands with each of the eight Brotherhood negotiators. Twelve years to the day after Randolph had launched the Brotherhood in Harlem's steamy Elks hall, the union of Pullman porters had its first contract with the powerful Pullman Company.

The mainstream press was so busy covering the railroad strike threat that it largely overlooked the Brotherhood's breakthrough. The *New York Times,* which had published ninety-three articles mentioning Pullman porters over the twelve years the Brotherhood was waging war, described the armistice agreement in just one paragraph on page twenty-eight. Stories in the black press were longer, but not much. It was preoccupied with a milestone of another sort as the boxer Joe Louis—the Brown Bomber and pride of black America—was defending his heavyweight title. The *Pittsburgh Courier,* which had considered the Brotherhood front-page news for years, gave the story five paragraphs on page seven. The *Chicago Defender* gave it a banner headline, but on page three, and the picture it ran of Brotherhood leaders took up slightly more space than its ten-paragraph story.

Although the media of the moment paid scant attention, the belated ballyhoo was breathtaking. For decades afterward, newspapers, magazines, and books offered a steady stream of superlatives to describe the porters' achievements. *Reader's Digest* told its 12 million subscribers that "to the Negro, the Brotherhood with its initial 18,000 members was a more significant organization than the United Automobile Workers with its then 400,000 members." The journalist Lester Velie credited Randolph with "the longest organizing drive in union annals, and from seemingly unpromising menial, frightened human beings—the humble porters he leads—he fashioned a disciplined union." Murray Kempton, one of New York's longest-lasting, widest-read columnists, called the Pullman porters "a little army unafraid." Of their triumph after twelve years of struggle, he wrote, "It is a measure of the Negro's circumstance that, in America, the smallest things usually take him so very long, and that, by the time he wins them, they are no longer little things: they are miracles."[72]

The NAACP explained that miracle in its *Crisis* magazine of November 1937. "As important as is this lucrative contract as a labor victory to the Pullman porters, it is even more important to the Negro race as a whole, from the point of view of the Negro's up-hill climb for respect, recognition and influence, and economic advancement," the political scientist G. James Fleming wrote. "The porters' accomplishment undoubtedly marks the first time that an all-Negro union has signed a contract with one of America's largest industrial organizations; this is the first time that Negroes have contributed so much of their own pennies (some million and one-half dollars) to push a fight for their economic betterment; this is the first time they have stuck together so long in a struggle in which there were so many odds against them; this is the first time that so important a step forward has been made under entirely Negro leadership."[73]

That was just the beginning of the list of "firsts." The Brotherhood was the first workers' organization of any color to displace a company union. It was the first black union admitted as a full-fledged member of the AFL and the most successful black union ever. Its auxiliary was the first international labor organization of black women. And when the Brotherhood thrashed the Pullman Company–backed union in 1935, the *New York Times* reported that "the election is said to be the first under the auspices of any governmental agency in which a Negro trade union has won recognition as spokesmen for the employe[e]s."[74]

That Negro trade union's spokesman and incarnation, A. Philip Randolph, won even louder acclaim. "Mr. Black Labor," they called him. A brilliant orator, brilliant and fearless leader, and great moral force, journals raved. He was dubbed "the Negro Mencken" and "an American Gandhi." New York mayor Fiorello La Guardia celebrated the porters' victory at city hall, proclaiming Randolph "one of the foremost progressive labor leaders in America." Others went farther, seeing him as a "modern messiah," "almost a God," and "Saint Philip of the Pullman Porters." The civil rights leader James Farmer named his Great Dane after Randolph, because man and dog shared "the majesty, the gentleness, the noble head, the supreme dignity, the grace of movement." When he told Randolph his pet's name, Farmer recalled, the labor leader "laughed with his regulated, patrician 'haw haw haw' and said, 'Jim, I don't know whether to be flattered or insulted. I don't know whether you're saying that I'm regal and majestic, or whether you're calling me a dog.'"[75]

The plaudits he would have appreciated most came from porters he never knew, many of whom had had misgivings about the radical outsider. But he won them over, slowly but forever. He played bid whist and inquired about their concerns. He stuck with them over twelve endless years that robbed him of his robustness but gave them the strength that comes with manhood. Some showed gratitude by signing up with a union they doubted could prevail. Others pointed to him in telling passengers why they no longer would respond to "George." A few named children after him. "Mr. Randolph was a gift to humanity when he lived on this earth. I call myself a disciple of Mr. Randolph," said Harold Reddick, who went to work as a Pullman porter two months before the first contract was signed in 1937.[76] The former porter Jewel Brown remembered his voice being "like a golden trumpet. A silver voice, a baritone but of silver. Sounded like a bell. A beautiful British accent."[77] To Dean Denniston, a waiter based out of Boston, the head of the Brotherhood of Sleeping Car Porters simply was "a 100-proof guy."[78]

No one could live up to that lionizing, but Randolph's first agreement with the Pullman Company did deliver major gains to the porters, maids, and attendants it covered in the United States and Canada. Minimum pay jumped from $77.50 to $89.50, the biggest hike ever. The new work month was the same 240 hours as for conductors, with anything over ensuring overtime. Three hours of sleep became the benchmark for any trip under twelve hours, four for any over, although that time was unpaid. Porters started getting paid for preparing cars, and seniority counted for more. Those called in as extras, hoping to land a job, were less subject to being exploited. And assurance was given that grievances would be handled more quickly and fairly. Taken as a whole, the agreement, which took effect October 1, 1937, gave porters for the first time a voice in their work life and a sense the Pullman Company was paying a fair price for their labor.

While all the porters in America stayed black, the Brotherhood eventually included non-Negroes as members. There were white barbers and Chinese maids, Filipino attendants and Mexican porters. And although busboys were not written into the 1937 agreement, they were part of the contract that took effect in June 1941. Those are parts of their history that Brotherhood officials liked to recount. They never mentioned that maids were an afterthought in 1937, getting two dollars a month less than the poorest-paid porter and fifteen dollars less than the highest. They exaggerated gains for porters by focusing on the lowest-paid among them. Their claim to have gone it alone added to the righteousness of their crusade, no matter that it ignored all the outside financial and political help they got over twelve years. And the Brotherhood did little to end the practice of porters doing the work of a conductor for the miserly pay of a porter.

Most of the black men and women who worked for the Pullman Company then were too busy celebrating to notice those gaps. In retrospect, it is clear that the Brotherhood began with certain built-in advantages that helped it take on the sleeping car giant. It was up against just one company, not a whole industry, the way many unions were. It represented as homogenous a workforce as there was, with Pullman porters sharing a single job, employer, race, and set of grievances. Getting to those men was easy, since they worked on a public conveyance rather than behind factory walls. Getting word around was even easier, since porters perpetually were on the move. Viewed that way, it might seem surprising, as the labor editor and columnist Kempton noted, that "there were only ten thousand porters to organize, but it took their Brotherhood almost ten years to win recognition from the Pullman Company and a little longer still to be admitted into the AFL as a union in good standing."[79]

There was another way to see things, however, one that suggests the enormity of the Brotherhood's accomplishment. Porters were as middle class a group of black workers as existed, in aspirations if not wages, which made them reluctant to join a union or any other controversial organization. They had grown up thinking of the AFL and other labor groups as lily-white, and of the Pullman Company as a benefactor of blacks. Twenty-five years of failed bids to organize had created a culture of defeatism. Scrubbing toilets and hustling tips created a self-image as subservient. Money, the law, and history were against them. Blacks were being thrown out of other jobs on the railroad, especially the position of fireman, and no railroad exercised as iron a grip over its workers as George Pullman's Palace

Car Company. All of this made the Brotherhood's long battle and ultimate victory an inspiration to blacks in fields as far-flung as red-caps and railroad car cleaners, tobacco workers and freight handlers.

"The importance of their victory cannot be minimized. It should have an inspiring effect on thousands of workers, white as well as black, who are deprived of their right to be represented by men and women of their own choosing and who heretofore have hesitated to throw down the gauge of battle," *Opportunity* magazine wrote in an editorial on the eve of the Brotherhood's first big success in getting recognized as the official bargaining agent for the porters. "To Randolph, Totten, Webster and their associates who for ten long years have fought unceasingly to establish the right of the [P]ullman porter to organize, great credit is due. They faced unbelievable obstacles and overcame them. They never faltered even when attacked by members of their own race who were weak in purpose and fearful of the far-reaching power of the Pullman Company. No labor leadership in America has faced greater odds—none has won any greater victory."[80]

Jewel Brown got an up-close look at the Brotherhood's impact on Pullman porters when he went to work as one the year of that first contract. "The union," he said, "took them off their knees."[81]

5

Behind the Mask

⠶

IT WAS THE only baseball they had. And now it was gone.

It was their only ball because in Freeport, Maine, of 1918, where boys gathered to play baseball every afternoon between school dismissal and chore time, the town could not afford a playing field, real bases, uniforms, or even a backup baseball. Not with fuel shortages, food rationing, and a flu epidemic infecting the nation. The spare change the boys could pull together totaled one baseball. One. But because Freeport was a baseball town, one ball was enough. Boys joined the team as soon as they were big enough to grip a bat. They played on the empty lot between the high school and town hall, using old sweatshirts as bases and battening down windows within range to keep the glass intact and ball in play. If the ball landed in tall grass, the game was suspended to ferret it out. If a batter connected hard enough to knock off the cover, the men at Dave Longway's garage stuck it back on with friction tape. During the frozen winter the boys painted their baseball yellow to see it in the snow.

And then on a lazy afternoon near the start of summer, the ball, the same one that the Freeport fry had played with for months, was lost. It sailed off Hank Soule's bat up over second base, cresting over the iron railroad tracks that ran through the outfield, descending like a rocket on a brilliant harvest night. Then it landed—*thwap*—right in the open palm of a Pullman porter on the Halifax-bound sleeping car. The porter was no more prepared to catch a ball than the boys were to lose theirs. But there it was, floating through the open vestibule of his parlor car, and he raised his open hand, instinctively, as any good American boy would know to do. And for a moment he was as stunned as they.

It all seemed like a dream as the boys reflected back. The old Maine Central work train motoring ahead on tracks just fifty feet behind second base, an empty Pullman sleeper in tow. The porter waving with his free hand, clasping the ball with his other. The boys were mesmerized—at the hit that sent their ball straight into the train door, and the ease with which the porter snagged it. Then they were enraged—that he had kept their only baseball, and there would be no more games till they could scrabble together enough dimes to buy another. Something had to be done. Perry Taylor got the number of the train from the stationmaster, Charlie Bailey, and wrote a letter to the president of the Maine Central. The other boys added their names. *Who was that porter,* they asked, *and could he bring them back their ball? Please.* They mailed the missive, then pooled their coins and bought a brand-new hardball at the sporting-goods counter of L.L. & G.C. Bean, the local department store that would make their town a destination.

By the time the sleeper came through again two weeks later, the boys had almost forgotten about their ordeal and letter. The same porter was aboard, and he waved from the steps of the vestibule. Then he tossed them a new ball clean of everything except some scribbling. The boys gathered around to read what they could see were signatures. There was Deacon Scott, the Boston Red Sox's sure-handed shortstop who set a record for consecutive games. The catcher Wally Schang, who during the off-season sewed covers on Pullman mattresses. And George Herman Ruth, the "Babe," who divided his time between first base, center and left fields, and pitching, and carried that 1918 Red Sox team to a world championship. It would be Ruth's next-to-the-last year in Boston and Boston's last World Series title in that still-young century, making it the stuff of legends and curses.

"It had the autographs of all the first-string players," John Gould, who was ten at the time and had just moved to Freeport, remembered eighty years later. "We never played with that ball. It was put in a small wood box with cotton batting, and the last I knew, Perry Taylor was its custodian." And there were more baseballs, one nearly every time that porter passed through. Some were autographed, others clean. Enough, in the end, to fill a bushel basket. "I think the porter was a baseball fan. He had friends and they'd either go to Fenway Park or Braves Field and sit in the bleachers and catch foul balls," Gould added. "We never needed balls after that. We had all the baseballs we wanted."[1]

They also had their first encounter with a black man. Everyone was white those days in Freeport, and in most of Maine. No one knew the name of the porter who brought them the baseballs, where he lived, or whether he had boys of his own. No one thought to ask. They were uncertain whether it had been his plan all along to return a signed baseball, or if that came in response to their letter to the railroad. Most believed the former, especially when the balls kept coming. To those boys, a black man *was* a Pullman porter, and their Pullman porter was magical. "This began an association with the only black man our town knew anything about in those days," concluded Gould, a columnist, historian, author, and dean of the Maine press corps. "And if nobody else feels it has historical importance, I do."[2]

And so it was for whites across the United States from the late nineteenth century through the middle of the twentieth. The Pullman porter was the only black man many of them ever saw. To some, he embodied subservience and obsequiousness. To others, dignity and mystery. Whatever their notion of him, it almost always was shrouded in mystery and born of ignorance. He remained a dark silhouette passing by at fifty miles an hour, the way he did through the Freeport outfield. Even if they rode the train with him, they never inquired about his life.

If they had, he would not have revealed much. That was how a Pullman porter insulated himself in a world filled with insults and indignities, one where he was called "George" or worse, and forced to beg for tips to support a family. He donned a mask as soon as he boarded the train, letting his white passengers see only his servant's face. The rest—his identity as a man, his humanity—was out of bounds. It was a matter of self-protection, the sort blacks in America got used to during generations on the plantation. It was a matter of survival.

IT WAS NOT necessary for a porter to ride into your life the way he did for John Gould and his friends in Freeport, or even for you to ride a sleeping car, to be introduced to the Pullman porter as man and mythology. Popular culture did that starting almost as soon as the first porter boarded a wooden Pullman in the 1860s. The exposure was built during the 1920s, the golden era of overnight travel, and was sustained through the union battles of the 1930s and the decline of the sleeper in the 1940s and beyond. In fact the less Americans rode Pullman cars and rubbed elbows with porters, the more they seemed to enjoy seeing, hearing, and reading about them.

Books were the first place the porter turned up, in fiction and non. Emma Goldman, the fabled anarchist and pacifist, recalled in her 1931 memoir how during a trip aboard a sleeper her companion Benny Reitman "had managed to unearth a couple of bottles in spite of Prohibition. He was an old hand at getting on the good side of porters, and he captured our darky's heart. Our porter had been busying himself about our room and sniffing the air all the time. 'Great stuff,' he grinned, closing one eye. 'Bet your life, George,' Benny admitted; 'can you get us a bucket of ice?' 'Yah, sah, a whole chest.' We had not enough bottles to fill a refrigerator, Ben told him, but he might 'come in on the swag' if he would bring an extra glass. The sly Negro proved to be a philosopher and artist. His observations on life were keen and his mimicry of the passengers and their foibles masterly."[3]

Goldman's observations, though supercilious, reflected a sympathy with the porter not always present in the literature of that era. They also astutely captured a porter's contradictory life on the train. Was he Goldman's gracious host? Her submissive servant? Like most Pullman passengers, she and Reitman could not quite decide,

A Pullman porter keeps a watchful eye on a vacationing family enjoying the scenery from a Canadian Pacific transcontinental train in the mid-1890s. *(Canadian Pacific Railway)*

BELOW: Robert Todd Lincoln, son of President Abraham Lincoln, succeeded George Pullman as president of the Pullman Company and served until 1911. *(Hildene/Robert Todd Lincoln Home)*

ABOVE: George Pullman founded Pullman's Palace Car Company in 1867 and soon after hired his first porter. *(David Perata Collection)*

Troops arrive in Pullman, Illinois, in 1894 to restore order during a factory-worker strike to protest declining wages and high rents. *(Chicago Public Library)*

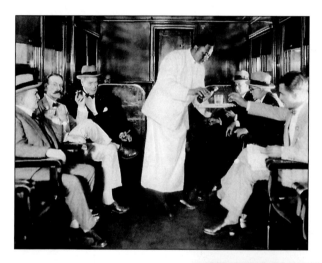

The New York Central's *20th Century Limited*'s extra-fare opulence earned it the moniker "Greatest Train in the World." During Prohibition, all the waiter could pour was near beer or a soft drink. *(Arthur D. Dubin Collection, Lake Forest College Library)*

Service on a Pullman car came complete with a porter willing to deliver telegrams and post letters. *(Arthur D. Dubin Collection, Lake Forest College Library)*

ABOVE LEFT: A Pullman porter hangs a heavy privacy curtain on a New York Central train in 1925. *(National Museum of American History, Transportation Collections)*

ABOVE RIGHT: These were the tools of the Pullman porter's trade. He used a whisk broom to give coats a final dusting before passengers departed—and to remind them that a tip would be appreciated. The Pullman Company dyed blue the blankets given to porters in the early years to distinguish them from brown blankets used by white conductors and passengers. A clothes brush helped porters keep riders' garments free of dust and grime. *(National Museum of American History, Transportation Collections)*

Pullman porter John Baptist Ford of New York with his family in 1924 after he delivered a lecture to students at Dartmouth College's Tuck School of Administration and Finance. *(Corbis)*

ABOVE LEFT: Pullman maids did at least as much work as their male counterparts—feeding and babysitting children and the aged, nursing the sick, doing laundry, and, as the photograph suggests, attending to white lady riders. *(Arthur D. Dubin Collection, Lake Forest College Library)*

ABOVE RIGHT: Minstrel players like these (identified only as Crumbley and Burris) typically portrayed porters as bumbling step-and-fetch-it characters. *(Corbis)*

Paul Robeson is Emperor Brutus Jones and Dudley Digges (left) is Smithers in the 1933 film adaptation of Eugene O'Neill's play *The Emperor Jones.* The play tells the story of Jones who, before he became potentate of a West Indies island, used his ten years as a Pullman porter to study the way whites wielded influence and power. *(Corbis)*

Porters and luggage-toting redcaps at New York's Grand Central Station show their affection for Joe Lewis as he arrives from Detroit for a 1941 bout against Billy Conn. *(Corbis)*

BELOW LEFT: Porter Parish Jones shines the shoes of sleeping soldiers in 1942. The "D" he marked on the sole helped him remember which berth to return that pair to. *(Corbis)*

BELOW RIGHT: A 1942 publicity photograph shows a porter holding his hand over a bugle used to wake troops. Porters were vital enough to the war effort that many were excused from the draft. *(Library of Congress)*

ABOVE LEFT: This Pullman porter is wearing the formal black cap and blue jacket required for receiving and discharging passengers. The company insisted that the hat's silver plate be shined so it sparkled. *(Corbis) Collection)*

ABOVE RIGHT: The Pullman Company began hiring Filipinos as porters in 1925 to discourage black porters from unionizing. Pictured here are porter Willie Williams, attendant A. B. Bates, and conductor D. R. Stump. *(National Museum of American History, Pullman Palace Car Company Collection)*

ABOVE LEFT: Three porters stand in white work jackets next to their Chicago, Burlington & Quincy train in Illinois in 1945. *(Photograph by Keith Harman, Trains Magazine Collection)*

RIGHT: A porter keeps watch outside his sleeping car in the formal pose used to greet passengers. His regal uniform and precise posture suggest the military air that the Pullman Company breathed into all its operations. *(Trains Magazine Collection)*

A dining car on the *Golden State Limited*, the Chicago-to-California luxury train run jointly by the Rock Island and Southern Pacific lines. *(Rock Island Lines, from Association of American Railroads Collection)*

RIGHT: Chef Melvin Pierson (center), and second cooks Cannis Elie (left) and Oliver Medlock, get ready for the rush of diners on the Southern Pacific's *Daylight* train in 1945. *(Southern Pacific News Bureau, David Perata Collection)*

1 **Pick the place** you want to go and *write for reservations*. When you get word there's room for you, see your railroad ticket agent and . . .

2 **Reserve Pullman space** for a trouble-free trip that will get you there *safely*—in *more comfort* than you'll get going any other way!

How to start on your vacation
(WITHOUT A WORRY IN THE WORLD)

3 **No worry** about weather, roads or mountains in an all-steel Pullman car. Pullman's been the *safest* way of going places fast for more than 80 years!

4 **No worry** about privacy or sleep. Your air-conditioned Pullman space is all your own, with big, comfortable beds it's a joy to stretch out in!

A 1946 ad promoting Pullman sleepers—and featuring the smiling porter who the company felt was crucial to selling its service. *(Bill Howes Collection)*

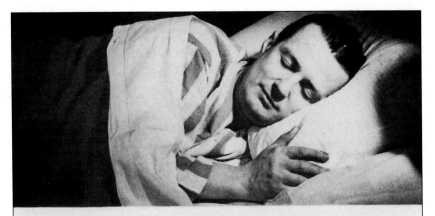

How many people make a good night's sleep?

1.
Your host, the friendly Pullman *Conductor*, supervises the other members of the Pullman crew and his greatest concern is a good night's sleep for you. (That's 1.)

2.
Then there's the attentive Pullman *Porter* who's proud of his art in serving you. He prepares your bed, makes sure you have everything you need, and sees that you're "up" at the time you want to be wakened. (That's 2.)

3.
Before you get on the train, a Pullman *Car Cleaner* goes over your accommodations "with a fine-tooth comb." She dusts and cleans everything in (and out of) sight—so that you can sleep in *pure* comfort. (That's 3.)

4.
When you slip between the crisp, clean sheets of that big soft bed, you can thank the Pullman *Laundress* for those spotless pillow cases and fresh blankets, too. (That's 4.)

5.
The Pullman *Repairman* also sees to it that you sleep well. He makes sure that all the mechanical parts of your car are working perfectly. (That's 5.)

6.
Finally there's the alert Pullman *Inspector* who checks every detail before he okays your car. He's the one who's responsible for that wonderful feeling of security you have when you're drifting off to dreamland. (That's 6.)

These are the six people directly responsible for the good night's sleep you get when you "go Pullman." Behind them are office workers, superintendents, electricians, car suppliers, and executives. In all, nearly 30,000 Pullman employees help make sure that some 60,000 Pullman passengers sleep well each night.

And here's a *fact* that helps you sleep. When you "go Pullman" you know you'll arrive, on dependable railroad schedules, right in town, convenient to everything!

Go Pullman
THE <u>SAFEST</u>, MOST <u>COMFORTABLE</u> WAY TO <u>GET THERE!</u>

1948. THE PULLMAN COMPANY

Another Pullman ad, which ran in *National Geographic* in 1948, suggests how important blacks were throughout the lower rungs of the Pullman organization. *(Bill Howes Collection)*

A. Philip Randolph, president of the Brotherhood of Sleeping Car Porters, leads a protest at the 1948 Democratic National Convention to demand an end to segregation in the U.S. military. *(A. Philip Randolph Institute)*

Randolph, in 1957, pledges solidarity with two other stalwarts of the civil rights movement, NAACP director Roy Wilkins (far left) and Martin Luther King Jr. *(Library of Congress)*

Edgar D. Nixon and Rosa Parks in 1955, following Parks's arrest in Montgomery, Alabama. Nixon, a Pullman porter, used the arrest to rally blacks to stay off the city's buses. The boycott helped launch the civil rights movement. *(AP/Wide World Photos)*

Princess Elizabeth ending a five-week tour of Canada in 1951. She bids good-bye to the Pullman porters who served her on the royal train, starting with Noel Mapp. *(AP/Wide World Photos)*

LEFT: Film legend Barbara Stanwyck samples the culinary fare on a Union Pacific train. Movie stars, baseball heroes, and celebrities of all stripes "went Pullman," which was shorthand for first class. (*Union Pacific Railroad, David Perata Collection*)

RIGHT: A Pullman porter poses with passengers in a double bedroom on a Chesapeake & Ohio train. (*Bill Howes Collection*)

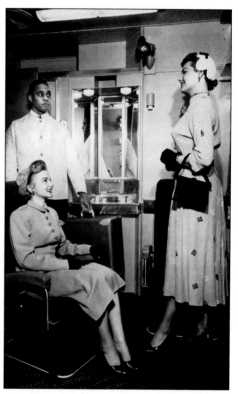

LEFT: A compartment is ready for night use. The door to the right in this publicity photograph is a wardrobe, the one next to it a toilet and lavatory. (*National Museum of American History, Pullman Palace Car Company Collection*)

Final preparations are being made for the departure of President Dwight D. Eisenhower's funeral train in March 1969. The Pullman Company had ceased operating sleeping cars nearly three months before, but it continued to lease and maintain them. Leroy Graham, pictured here, was one of twenty-one former Pullman porters hired full-time by the Chesapeake & Ohio and Baltimore & Ohio railroads. *(Bill Howes Collection)*

ABOVE LEFT: Lawrence "Happy" Davis went to work for the Pullman Company in 1925 and stayed on the job until the company ceased operations in 1969. He is shown here outside his home in Washington, D.C. *(© 2003 Lee Wexler)*

RIGHT: The Reverend Jimmy Kearse spent eighteen years as a waiter with the Baltimore & Ohio Railroad. Here, he is shooting pool in the retirement complex where he and his wife live in Maryland. *(© 2003 Lee Wexler)*

LEFT: Ernest Porter, at age 102. He grew up on a farm in Tennessee and went to work for the Pullman Company in 1947, staying until 1964. (© 2002 Lee Wexler)

RIGHT: Virgil Orite Smock was part of a Pullman family, with an older and younger brother also working for the company, as had his father and grandfather. Virgil started with the Pullman Company in 1936 and stayed until 1960. (© 2003 Lee Wexler)

Garrard Wilson "Babe" Smock, Virgil's younger brother, worked for Pullman from 1937 until 1960. Babe is pictured here outside his home in southern California with his daughter, Errica. (© 2003 Lee Wexler)

Samuel Turner worked as everything from dishwasher to cook, waiter to attendant, during his four decades with the railroads. *(© 2003 Lee Wexler)*

Maggie Hudson, just the third porterette with the Baltimore & Ohio Railroad when she began work in 1943, remained on the job until 1970. She is shown here at work, and, some half century later, donning her old railroad hat. *(© 2003 Lee Wexler)*

Tony Fulton has been a member of the Maryland House of Delegates since 1987. He says he learned his most telling lessons about politics and life from his father, a longtime chef for the Baltimore & Ohio Railroad. *(© 2003 Lee Wexler)*

Elaine Jones ran the NAACP Legal Defense Fund, the nation's most esteemed civil rights law firm. Jones's father, her role model, spent nineteen years working as a Pullman porter. *(© 2003 Lee Wexler)*

so they had it both ways. They let him in on their law-breaking, even inviting him to become a coconspirator by taking a prohibited drink. But they called him "George," suggesting he was George Pullman's property, and saw him more as entertainment than as a social equal.

Most authors were more biting and less nuanced. "Somebody has said that Pullman porters are black so they won't show the dirt, but they certainly show the heat," Mary Roberts Rinehart wrote in her mystery-adventure novel *The Man in Lower Ten*.[4] That was natural enough dialogue for her hero back in 1909. So was having Sinclair Lewis, thirteen years later, put these words into the mouths of characters in *Babbitt*: "'How late are we, George?' growled the fat man. 'Deed, I don't know, sir. I think we're about on time,' said the porter, folding towels and deftly tossing them up on the rack above the washbowls. The council stared at him gloomily and when he was gone they wailed: 'I don't know what's come over these niggers, nowadays. They never give you a civil answer.'"[5]

A Pullman porter christened Epic Peters—and called Hop Sure—got a starring if less stately role in Octavus Roy Cohen's 1930 *Epic Peters: Pullman Porter*. A regular contributor to the *Saturday Evening Post*, Cohen was known for his humorous Negro detective stories. In one, Epic helps a destitute friend named Foster make it to Atlanta without paying a fare, but worries the conductor will find him out. "Bet was he to 'scover 'bout Mistuh Foster I would git kicked out of my job so hahd my ancestors would starve to death," Cohen writes. In another, Epic turns bard: "I plays my cards against my chest, I nusses all my chips; I never joke an' Ise never broke, 'Cause Ise hell on gettin' tips."[6]

Goldman, Rinehart, Lewis, and Cohen wrote in different genres and placed their porters in different roles. All, however, saw him through the same filter—that of a white writer—which explains why the view was foggy and one-dimensional. And given how widely read their books were, these authors' portraits, with all their misconceptions and condescension, helped shape America's perception of the subalterns of the sleeper.

Black writers were more illuminating, but not by much. Many had the advantage of having lived in the same black neighborhoods porters did, but Jim Crow too often kept them off the sleeping cars that defined so much of a Pullman porter's life. James Weldon Johnson lifted the porter to hero's status—then brought him crashing to earth as a lowlife—all within twenty pages of his 1912 *The Autobiography of an Ex-Coloured Man.* It was the first first-person novel by a black, and one of nearly fifty books by this lyricist, teacher, diplomat, and civil rights leader. His protagonist's trunk is pilfered at a rooming house, and his money is stolen, along with his favorite necktie, a black and gray one. He confides in the Pullman porter he met in a dormitory the night before, and is taken aback when the porter lends him fifteen dollars and offers to hide him in a linen closet so he can ride free from Atlanta to Jacksonville. Later, at a dancing pavilion in Pablo Beach, "[I] saw the Pullman-car porter who had so kindly assisted me in getting to Jacksonville," Johnson's narrator explains. "I went immediately to one of my factory friends and borrowed fifteen dollars with which to repay the loan my benefactor had made me. After I had given him the money, and was thanking him, I noticed that he wore what was, at least, an exact duplicate of my lamented black and gray tie. It was somewhat worn, but distinct enough for me to trace the same odd design which had first attracted my eye. This was enough to arouse my strongest suspicions, but whether it was sufficient for the law to take cognizance of I did not consider. My astonishment and the ironical humour of the situation drove everything else out of my mind."[7]

Forty years later Ralph Ellison wrote his own first-person novel about a black man's journey through racist America, *Invisible Man,* and like Johnson's, it included a porter. Ellison recalled a story a porter told him in Eddie's Bar in Harlem. In a book filled with memorable quotes, perhaps the most remembered is the one Ellison borrowed from that porter: "I'm in New York, but New York ain't in me, understand what I mean. Don't git corrupted."[8]

Pullman porters were a favorite of nonfiction writers, too, who saw them as gritty, well-traveled representatives of both black America and the exotic world of the railroads. That is why Studs Terkel included the porter Edgar D. Nixon in *Hard Times,* his oral history of the Great Depression. "A Pullman porter can always get into a conversation anywhere. He walked into a barber shop, some-body'd say, 'I didn't see you around here,' or maybe they'd notice his pants with the stripe," Terkel quoted Nixon as saying. "Every-body listened because they knowd the porter been everywhere and they never been anywhere themselves."[9] That also is why President Franklin Delano Roosevelt's Federal Writers' Project collected so many porter stories, including the following one in 1939 from Leroy Spriggs, a Pullman dining car worker from New York.

> We all knew that Chef Watkins was killing the Company for every-thing he could steal. He had bought a huge rambling old country house down in Maryland and a large breeding farm for jumping horses and prize stock. And you can't do that on what the Pullman Company pays you even if you have worked for them twenty years and have full seniority rating. Nothing was too big or too small for him to steal. He had worked out a system with the commissary stew-ard and between them they did an awful lot of bill padding. In addi-tion to that, he used to throw hams, chickens, legs of lamb and anything else off to his wife or children whenever he passed his place near Bowie. . . .
>
> Well, the boys got together and decided that old Cheffie had to go. So what we did was to drop a little hint here and there to Mr. Palmer, our chief steward, that if he'd just happen around the kitchen when we were nearing that Seaboard crossing, he might find out what was happening to all our missing supplies that he was catching hell about back in the New York commissary.[10]

Porters lived on in books long after Pullman's sleeping car service died in 1969. More enlightened attitudes about race made it easier for authors to sympathize with them, although not having lived through the era made it more difficult to capture the sleeping car's flavor and dialogue. Alice Walker, in her 1989 novel *The Temple of*

My Familiar, got right the lexicon and compromised circumstances in her character Uncle Rafe.

> Fifty years he'd been a porter. Carrying, mainly, white people's bags. Sometimes, for his "vacation" on the job, he'd snuck up behind some pretty "brownskin" with "a shape on her hittin' ninety-nine," on her way to the sooty Jim Crow car, and insisted on carrying her bag. These were the moments that made his work bearable, and he learned to create such brief encounters, small moments of delight for himself, as the train barreled down the tracks. He got on well with small children (they almost immediately referred to him as "uncle") and their pets. Young mothers traveling alone doted on him. He was helpful, modest, quick, and definitely knew his place—they could read this easily in his demeanor—because he, like so many colored men, had perfected the art of doing the most intimate things to and for white people without once appearing to look at them. It was an invaluable skill.[11]

Another veteran Pullman porter, forty-three years on the job, did not fare as well in James Alan McPherson's 1968 short-story collection *Hue and Cry.* A woman from Dearborn complained to the conductor that she would never be able to sleep in her roomette knowing that a black man was sitting just outside in the corridor. "The porter," McPherson wrote,

> who stood all the while like a child waiting for punishment, seemed to droop and wither and grow smaller; and his eyes, which had only minutes before flashed brightly from the face of the conductor to the enraged face of the lady, now seemed to dull and turn inward as only those who have learned to suffer silently can turn their eyes inward. He was a very old man and he grew older, even older than his occupation or the oldest and most obsequious Pullman Porter. . . . It was finally decided that the Dearborn lady would take a seat in the coaches for the night. She wanted it that way. The porter would sleep as he had always slept: sitting up in the back of the car with his eyes closed and his mind awake and his coffee can by his side and the small bright night-light over his bowed head, and his ear next to the buzzer in case someone should

ring. Everyone agreed that it was the way things should be; it was necessary for comfort, and besides, it was his job.[12]

Children's writers were equally captivated by porters, although their characters often were as unflattering and hidebound as those aimed at older readers. *Francie,* the popular 1999 book by Karen English, features a small black child of that name whose porter-father abandons the family. Which is not surprising since, as a gossipy neighbor tells Francie's mother, "Pullman porters had some of the worst reputations. Some even kept two families, one down South and one up North." Francie refuses to believe it for as long as she can. But each time her father is supposed to visit, something prevents him; and each time he is about to move Francie, her brother, and mother up North with him, there is a last-minute glitch. In the end, he writes one too many letters putting off his promises for even his adoring daughter to stay faithful. "I finished all the pointless stuff about how hot and humid Chicago was, how hard Daddy's last run was. How tired he was," says Francie. "And I thought, maybe he did have another family. Mama held out her hand. I put the letter in it and watched her fold it in half. She got up and put it on the pantry shelf in the little box with all the others."[13]

Why have authors been so drawn to the Pullman porter? Because his story is compelling. Whether it was abandoning his first family in the South for a more urbane one in Chicago, the way Francie's father presumably did, or passively absorbing the verbal abuse of McPherson's racist rider from Dearborn, a porter's tale was packed with tension and pathos. It also was a story that book-buying whites could relate to from their time riding the sleeping cars. For an author interested in holding white readers while introducing a black character, the safest approach was to make it one whites knew, or thought they did. Lastly, the porter brought with him the backdrop of a train, an ideal setting for romance and tragedy, murder and other mysteries.

Those backdrops worked even better in film, first the silent kind, then the talkies. The porter generally was a prop, a smiling, obliging figure who evoked images of the elegant sleeping cars he oversaw and the slaves from whom he came. He rode with *The Girl on the Pullman* in 1927. He was back with Nick and Nora Charles as they shuttled between the coasts in the 1930s *Thin Man* series. And he kept watch over Claudette Colbert as she headed to Florida to nab a rich husband in Preston Sturges's 1942 *Palm Beach Story*. That nameless porter's early dialogue consists of three "no mam's." He becomes a bit more loquacious when Colbert, frantic at finding that the stateroom car with her suitcase has been decoupled from her sleeping carriage, insists he must not have looked carefully enough. "Oh yes, mam, I looked, but I didn't see it. But it weren't there, that why I didn't see it," he says staccatolike. He proceeds to describe where the conductor ordered the cars unhinged, but she cuts him off, saying, "Never mind the geography." Colbert repeats that the bags are lost, but the porter stands tall, as always, for his employer, insisting, "Nothing ever gets lost on a Pullman. They's safe alright. I recollect one time a lady left . . ." She cuts him off before we learn just what it was the lady left.[14]

Scenes like those seem innocent enough, no matter that the dialogue is truncated and the racial interactions stilted. It was the way things appeared then, at least through the white filmmaker's lens. But even more than with books, the portrayal of porters on film did more than reflect reality. It reinforced it. Especially in places like Montana and Maine, Oregon and Idaho, where the only blacks most whites saw were on the big screen. And where, in the *Palm Beach Story* and scores of other movies, the black man took the form of a shuffling, stammering Pullman porter.

The porter takes on a more human, multidimensional form in the stage and film versions of Eugene O'Neill's *The Emperor Jones*. Brutus Jones certainly is the most renowned, if not regal, Pullman porter ever. But although real porters relished Jones's rise from second fiddle to lead violin, and delighted in one of their own being played by the majestic Paul Robeson, the playwright reveled in his character's seamy side. Jones spends ten years on the Pullman sleepers listening carefully to his influential white passengers, learning how they amassed and maintained power and wealth. He draws on those lessons to crown himself emperor of a West Indies island, where, in a betrayal reminiscent of his namesake Roman general, he is as merciless as a white slavemaster in ruling his black subjects. He also hides his past misdeeds, which include killing a man during a crap game, then murdering a guard while escaping his chain gang. "For de big stealin' dey makes you Emperor and puts you in de Hall o' Fame when you croaks," Jones explains from his island palace. "If dey's one thing I learns in ten years on de Pullman ca's listenin' to de white quality talk, it's dat same fact. And when I gits a chance to use it I winds up Emperor in two years."[15]

O'Neill tried to create parts for blacks that rose above the condescending, New York columnist Murray Kempton wrote in his 1955 memoir. In the end, however, "O'Neill's heroes were Negroes whose disaster was that they wanted to be white men. But they were not like ordinary Negroes and Brutus Jones was not an ordinary Pullman porter. The Pullman porter rode his car, silent with all the chaff around him, always most agreeable when he was of the old school, accepting the generic designation of 'George' as though it were a balm instead of an affront, a domestic apparently unaltered by the passage of time or the Emancipation Proclamation. A sensitive white man might look at him, at once deferential and removed, and wonder what he was really like. There was a certain thrill to the notion that he might be a Communist or a murderer or even an emperor—a doomed emperor of course—if his chance came and the constituency were inferior enough. But he was, after all, only a man beneath his station, as every servant is a man beneath what should be his station."[16]

However demeaning Kempton and others judged the role of Jones, James A. Bridges saw it differently, especially when Robeson played Jones. A porter for more than thirty years, Bridges said he aspired to the job from the moment he watched Robeson in the 1933 film adaptation of O'Neill's play. "He was a Pullman porter and uh, I saw that and I wanted to be a Pullman porter."[17] For Eddie

Anderson, it was pretending to be a Pullman porter that launched his career. It happened during a skit one Sunday night on Jack Benny's national radio broadcast, with Anderson playing the part of porter Rochester Van Jones. He was such a hit that scriptwriters had Benny "hire" Rochester away from the railroads, dropped the Van Jones, and made him just plain Rochester, a gravel-voiced valet and one of America's favorite comedians from the 1930s through the early 1960s.[18]

An American in the first half of the twentieth century did not have to read books, or even go to the theater, to hear about Pullman porters. They were right there on the radio, in songs and ballads. In most, like the 1932 "Shuffle off to Buffalo," the reference was casual. It imagines heading to that honeymoon destination Niagara Falls on a slow train, where "For a little silver quarter, We can have the Pullman porter Turn the lights down low." Written for the 1933 musical *Forty-Second Street,* the tune was an even longer-lasting hit than the play.[19] "Been on the Cholly So Long," by contrast, was largely ignored in its original form, when it contained the line "On de pilot lay po' Jimmie Jones, He's a good ol' porter, but he's dead an' gone, Dead an' gone, dead an' gone, Kaze he's been on de Cholly so long." It became a classic, however, after the railroad engineer Casey Jones died in a wreck and replaced Jimmy Jones on the train, or Cholly, and in the song.[20] All it took to make a folk classic of Steve Goodman's "The City of New Orleans" was having Arlo Guthrie record it in 1972. "And the sons of Pullman porters and the sons of engineers," Guthrie sang, "ride their fathers' magic carpet made of steel."[21]

Porters also claimed as their own the ballad "Hot Time in De Ole Town." They said a porter's wife was seething when she went looking for her husband at his favorite tavern in Colorado. "When ah gits mah hands on dat niggah," she fumed, "deh's gonna be a hot time in de ole town tonight." A songwriter supposedly overheard her and was moved enough to turn her words into the popular ballad.[22] While that story is impossible to confirm, it is a sure bet that porters inspired the song "Pullman Porter." It captures the spirit of their work, and the despair.

Runs from California
Plumb up to Maine.
I's a Negro porter
On de pullman train.
  Pullman train,
  Pullman train,
I's de Negro porter
On de pullman train.

Braid on the cap an'
Buttons in a row,
On that blue uniform
Right down the fo'.
  In pullman train,
  Pullman train,
I's a Negro porter
On de pullman train.

It's a tip right here
An' a tip right thar,
Tip all along
Up an' down de pullman car.
  Pullman train,
  Pullman train,
I's a Negro porter
On de pullman train.

Pocket full o' money,
Stomach full o' feed,
What next in the worl'
Do a fellow need?
  Pullman train,
  Pullman train,
I's a Negro porter
On de pullman train.[23]

Newspapers, too, were fascinated by the Pullman porter. The *New York Times*, America's paper of record, covered weighty matters, from their union drive to strike threats. But it, like the country it was covering, also was fascinated with porters as men and as mirrors of the world they traveled. It wrote about one porter dreaming about, betting on, and winning with his lucky number, and another chartering a private Pullman car after he won the Irish Sweepstakes.[24] It was not just American reporters who found porters compelling subjects. In 1932 Paul Scheffer, the British correspondent for the German paper *Berliner Tageblatt,* gave a speech at London's Royal Institute of International Affairs on Europe's heavy burden paying off its debts from World War I. "[It] is the conviction of even the most simple people in the United States that Europe is lost," he said, adding—in case anyone still was unconvinced—"I can assure you that this is the opinion of any Pullman porter."[25]

Although the spotlight generally was welcomed, that was not the case in 1949 when the *Saturday Evening Post* quoted a porter on how much he made in tips; whether or not readers paid attention, the Internal Revenue Service did, and began scrutinizing with new fervor porters' tax filings.[26]

Too little limelight was the issue with Matthew Henson. The explorer Robert E. Peary became famous overnight in 1906 when word got out that he had "discovered" the North Pole, but it took nearly eighty years for honors to be bestowed on the ex-Pullman porter who was at Peary's side on that trek to the top of the world. Henson died in obscurity after working until he was seventy as a messenger, then retiring on a pension of just over one thousand dollars a year. Finally, thanks to pressure from a Harvard scholar and others, Henson's remains were dug up in 1988 from a modest grave in the Bronx, New York, and reinterred next to Peary's at Arlington National Cemetery in Virginia. Over the next decade the black pioneer had a navy explorer ship named after him, received the National Geographic Society's most prestigious medal, and was memorialized in a series of books, on a U.S. postage stamp, and in a made-for-TV movie.[27]

Those notions of the Pullman porter as everyman, or no one, stand in dramatic counterpoint to the porter's standing in his own world back then. To whites who watched him on the train or film screen, he epitomized servility. To black neighbors and friends, he personified sophistication and urbanity. He was a man of worlds they would never see or experience. And the porter did more than pass through those worlds. He helped disseminate the culture he saw and tasted to black Americans and whites, in ways that writers and moviemakers seldom appreciated or reflected. He picked up, read, and passed on newspapers and magazines that passengers left behind. He did something similar with music. In cities like Chicago and New York, the porter would buy dozens of the latest albums of sultry Bessie Smith and Mother of the Blues Ma Rainey. He resold them, often for twice the price, in communities across the South where the local department store, if there was one, did not stock black artists. Buyers got not just the records but their first look at revolutionary music forms like jazz.[28]

Porters and dining car men also got to mingle with musicians like Duke Ellington, Benny Goodman, and Louis Armstrong. They traveled the country on Pullman sleepers and played their pianos, clarinets, and trumpets late into the night in the club car, where porters listened, learned, and passed on what they picked up. It worked in reverse, too: porters spent time in the hamlets and villages of rural America, where the blues and bluegrass were born, and they recounted what they had heard when they got home to the city or talked to troubadours on the train. "When we would go South we'd go into black neighborhoods and talk to the people we were dancing with," recalled Joseph Strowder, who spent thirty years as a waiter on the trains. "The music there was different, they had a whole lot of blues, whereas we were used to swing and jazz and all that."[29]

Gossip was yet another porter specialty. They picked up tidbits about everything from politics to finances, and knew which to keep alive and which were privileged. One porter overheard President Roosevelt saying, "Byrnes! Byrnes! Byrnes!" as he made clear his preference for former senator James F. Byrnes over Harry Truman for vice president in 1944. (Byrnes lost out there but ended up as Truman's secretary of state.)[30] Porters who served on FDR's train also knew how crippled he was long before the public did. Others tracked down stock quotes midroute for ex-president Hoover, who had presided over the Great Crash, kept Richard Nixon's secret that his staffers were fudging his signature on menus handed out during his whistle-stop campaigning, and only whispered among themselves when a priest went on a drinking binge. They knew that the Duke of Windsor liked Budweiser, and kept a case on hand for him. And they knew, before it happened, about President Kennedy's doomed invasion of Cuba's Bay of Pigs, or at least suspected something was up as they watched the unusual transport of troops. "We moved a lot of soldiers," recalled the former waiter Edward Roland Exson. "We got them from Washington and from Richmond and carried them to a base in Georgia. We thought it was a funny thing."[31]

Sometimes what they had seen or heard gave them the power to send people to jail or save them from it. "I am getting into bed, my leg hanging out as I am sitting down taking off my shirt and tie, and I see this woman carrying her young child who is sleeping back to a roomette," remembered Robert McGoings. "There's a man there with that roomette, and she reserved a lower berth for her and the kid where there's more room. So the male gets into the lower berth with her, and the kid is back in the roomette. The man wasn't her husband. I knew he had picked her up because they had been drinking in my car. That's common. The next morning they got off in Washington. On another trip I was met by the police, the Navy, and my superintendent out of Washington saying they wanted to talk to me about that woman. 'What do you know about her claiming she was raped?' they asked. 'She came out of San Diego. Her husband is in the Navy, and she was going to Annapolis.' I said it wasn't no rape. It turned out she was afraid she might get pregnant. Once I told them that story about her moving the child I didn't hear no more about it."[32]

Benjamin McLaurin, a porter and longtime Brotherhood leader, recalled in 1960 how the Pullman porter's seamless network made it easy to get union literature or anything else across the country almost instantaneously: "We didn't have to wait on airmail—we gave it to a porter, and it got there. Occasionally, even now, when we have to get information to someone or get things delivered quickly, we resort to the porter."[33]

Books were another thing porters picked up on the train, and while they often handed them off to their children or even strangers, sometimes they held on. George Young, who spent nearly twenty years as a porter, ran Young's Book Exchange on West 135th Street in New York and became what the *New York Times* called "one of the best-known Negro bibliophiles." Everywhere he traveled he met with secondhand dealers and rummaged through stores in search of manuscripts about blacks. "Young's aim is to show the world that the negro is something besides a laborer and a domestic servant; to give the Caucasian proof of negro intelligence, ability and intellectuality," the *Times* wrote in 1921. "Whether he accomplishes his ends or not, it is a remarkable thing to realize that a colored man, a score of years a Pullman porter, should harbor such ideals and ambitions."[34]

There was one more way Pullman porters left a mark on American literature and music, film, and other culture: making it themselves. The former porter William "Big Bill" Broonzy did it with his recordings of the blues, including his post–World War II favorite "Black, Brown and White Blues," which laments that "if you's white, you's right, but if you's brown, stick around, and if you's black, oh brother, git back, git back, git back." It was a lesson he learned, or at least had reinforced, on the sleeping cars. Although Broonzy toured and turned out records for thirty years, it was not until 1953 that his income was sufficient as singer, guitarist, fiddler, and songwriter for him to give up his work as cook, janitor, and porter.[35]

Oscar Micheaux, another former Pullman porter, published seven novels and produced forty-four movies. Dubbed the "Spike Lee of the silent era," his 1919 *The Homesteader* was the first full-length film made by a black. A year later, in *Within Our Gates*, Micheaux hit back at D. W. Griffith's racist classic *The Birth of a Nation*. Where Griffith portrayed drunken Negroes raping white women, Micheaux used nearly identical lighting, blocking, and scenery to show a white man attempting to rape a black woman.

Gordon Parks was equally multidimensional in his artwork, and like Micheaux, he drew early inspiration from his days on the railroad, in his case as a dining car waiter. Parks was fascinated by photographs in magazines that his riders left behind, and eventually started taking his own. By 1940 he was working for *Life* and *Vogue*, shooting subjects as varied as glamorous models in Paris and warring gangs in Harlem, and earning distinction as America's first mainstream black photojournalist. He wrote an autobiography, too, and painted, played the piano, composed, and directed a series of Hollywood films including, in 1971, the blaxploitation classic *Shaft*.

Then there was the poet and novelist Claude McKay, whose days on the sleeper schooled him in how porters talked and thought, and convinced him their story had to be told. Finding the time to tell it was not easy. Working on the dining car "sometimes I carried lines in my thoughts for days, waiting until I found time to write them down," he explained in his memoir. One time "I was possessed with an unusually lyrical feeling, which grew and increased into form of expression until one day, while we were feeding a carload of people, there was a wild buzzing in my head. The buzzing was so great that it confused and crowded out all orders, so much so that my mechanical self could not function. Finally I explained to the steward that I had an unbearable pain in my belly. He excused me and volunteered to help the fourth waiter with my two tables. And hurrying to the lavatory I locked myself in and wrote the stuff out on a scrap of paper."[36]

That surreptitious note-taking paid off in his 1928 novel *Home to Harlem*, where McKay captures the real-life pulse of the rails. "Two Pullman porters came into the dining-car in the middle of the waiters' meal," he wrote. "'Here is the chambermaids,' grinned the second cook. 'H'm, but how you all loves to call people names, though,' commented the fourth waiter. The waiters invited the porters to eat with them. The pantryman went to get them coffee and cream. The chef offered to scramble some eggs. He went back to the kitchen and, after a few minutes, the fourth cook brought out a platter of scrambled eggs for the two porters. The chef came rocking importantly behind the fourth cook. A clean white cap was poised on his head and fondly he chewed his cigar. A perfect menial of the great railroad company."[37]

IT WAS PRECISELY because he was the ideal menial, or must seem to be, that the porter had to work so hard behind the scenes to keep his dignity intact. His newly recognized union helped, winning for him better working conditions, heightened job security, and the self-respect that comes from forging a brotherhood. But there was no way to write into a contract protections against racist riders, brutal bosses, or the perpetual assault on his pride. He needed more to get by day-to-day, as porters had from their earliest days on the sleeper. He needed to don a mask.

It was a mask of pliancy, and it went on whenever he came into contact with white passengers. Gleaming white teeth were part of the disguise, along with a never-fading smile. It protected his true feelings by camouflaging them. Pullman customers and the Pullman Company got the anonymous servant they sought, and he saved what he really felt and thought for home, or Baker Heater League sessions with fellow porters. It was his secret, a side of his life as a Pullman porter that never made it into the ballads, the books, or the consciousness of boys playing baseball in towns like Freeport, Maine. That was image; this was reality.

Pullman porters were not the first blacks to change faces when they entered a white world. The tradition traced to their slave ancestors, who risked beating and even death if they bared true emotions. So they willed themselves into a sphinx and stayed that way as long as they were in the Big House. Black maids and nannies employed a similar protective technique, becoming so absorbed in work their white employer barely noticed they were there. Clowns and minstrels had been using actual masks for hundreds of years to transform their personalities, or hide them, while Jews, Catholics, and blacks of all ages did the same thing—without a mask—when dealing with the dominant culture.

But no one donned a disguise as often, over as many years, as the

Pullman porter. The Pullman Company exploited that image of the dark-skinned, white-toothed servant in newspaper and magazine ads marketing its sleeper service, and in promotional films like *The Lady Said Thanks.* Black washerwomen, gardeners, and other domestic workers who went home every evening could let down their guards; porters, like live-in servants, remained in their all-white world on wheels for days at a time, in quarters too close to relax. Which is why, as the Brotherhood's McLaurin explained in 1960, "porters actually carried two faces, and this is perhaps true—even now— because after all, the Negro has to try and survive, and he might say one thing to you and mean something altogether different."[38]

Porters had different ways of describing those two faces and justifying them. "It was amazing how inhuman the passenger population was. They wouldn't respect you as a man," said the veteran porter Harold Reddick. He and his porter brothers responded by "becoming the best trained men in the world at maneuvering, at getting over it. You survived by knowing that at the end of the road, when payday came, you could buy your steak and cut it as thick as you wanted it cut."[39] William Howard Brown agreed that training was key, and said the Pullman Company schooled porters like him in how to acquiesce in the abuse: "When you were hired, you had to go through routines to see how you would react. They'd never address me as 'Mr.'; they'd call me 'Brown.' They'd say, 'Brown, when a passenger gets on and calls you "nigger," what would you do?' You knew the answer you were supposed to give. It was never to tell the passenger what you were thinking. I said that I would resent it but never hit back. I'd just take it and go on about my business."[40]

Having a union of his own helped Happy Davis, who went to work for the Pullman Company just as the Brotherhood of Sleeping Car Porters was beginning its organizing drive. "The BSCP was the greatest organization known to mankind," said Davis. "We even had our name card to put up on the front of the car, with your name on it so the passengers wouldn't call you 'George' or something. He had to refer to you by your name that was on your name card. All before then, a porter was liable to be any damn thing. . . . Passengers called me everything but a child of God! But I laughed it off. I don't get insulted long as you got some money, you understand what I mean. Porters didn't like it, though. You'd be surprised how proud the Pullman porter is. Pullman porter's a proud man."[41]

Davis called it "laughing it off." Other porters had other expressions for that hard-learned habit of maintaining their pride while suppressing their feelings. One referred to it as learning to keep his cool. Another said it was hardening his skin so nothing could get under it. Samuel Turner, a pantryman, second cook, and waiter, boiled it down to this: "A lot of time we'd feel like crying but we'd laugh, you know, and finally that stage passed over."[42]

For A. C. Speight, simply ignoring insults from passengers became so instinctive during his years as a porter that he and his friends developed their own expression for it: *ig.* "Coming out of Texas," Speight explained, "the man, he called me 'nigger.' His wife says, 'Don't say that.' He said, 'He's just a nigger, ain't he?' I didn't say nothing, just kept on going, just igged him, that's all. Some things it's better off not saying anything, because wherever you were, you'd get in trouble, see. You learned that as part of the game. Ig him."[43]

It was even tougher for Pullman maids. They were subjected to sexism as well as racism, and there were too few of them to develop their own lexicon or other concerted responses. "One incident I remember is there was a fellow sitting over there and looking around at me. He said, 'You would be a pretty little girl if you wasn't a nigger,'" said Maggie Hudson, one of the first porterettes on the Baltimore & Ohio line. "I didn't get angry. I expected it at that time; there wasn't even Martin Luther King around then."[44] Maggie and her colleagues, male and female, took the bullying because they were accustomed to it and had become numb. They took it because, as Edward Exson explained, "you love your family so much that you will accept perhaps being abused a little more than if you were independent."[45] They took it because they had to to keep the job, and knew any new job would carry its own forms of mistreatment.

But each porter had his limit. To the Reverend Jimmy Kearse, just about any behavior by passengers was okay as long as they didn't touch him.[46] To George Smock, it was, ironically, being called "George." "The passenger called me 'Gawg' and I tried to explain to him that the name was spelt G-E-O-R-G-E, and not G-A-W-G, or however he might want to pronounce it," Smock explained. "And being told he would call me what he wanted to, I laid one on him. . . . Sometimes it didn't take more than two or three words to be exchanged before the fire [in me] rose."[47] Lester Arnold was more Machiavellian: "I had to take it unless there was nobody there but me and him. Then I could let him have it."[48] Ernest Porter, whose grandfather was a slave, retired from his job as a Pullman porter a mere two months shy of qualifying for a full pension. He had had a run-in with a white steward, he recounted at age 102; "if I had made another trip, I would have gotten into something worse. I thought, 'I'd better go when things aren't no worse than they are.'"[49]

Extending those limits, and managing that anger, became a crucible to many porters, a sign of their self-awareness and ability to master the often-hostile environment of the sleeping car. All porters had to be diplomats. But many took the challenge several steps farther, becoming students of human behavior and sages in psychology, even if they had no degree to prove it. "One day I was talking to a young lady, and she just asked a lot of questions. I don't know why, but I had to answer; we were conversing," recalled Joseph Strowder, whose first run as a waiter was in 1937. "One of the men at the table just across the aisle said, 'Boy, ain't you got anything else to do?' He couldn't appreciate me talking to this white woman in a friendly manner. The lady rebuked him, but I couldn't afford to say nothing. If he made any kind of a report on me, I'm gone. I'm fired automatically. So I had to take it all, then go find something else to do rather than talking to this lady, because that fella held my job in the palm of his hand. It was an accomplishment. I kept from hating passengers like that. I called myself outsmarting them."[50]

The black nationalist Malcolm X learned his own lifelong lessons in reading people, and coping with personal crises, as a teenager working on the train: "I remember that once, when some passenger complaints had gotten me a warning, and I wanted to be careful, I was working down the aisle and a big, beefy, red-faced cracker soldier got up in front of me, so drunk he was weaving, and announced loud enough that everybody in the car heard him, 'I'm going to fight you, nigger.' I remember the tension. I laughed and told him, 'Sure, I'll fight, but you've got too many clothes on.' He had on a big Army overcoat. He took that off, and I kept laughing and said he still had on too many. I was able to keep that cracker stripping off clothes until he stood there drunk with nothing on from his pants up, and the whole car was laughing at him, and some other soldiers got him out of the way. I went on. I never would forget that—that I couldn't have whipped that white man as badly with a club as I had with my mind."[51]

While their tolerances varied on many topics, there was a consensus among porters, waiters, and other black workers on the sleepers when it came to *Tomming:* It was taboo. Okay to work hard, doing jobs most would consider menial like scrubbing toilets and polishing cuspidors. Okay, too, to whisk off a customer's jacket and spitshine his shoes in search of an extra tip. Even to ignore the ignominy of being addressed as "boy," "nigger," or "George." But not to behave like that old slave in Harriet Beecher Stowe's 1852 novel *Uncle Tom's Cabin.*

The problem came in defining just what qualified as Tomming, which generally turned out to be something the other guy did, not you. Samuel Turner said he was willing to do just about anything to earn "a nice big fat tip" that would help support his family. "Some of the colored boys said it was Tomming, but it wasn't Tomming," Turner insisted. "It was just making the people happy. It wasn't Tomming. It wasn't that you were bowing to them. You were hustling and making you some money. Give them a little extra service. It didn't hurt you to give them a little extra service."[52] Leroy Richie, who was born in North Carolina at the turn of the century and went to work as a porter in 1926, said, "If you think you are an Uncle Tom, you are an Uncle Tom. Whether you're a

Pullman porter or whatever you are. So I never thought that I was an Uncle Tom."[53]

Robert E. Turner had his own ideas on that thin line between being obliging and being unctuous, and he laid them out in a 1945 treatise addressed to his sister that he called *Memories of a Retired Pullman Porter*. As he saw it, every porter was forced by the Pullman Company to do at least some of the bootlicking and back-scratching that conjured up memories of Uncle Tom. "All porters," for instance, "were supposed to drop everything when they were called by the Pullman office. They were supposed to stand by their phones, ready to report for duty and cheerfully willing to go any place they sent him. This became so monotonous that porters would not answer their phones when they rang, unless there were no one else to answer them. Then the company introduced another method equally bad if not worse than the plan of standing by their phones. Whenever a porter was called, whoever answered the phone was to tell the porter to report at a certain time and place for service or take a certain car to a certain place. If the porter failed to do either, he was severely penalized by being pulled off his line or losing several trips. This method of penalizing the porters kept them all frustrated and forced them to worry, which lowered their efficiency and robbed them of their happiness. But the porter was always expected to keep smiling, and if he did not display some of that Uncle Tom stuff, he was considered a surly porter."[54]

All that smiling took a toll on porters. So did seeing themselves portrayed as simple-minded, kowtowing characters in films like *Palm Beach Story* and books like *Epic Peters*. Worst of all was having to retreat behind a mask. Some began to hate themselves. Others developed so many layers of rationalizations they no longer recognized when they were demeaning themselves. How could you remember what you really felt or thought if you spent day and night deceiving people, smiling when you should be scowling, and turning the other cheek when you should be punching a passenger in the nose? The price George Smock paid for doing just that was losing his job, more than once. But at least, as he said, "running my fury upon someone" was a way to vent pent-up frustrations.[55]

Pity the porter like John R. Merritt who held it in. "I dropped my head and walked away. That's all. If somebody called me 'Sam,' I didn't bother. When I was called 'Tom,' I just walked away," Merritt said, sounding convincing. But it was not quite that simple. "It sometimes did churn," he admitted. "You sometimes couldn't sleep at night with all that is on your mind. You wondered what was going to happen tomorrow. You were always in an uproar."[56]

Once they bid good-bye to their last passenger, porters finally could peel off their masks and begin to ease the uproar. It helped to talk things over with fellow porters and, where possible, laugh about all they been through. "They'd come back and tell these stories about the stupid white people they had encountered. Some acted as if black people couldn't understand English," recalled Roger Wilkins, whose uncle, grandfather, and granduncle were railroad men. "They had to put on faces that acquiesced to white power, but in their real lives they carved out more freedom for themselves, psychic and otherwise, than white people could imagine."[57]

Happy Davis tried to tap that psychic freedom on the job as well as off, which is how he survived forty-five years with the Pullman Company. He did it by donning the very smile the company demanded of him, and by actually enjoying the job despite the abuses and humiliations. "Some of them people were pretty rough, but I tried to keep smiling. There were miles and miles of smiles," he recalled from his living room in Washington's Mount Pleasant section, a neighborhood once filled with Pullman porters.* Anytime he was tempted to yield to temptations of the flesh or strike back against his abusers, he remembered the seven children he had at home. Yet even he had his limits, as he showed after his last run back to Washington

---

*Davis said his nickname, "Happy," came not from smiling on the train but from his days as a sandlot baseball player. "I was a dirty ballplayer," he recalled. "I tried to copy Ty Cobb. I used to sharpen my spikes like him. I tried to hurt you, and I would laugh at it."

from Cincinnati: "I took a rope out of one of the linen bags and tied up my shoes. I threw those shoes into the Potomac River and said, 'No more work.'"[58]

NEVER WOULD PULLMAN porters enter the public consciousness more than they did during World War II, as they hauled hundreds of thousands of GIs across the United States. And never did they have more reason to don their masks in a bid to safeguard their self-respect.

The war itself was a godsend to the railroads, and especially to the Pullman Company, which had gone into a tailspin during the depression. The best of times for the company was 1925, when it earned $16.8 million and carried 35,526,000 passengers, or the equivalent of a third of the U.S. population. In 1932 it had its first unprofitable year ever, and by 1935 it was $502,000 in the red and carrying just 15,479,000 riders. George's once-sacred dividends were suspended from 1931 through 1933. Rates were cut, parlor cars decoupled, and as of 1932 there were just 8,658 porters on the payroll, down from 12,526 two years before. Those who remained were lucky to get a nickel tip, as passengers simply had less to give. The depression was partly to blame, as even business moguls temporarily downsized to coach; much worse, for the long haul, was the quick rise of the automobile, bus, and fast-stepping day trains, and the creeping advance of commercial airlines. But just when things looked most dismal, the economy began to turn around and Americans started taking a keen interest in the war raging in Europe.[59]

U.S. entry into the conflict meant a frenzied effort to transform farmers, factory workers, and other civilian laborers into military men. That meant moving them first to training camps, then to the hulking gray Cunard ships that ferried them to the front lines in Europe. Ninety-seven percent of troop movements within U.S. borders were done by the railroads, and 66 percent of that by Pullman. It was an arresting image worthy of George Pullman: an army being driven to war in a sleeping car. Soldiers got to ride a Pullman sleeper on any trip longer than twelve hours. Thirty thousand men qualified each night in 1944, taking up fully half the company's berths and requiring the dispatch of a sleeping car every two minutes and forty-eight seconds. To handle the surge, the company pulled nearly two thousand mothballed cars back into service, built twelve hundred new ones for the government, and hired back more than one thousand porters.[60]

The war helped Pullman porters in more ways than just creating work. It kept scores of them out of the draft. Some local draft boards considered railroads vital enough to the war effort, and Pullman porters so vital to troop trains, that it regularly freed them from military service. "They gave me six deferments," said Philip Henry Logan, who went to work for Pullman during the war. "The first was for about six months. The last one they told me was my last time, but before it ran out the war was over."[61] Leroy Graham started on the sleepers in 1941, and got three deferments. In the end he was drafted into the army; "but we had V-day, and I didn't have to go."[62] Joseph Strowder was less lucky: "I was drafted from the railroad. I went in in 1941 and came out in 1945. I was in the first draft in Washington, D.C. They kept some people out, but my railroad job didn't keep me out."[63]

Being considered critical to the war effort was not always an asset. Even more high-paying jobs in factories opened to blacks during this global conflict than the first one, as orders picked up in workplaces at the very moment workers were leaving for the battlefront. Many porters would have jumped at the chance for a job closer to home with a higher salary, but Uncle Sam said they had to stay on the train. "I have just returned from a business trip to the Pacific Coast, where I saw all the splendid work our shipyard workers are doing there to win the war," Wallace C. Speers wrote in a letter to the editor of the *New York Times* in July 1943. "En route I came in contact with another war effort which in some ways is just as remarkable but which has not received much publicity. I refer to the work the Pullman porters, both sleeping car and dining car, are doing. These men have been frozen in their jobs, and hence cannot try for perhaps more lucrative employment in war industries. This alone might well sour an ordinary man's point of view. They have to handle more regular business than ever in their history before and, in addition, take care of hosts of service men. . . . I suppose they can't award the Navy or Army 'E' to a group of men like that, but I would like to nominate them for a good rousing cheer from an appreciative country."[64]

If Speers only knew. To most porters, soldiers were hell on wheels. They got drunk and rowdy, and stayed up all night playing poker or shooting craps, which was understandable since they were kids on their own for the first time with what might be a one-way ticket to the battlefront. They had little inclination to tip, and little money if inclined. Some were physically sick, others just war weary; both types required extra care from the train crew, if only to keep them from drinking the rubbing alcohol intended to salve their wounds. And while porters say they were proud to do their part for the national war effort, they remember the GIs as testing their patience more, even, than baseball players, boarding school brats, and that penny-a-pop tipper John D. Rockefeller.

"They really raised a lot of hell. They was disgusted, and of course they had reason to be, going to fight a war they knew nothing about. I would just fix their beds and go back and sit in the smoking room and let them raise hell all by themselves," remembered Leroy Parchman of Chicago. Many of the military men, he added, were also racists and were not afraid to make that known: "I never will forget this soldier, he was escorting a body back to Whitefish, Montana, and he was very abusive to the crew. He called them niggers and everything. This fella [a porter], he's dead now, was on his car when the soldier come through with all his nasty remarks. Nobody said nothing, but this fella said, 'I can't take it no more. I'll fix him.' He went in the soldier's locker and got all his orders, a big envelope, and when we passed Whitefish River he threw all the orders in the river."[65]

To Jimmy Kearse, it was logistics that made troop trains most daunting. "Sometimes we'd have on one train six or seven hundred soldiers and we'd have to feed all of them," he said. "Feed all of them three meals per day, and we managed to do it. . . . It was my job, most of the time, to bring the coffee. I remember on a special troop train, we were coming from Chicago, and we were coming through Martinsburg, West Virginia. Just as we were coming up the hill into Martinsburg station, I had eighteen cups of coffee on my tray with no saucers under. Eighteen cups of coffee that were just about filled to the brim and somebody pulled the emergency cord. It stopped the train. The train went into lock. Now, what am I going to do with this coffee? I've got to think fast. So I'll tell you what, I would get some gyration. I would move. I just held the tray like that and got down on one knee and twisted and brought it down like. Brought it across my body and down. Not a drop spilled and those guys gave me a standing ovation just like I was Sammy Davis Jr."[66]

In this world war, like the first one, what upset porters far more than troops acting up was the way the conflict underlined the racial insensitivity of the Pullman Company—and the nation. A white flagman was assigned to every car with WAVEs or WACs, as if black porters could not be trusted with these white women from the navy and army. Black soldiers got second-class treatment from nearly everyone but the porter. And, as the longtime porter Ollis Fellows recalled, "German prisoners of war on our train could go in restaurants in the South and eat, but we couldn't. We went in the back door and got a sandwich and stuff."[67]

There were some rewards that came with carrying soldiers. They often made their own beds or did not care if they went unmade. Sergeants on occasion took up generous collections for a tip. And incessant appeals to porters to help them buy liquor at each stop could net a handsome profit, as Virgil Smock recalled: "When we got to Santa Barbara or Phoenix, porters would go up and get the guys a bottle. The guy would give you $5 for a half pint which cost $1.70."[68]

The money was nice, but World War II's most lasting impact was how it made people notice Pullman porters for what seemed to be the first time. Military personnel accounted for more than a million trips a month during the heyday of the conflict, which meant a lot of troops getting their first taste of Pullman travel. The soldiers, of course, were preoccupied with the battle they were about to join, and many of the specially designed troop cars were anything but glamorous, with three tiers of crosswise bunks that earned them the slur of rattletrap. Still, the young warriors would remember what often was their maiden trip on a train of any kind, and their first time getting waited on as if they were somebody special. Those wartime experiences did at least as much as movies and books to make the Pullman car and the Pullman porter part of America's popular culture.

6

Train to Freedom

::

MARTIN LUTHER KING JR. was not the first choice to lead the Montgomery bus boycott that catapulted him to glory and kickstarted the civil rights movement. Nor was he a logical choice, at just twenty-six, with no track record in race politics and only a year out of graduate school. He was not even a willing choice.

But Edgar D. Nixon never gave him a choice. It was December 2, 1955, the day after Rosa Parks was arrested for refusing to yield her bus seat to a white rider. It was a day that would change the course of American race relations, and Nixon was up before the sun rallying black leaders behind his radical proposal to boycott the segregated buses. "Number one, I called Ralph D. Abernathy. And he said he'd go along with it," Nixon recalled later. "Second, I called the late Reverend H. H. Hubbard. And I called Reverend King, number three. Reverend King said, 'Brother Nixon, let me think about it awhile and call me back.' Well, I could see that. He's a new man in town, he don't know what it's all about. So I said, 'Okay.' So I went on and called eighteen other people, and I called him back and he said, 'Yeah, Brother Nixon, I'll go along with it,' and I said, 'I'm glad of that, Reverend King, because I talked to eighteen other people, I told them to meet at your church at three o'clock.'"[1]

That fortuitous assignment, based more on the size of his church than his capabilities, would recast King's life and launch him into the American orbit. The obvious choice to have presided over that first meeting and the wider boycott, as King himself said afterward, was Nixon. This tall, raw-boned son of an Alabama sharecropper, with fists as thick as boxing gloves and skin the color of midnight, was the black activist whom whites in Montgomery knew best and blacks trusted most. He was a past president of the Montgomery and Alabama branches of the NAACP, which he helped found, and the current president of the Progressive Democratic Association, a black alternative to Alabama's all-white Democratic Party. He was the first black in the twentieth century to seek elective office in the city that was the first capital of the Confederacy, losing by just ninety-seven votes.* When the civil rights battle heated up, Nixon's home was the first to be bombed. He knew every local cop and sheriff, lawyer, judge, and jailer, which is why his telephone rang so often in the dark of the night when a black needed bailing out. Perhaps his greatest advantage in building contacts and confidence— and greatest contrast with the callow Reverend King—was Nixon's thirty-two years as a Pullman porter, including founding and serving as the only president of the Montgomery division of the Brotherhood of Sleeping Car Porters.

That was also Nixon's greatest liability. His travels on the sleeping car meant he would miss the session he had scheduled at King's Dexter Street Baptist Church and other meetings like it. So he took himself out of the running to be president of the Montgomery Improvement Association, the group created to manage the boycott, opening the way for King's selection.

Still, everyone at Dexter Street knew it was Nixon who had given birth to the notion of a boycott, which he saw as the quickest way to move the nascent civil rights struggle from the courthouse to the streets. Only a year before, the U.S. Supreme Court had handed down its momentous *Brown v. Board of Education* ruling outlawing segregation in public schools, but progress in applying it was slow and there was little sense of how to foster integration outside the classroom. Nixon saw public buses as the adult counterpoint to the

---

*Nixon was running for the Montgomery County Democratic Executive Committee, the local party's top decision-making body. He won 42 percent of votes cast in a district where just one in four voters was black.

schools, and he knew from his days battling for the Brotherhood the broad strategy and rough-and-tumble tactics needed to take on a transportation monopoly. Jim Crow was sinister everywhere, but nowhere more than on buses. Blacks had to seat themselves from back to front, whites front to back; when there were no more seats for whites, drivers would shout, "Niggers, move back!"*

Nixon knew the system was ripe for a challenge, but he knew the choice of a test litigant could be decisive. Not the minister's daughter, who, though she was brave enough to get arrested, might not stand up under pressure. No, too, to the schoolgirl he thought too promiscuous, and another woman whose father supposedly was a drunk. The fourth person jailed for refusing to be moved was Rosa L. Parks, who Nixon knew right away "was the person." Married but childless, she supported her invalid mother by sewing, a skill she learned at Miss White's Industrial School for Girls. Frail and middle-aged, with a passion for Bible reading and disdain for dancing, Parks was well known to Nixon from a dozen years managing his NAACP and Brotherhood offices. She also was well prepared for her role, having recently attended a two-week course on "radical desegregation," and having been ejected before by the same driver although not arrested.[†] This time two policemen took her to the city jail, where Nixon arrived a few hours later to post bond.

The next critical step was picking someone to orchestrate the boycott. Nixon had made sure no decision was made at the first meeting in his absence. Before the second, he and two leading ministers—Abernathy and E. N. French—met to set the script. "Abernathy was sittin' as close as me in here to you, and he leant over," Nixon remembered. "He said, 'Brother Nixon, now you gon' serve as president,

---

*Every bus had thirty-six seats. The first ten were for whites. The last ten were for blacks, unless whites needed them. The middle sixteen were up to the driver, who carried a gun. Douglas Brinkley, *Rosa Parks* (New York: Viking, 2000), 57.

[†]Parks's driver, James F. Blake, was a "vicious bigot who spat tobacco juice out of his bus window and cursed at 'nigras' just for the fun of it," the historian Douglas Brinkley wrote. "His favorite sport was making African-Americans pay in front and walk back to board in the rear, then leaving them with a faceful of exhaust as he gunned the bus away before they could get on." Brinkley, *Rosa Parks*, 58.

ain't-chya?' I said, 'Naw, not unless'n you all don't accept my man.'
He said, 'Who is your man?' I said, 'Martin Luther King.' He said,
'I'll go along with it.' French said, 'I'll go along with it.' So then we
had not only our recommendation, our resolution, our name, we had
our president."[2]

Nixon tapped King because his was the wealthiest and most influential black church in Montgomery, he had not been in town long
enough to make enemies, and he was almost as eloquent as Nixon's
mentor, A. Philip Randolph. King had one other trait that must have
made him attractive: he was impressionable enough to let Nixon pull
his strings, at least at the beginning. Nixon did so generally to King's
benefit, mobilizing working-class blacks around a boycott that
required many to walk for miles. He traveled the country spreading
word about the protest and raising what he said was more than
$400,000. And, at the meeting where King was elected president and
he was named treasurer, Nixon confronted head-on those who were
unnerved by the prospect of riling white Montgomery.

"I said, 'How you gonna have a mass meeting, gonna boycott a
city bus line without the white folks knowing it?'" Nixon recounted.
"I said, 'You guys have went around here and lived off these poor
washerwomen all your lives and ain't never done nothing for 'em.
And now you got a chance to do something for 'em, you talkin'
about you don't want the white folks to know it.' I said, 'Unless'n
this program is accepted and brought into the church like a decent,
respectable organization. . . . I'll take the microphone and tell 'em
the reason we don't have a program is 'cause you all are too scared
to stand on your feet and be counted. You oughta make up your
mind right now that you gon' either admit you are a grown man or
concede to the fact that you are a bunch of scared boys.'"[3]

What Nixon was doing in Montgomery in the 1950s, other Pullman porters were doing across the United States. They promoted
antilynching campaigns, helped plot the first "freedom rides,"
spearheaded the March on Washington, and jumped into other big
battles in the courts, voting booths, and on the street. They put up
their money and manpower and turned over their union halls for

meetings. They knew how to battle the white power structure, having taken on and beaten the infamously antiunion Pullman Company, and shared those lessons in building support for broader economic and political rights. And porters carried the civil rights message across America the same as they had the Brotherhood's, by delivering black newspapers and jawboning with everyone they met.

There was one more thing that Nixon and his fellow porters shared when it came to the civil rights movement: their contributions have largely been forgotten by scholars, the public, and even their own families.

History has acknowledged Montgomery's place as a bookend in the struggle for civil rights, with the movement seen as starting with the boycott and ending with passage of the Voting Rights Act of 1965. "Until Montgomery, the white South never thought it had an adversary. At Montgomery, blacks showed not only that they could come together for the struggle, but knew how to win," the historian Milton Viorst wrote of the yearlong boycott, which culminated in the city's bus segregation ordinance being declared unconstitutional.[4] But although Martin Luther King Jr.'s role seems to grow with each retelling of the Montgomery story, Nixon is relegated to a diminishingly minor character. Or not mentioned at all. "I'm called an Uncle Tom now because I can deal with the power structure," Nixon, known as all porters were by his initials, "E. D.," said two decades after the boycott ended. "So many people got famous out of it and I was still left here. And I'm still here servin' the people and the rest of 'em gone."[5]

The older he got, the more embittered he became toward "the rest of 'em," especially King. "I was on an airplane coming down from New York some time ago, sittin' beside a lady, and she asked me who I was," Nixon recalled. "I told her. She said, 'Oh, you're down in Montgomery, Alabama.' She said, 'Lord, I don't know what'ud happened to the black people if Rev. King hadn't went to town.' I said, 'If Mrs. Parks had got up and given that white man her seat, you'd never ahead of Rev. King.'"[6]

King, however, did not forget. He called Nixon "one of the chief voices of the Negro community in the area of civil rights, a symbol of the hopes and aspirations of the long oppressed people of the State of Alabama." Regarding that inaugural planning session for the boycott, the civil rights legend continued, "had E. D. Nixon been present, he would probably have been automatically selected to preside, but he had had to leave town earlier in the afternoon for his regular run on the railroad." As for Nixon's "scared boys" speech, King's recollection of the wording was slightly less colorful than Nixon's, but he wrote that "with this forthright statement the air was cleared. Nobody would again suggest that we try to conceal our identity or avoid facing the issue head on. Nixon's courageous affirmation had given new heart to those who were about to be crippled by fear."[7]

IF E. D. NIXON nudged the Reverend King into majesty, it was A. Philip Randolph who tutored him on wearing his cloak of command. Which was only appropriate, since Randolph had been the de facto leader of America's civil rights movement since before it was recognized as a movement. He was the Martin Luther King Jr. of an earlier generation, or two. He met with more American presidents than any black leader before, called and carried off bigger demonstrations, and recorded more victories that touched average blacks. He jumped into the fray earlier, and stayed longer, than anyone, including King, whose participation was curtailed and immortalized by the bullet of an assassin.

Randolph's passion for civil rights came from his parents, James and Elizabeth, and he knew it would become his calling even before he left Jacksonville in 1911. Black rights and racial justice were the driving forces in his days sermonizing on street corners in Harlem, trying to organize ship hands and elevator operators, and writing and editing the *Hotel Messenger,* then the *Messenger.* While other speechmakers, black and white, were rallying the country to war in 1918, he was congratulating his listeners "for doing [their] bit to make the world safe for democracy—and unsafe for hypocrisy." It was a line that stirred the crowd by reminding them of racial intolerance on the home front, and stirred federal agents to arrest him after he delivered it in Cleveland.[8]

The twelve-year battle to get the Pullman Company to negotiate with the Brotherhood of Sleeping Car Porters also was framed around racial issues along with union ones. That was partly a matter of strategy: it helped rally the black community to the porters' cause and unmask the Pullman Company's paternalism. But to Randolph, civil rights mattered as much as his porters, sometimes more. He never hid that from porters, telling them from the start that the immediate battle was to get more money and fairer working conditions for them, then to win the same for other blacks. In 1927, just two years after launching the union bid, he published in the *Messenger* this imaginary exchange between the racially aware New Porter (NP) and the Uncle Tom Porter (UTP):

NP: White folks are no different from any other kind of folks, pop. It all depends on how much *power* you got, and you can't get power unless you are *organized*. You know the old joke about the farmer not bothering *one hornet* because of fear of the *rest* of the *hornets standing behind him*. Well, that's all we porters got to do. That's all the Negro race has got to do—*stick together*; be *all for each and each for all*.

UTP: But, son, you know des *"niggers"* ain't like *hornets*, dey ain't gwine to *stick*.

NP: That's nothing but the slave psychology in you, Pop. You don't think a black man can do anything a white man can do. That's all bunk, pop. Get that stuff out of your noodle. This is the 20th Century. Understand that "a man's a man." A Negro can do anything he is big enough to do. When you're right, pop, and got "guts," you can stand up and look any man in the face and spit right square in his eyes if he tries to give you any *hot stuff* about your rights.[9]

Randolph's willingness to spit in the eye of the establishments, white and black, became clear in 1935 when he helped launch the National Negro Congress and became its first president. The congress said it aimed to unite all black organizations behind a progressive agenda, but it actually meant to challenge that most Brahmin of black power centers, the National Association for the Advancement of Colored People. Founded twenty-six years earlier, the NAACP had an impressive record of attacking racism in the United States— generally by filing lawsuits, lobbying the president and Congress, and gingerly appealing to the conscience of white America. Its members were white along with black; its benefactors the elites of both races. The National Negro Congress embraced a more militant and populist program that included picketing and boycotts, and that relied exclusively on black workers and black money. Although Randolph eventually grew wary of a growing Communist influence within the congress and resigned his presidency, his five-year involvement left him believing in the power of the worker, the primacy of mass action, and the need for blacks, at times, to go it alone.[10]

Such early struggles proved his passion, but Randolph's clearest impact on the civil rights front came during the decade after the Brotherhood won its first contract in 1937. The union at that point focused less on political battles and rhetorical flourishes and more on securing pensions, arguing grievances, and other nuts-and-bolts matters that had always been the bailiwick of Milton P. Webster and the bane of A. Philip Randolph. So Randolph more than ever left those union tasks to his deputies and, armed with the cachet of having stage-managed America's most successful black labor drive, zeroed in on the second half of his union-race agenda. And while he took on so many civil rights leadership roles that it sometimes diluted his impact, his commitment was clear-cut and his focus razor-sharp when it came to the March on Washington movement.

It was not a movement to start with, nor even a campaign. More a tactic born of frustration. America's depressed economic outlook finally seemed to be brightening by late 1940, as defense industries were gearing up to supply Britain and its allies with ships, guns, tanks, and anything else they needed to turn back Adolf Hitler's armies. Blacks, however, were not part of the plan. On the eve of the war there were fewer than 5,000 black troops in a U.S. Army of 230,000, and fewer than a dozen black officers.[11] Most of the new defense jobs, even unskilled ones, were open only to whites. So pervasive was the paranoia about whites being contaminated by contact with blacks that the War Department at first refused to accept any blood drawn from blacks, then in 1942 began a segregated system for collecting and dispensing plasma and platelets for its soldiers. Randolph and other black leaders had tried redressing such injustices by writing letters, convening conferences, and even holding a face-to-face meeting with President Roosevelt in the fall of 1940, but nothing worked and they were running out of patience as well as ideas.

That was Randolph's state of mind when he left by train around New Year's with his top lieutenant, the fiery Webster, to visit Brotherhood offices across the South. "On that particular day as we crossed the Potomac River, Brother Randolph said to me, he says, 'You know, Web, you know we got to do something about these jobs around here.' He said, 'We're going to hold a lot of conferences but we're not getting anywhere,'" Webster remembered fifteen years later. "Of course, knowing Brother Randolph, I said, 'Well here comes something else. What do you suggest that we do?' 'Well,' he says, 'I think we ought to get ten thousand Negroes and march down Pennsylvania Avenue, and protest. What do you think about it?' I said, 'I think it's all right. Where are you going to get the ten thousand Negroes?' He said, 'I believe we can get them.'"[12]

Whether or not he actually could have assembled ten thousand Negroes is uncertain and probably unimportant. It was the threat that counted, and Randolph repeated it in speeches as he and Webster sped through the South and in articles in any journal that would publish them. He coined a slogan: "We loyal Negro American citizens demand the right to work and fight for our country." The March on Washington Committee was created, with him at the helm, branches were set up in eighteen cities, and the NAACP was enlisted along with other mainstream black groups. It was not just the upper crust that was mustering around a march for racial justice. The protest had become topic number one in bars and pool halls, jitterbug parlors and black churches. Randolph had touched a nerve, tapping into the ire and exasperation of the black masses and, in the process, fanning fears in white America. In May of 1941 he upped the ante by a factor of ten, vowing to turn out 100,000 marchers. And while he thanked his white supporters, Randolph made clear that the marchers and even the money must come from blacks alone.

His antics were working, grabbing the attention of groups as diverse as the FBI and the Communist Party. "There is some indication that the Communist Party will endeavor to convert the March into a Communist demonstration," FBI boss J. Edgar Hoover reported to the White House in June 1941. A rash of memos made clear the bureau was following every iteration of the planning.[13] That the president, too, was paying attention became apparent when he dispatched his wife, Eleanor, black America's strongest ally in the White House, to press Randolph to call it off.

He refused, leading an increasingly annoyed Roosevelt to the one tried-and-true tactic left: his capacity to enchant. He invited to the White House Randolph and NAACP chief Walter White, along with such senior federal officials as the secretary of war and the heads of the wartime Office of Production Management. It was Randolph the president zeroed in on as the meeting began. "Hello, Phil," Roosevelt began, "which class were you in at Harvard?" Randolph explained he never went to Harvard, to which the president replied, "I was sure you did. Anyway, you and I share a kinship in our great interest in human and social justice." The president continued his banter until Randolph, realizing the meeting could end without resolution, interrupted: "Mr. President, time is running on. You are quite busy, I know. But what we want to talk with you about is the problem of jobs for Negroes in defense industries. Our people are being turned away at factory gates because they are colored. They can't live with this thing. Now, what are you going to do about it?"[14] Roosevelt refused to issue the order Randolph wanted barring discrimination in defense plants; Randolph refused to accept anything less as a precondition for calling off his march. New York mayor Fiorello La Guardia, a friend of both men, broke the deadlock by suggesting that Randolph meet with White House staffers to hammer out a compromise. It worked, and the president signed

Executive Order 8802 on June 25, 1941, just six days before the march was due to be held.

The presidential order made it U.S. policy "that there shall be no discrimination in the employment of workers in defense industries or government because of race, creed, color, or national origin." The Fair Employment Practice Committee (FEPC) was created to investigate and redress allegations of bias. Webster, the most defiant of Randolph's lieutenants, was named to the committee. While militants slammed Randolph for calling off the march and failing to win a promise of integrating units within the armed forces,* Order 8802 generally was recognized as a milestone in racial reconciliation, maybe even the second Emancipation Proclamation that Randolph and his associates claimed. He had pried open the lucrative defense industries to admit black workers and pushed the U.S. government to its most decisive civil rights stance since Reconstruction. He had gone eyeball-to-eyeball with the most charismatic, powerful American president of that era, or any, and made him blink. He was, for now, the supreme civil rights leader in America.

"The Negro did not come out of the war as a free worker in an open economy. But the FEPC had given him a place in the basic industries which he had never held before," the Pulitzer Prize–winning columnist Murray Kempton wrote in his memoir. "In the future, whites and Negroes would work together in factories where the Negro had never existed as a skilled worker. There were many factors in this revolution, but none were more important than Philip Randolph and his Pullman Porters and their March on Washington."[15]

---

*Some dissenters had long memories. During the Harlem riots of 1943, two years after Randolph called off the march, "one of the first things destroyed was the March on Washington headquarters on a hundred and twenty-fifth street," recalled Bayard Rustin, Randolph's aide and friend. "The destruction was intentional. Scrawled on the wall was, 'Randolph, why don't you march?' I think the writers were trying to say to him, 'Get on with it. We're in a bad state. Do something!'" Milton Viorst, *Fire in the Streets: America in the 1960s* (New York: Simon and Schuster, 1979), 206.

The *Amsterdam Star-News,** New York's most influential black newspaper, rendered a similar verdict in an editorial titled "A. Philip Randolph, Leader." It began by noting, "[Randolph] is being ranked along with the great Frederick Douglass," and "his name is rapidly becoming a household word." It continued: "For many years the Negro has been groping for a leadership that could be trusted. It seems, now, that that leadership is being ushered in. We regard A. Philip Randolph as the man of the hour. His sacrifices in the past, which were made in times of stress and want, would seem to indicate he cannot be bought. On his record we heartily endorse his program and commend him to the Negroes of America, who look for and hope for a better day."[16]

So successful was the Washington march, or rather the threat of one, that Randolph kept alive both the march and the movement around it. Even as he went on national radio to cancel the July 1 demonstration, he made clear that it was his aim "to broaden and strengthen the Negro March-on-Washington committees all over the United States, to serve as watchdogs on the application of the President's executive order." And so he did. During the summer of 1942 he staged rallies in Chicago and St. Louis to pressure the Fair Employment Practice Committee into delivering on its promise and to remind the president that America's blacks, having realized the potency of their protest, would keep speaking out. The biggest and most successful spectacle was in America's premier public arena, Madison Square Garden, where twenty thousand people watched as Randolph was led in by a chef in a white hat and one hundred uniformed Pullman porters, with fifty maids forming the rear guard. "All walks of life were represented, some of our most prominent women doctors, lawyers, school teachers, social workers, housewives, and even 'ladies of the evening,'" wrote the *Amsterdam News*. "Between 7 P.M. and 1 A.M. Tuesday night, in the area from 110th

---

*This is the same publication as the *Amsterdam News*. It was called the *Star-News* in 1941 and 1943.

St. to 126th St., sometimes called 'Harlem's red light district,' these 'ladies' were conspicuous by their absence."[17]

As for an actual march, it did happen, but not for another twenty-two years. Again, blacks had their hopes raised by a new Democratic president, this time John Fitzgerald Kennedy. But all they saw were unemployment rates twice the national average, wages barely half as high as those of whites, and protests quashed by the likes of Birmingham police commissioner Eugene "Bull" Connor, who called out the attack dogs and high-pressure hoses. Again, J. Edgar Hoover tried to scuttle the march. Like Roosevelt, Kennedy sought to charm Randolph into backing off, but the result was the same. The black leader stood his ground and went away the winner. As the Kennedy chronicler Arthur M. Schlesinger Jr. writes: "A. Philip Randolph, speaking with the quiet dignity which touched Kennedy as it had touched Roosevelt before him, discussed the attempt to shift the civil rights drive from the streets to the courts. 'The Negroes are already in the streets,' Randolph said. 'It is very likely impossible to get them off. If they are bound to be in the streets in any case, is it not better that they be led by organizations dedicated to civil rights and disciplined by struggle rather than to leave them to other leaders who care neither about civil rights nor about non-violence?' . . . When asked about the march at a press conference in mid-July, Kennedy, noting that the participants intended 'a peaceful assembly calling for a redress of grievances' and that it was 'not a march on the Capitol,' said, 'I think that's in the great tradition.'"[18]

The march, on August 28, 1963, brought 250,000 blacks and whites to the sprawling green mall in front of the memorial to Abraham Lincoln, which seemed just the right backdrop. Turnout was two and a half times more than organizers dared hope for. It was more people than had ever gathered in Washington or anywhere else in America to raise their collective voice for human rights, for civil rights. Randolph, godfather of the march and movement, began the program by telling listeners they were "the advance guard of a massive moral revolution for jobs and freedom." He was followed by civil rights leaders John Lewis, Roy Wilkins, and Martin Luther King Jr., with King captivating the crowd by sharing his dream that his "four little children will one day live in a nation where they will not be judged by the color of their skin but by the content of their character."

While the eloquence of that "I have a dream" speech, and the performances of entertainers like Marian Anderson, Joan Baez, and Bob Dylan, were what most in the audience would remember, the march's lead organizer took away something different. "It wasn't the Harry Belafontes and the greats from Hollywood that made the march," said Bayard Rustin. "What made the march was that black people voted that day with their feet. They came from every state, they came in jalopies, on trains, buses, anything they could get—some walked. There were about three hundred congressmen there, but none of them said a word. We had told them to come, but we wanted to talk with them, they were not to talk to us. . . . The march ended for me when we had finally made sure we had not left one piece of paper, not a cup, nothing. We had a five-hundred-man cleanup squad. I went back to the hotel and said to Mr. Randolph, 'Chief, I want you to see that there is not a piece of paper or any dirt or filth or anything left here.' And Mr. Randolph went to thank me and tears began to come down his cheeks."[19]

The tears were of joy for finally seeing his march happen. But they also sprung from a recognition that, when he introduced King to the crowd that afternoon, a mantle was being passed. King was "the man who personifies the moral leadership of the civil rights revolution," Randolph had said. And so he was. What went unsaid was that Randolph had been that man for most of the previous half century.

Ironically, Randolph's real March on Washington produced less definitive results than his threatened one twenty-two years before. The outpouring on the mall probably speeded passage of the land-mark Civil Rights Act of 1964, but the civil rights movement by then was operating on so many fronts that it was impossible to establish cause and effect. It certainly eclipsed any earlier mass demonstration, but blacks already had demonstrated their determination in protests from Montgomery to Birmingham. The march's most lasting contri-bution was that millions of Americans who watched it on TV or read about it in the papers "witnessed for the first time black people and white united, marching and celebrating side by side," Juan Williams wrote in *Eyes on the Prize*, a history of the civil rights struggle. "The march brought joy and a sense of possibility to people throughout the nation who perhaps had not understood the civil rights movement before or who had felt threatened by it."[20]

To most men, the March on Washington movement would have been overwhelming, especially if, as with Randolph, it came on top of a full-time job as president of the Brotherhood of Sleeping Car Porters. But civil rights was even more consuming for him, a rapture as well as a responsibility. So even while plotting out marches he was testing a series of other strategies to promote racial justice.

At the top of his agenda was convincing the House of Labor to open its doors to other black workers the way it had to his Brotherhood. Randolph understood that labor was a central pillar of the American power structure, one constructed around the lofty principles of equality and democracy. He also knew that organized labor's racist treatment of black workers made a mockery of its founding precepts. Exposing that hypocrisy, Randolph believed, not only would change the American Federation of Labor but could begin to reform America itself. So he goaded the organization from the outside, launching the Negro American Labor Council in 1959 to agitate for greater black participation in the union movement. And he pressed from the inside, pushing year after year for the AFL to banish unions that maintained color bars. Although others were intimidated by George Meany, who ruled the newly united AFL-CIO with a razor tongue and steel fist from 1955 to 1979, Randolph took him on directly and publicly on the issue of integration. In one exchange at the federation's 1959 convention, Randolph told the labor boss that letting unions segregate was as "immoral" as it would be to let them be taken over by Communists or racketeers. Meany shot back that black workers preferred all-black locals and demanded of Randolph, "Who the hell appointed you as the guardian of all the Negroes in America?"[21]

It was not just union members Randolph was trying to guard,

but men like Odell Waller of Virginia. The black sharecropper had killed his landlord—claiming it was in self-defense—but was convicted by an all-white jury and sentenced to die in the electric chair. Randolph understood before most the built-in bias of racially exclusive juries. While it would take another three decades for American courts to begin fulfilling the promise of a "jury of one's peers," Randolph tried to undo the Waller panel's harsh edict by getting his sentence commuted. The union leader orchestrated a national drive that generated seventeen thousand letters to Virginia governor Colgate Darden, including a delicately worded one from President Franklin Roosevelt. Although that campaign failed and Waller was executed, it was one more instance of what Randolph said was blacks "learning to use pressure."[22]

The Brotherhood president also became expert at courting and cajoling American presidents to do more than they felt comfortable doing for blacks. His first presidential encounter was in 1925 as part of a delegation urging Calvin Coolidge to support anti-lynching legislation. Lynching had become epidemic, with nearly twenty-five hundred black men, women, and children being hung or otherwise executed by white vigilantes since 1880. It was not just the mob violence that enraged Randolph, but the way the white establishment endorsed it by failing to prosecute the perpetrators. President Coolidge listened as Randolph and two dozen other black leaders made their case for a crackdown. But, as Randolph later recalled, Coolidge's reaction suggested "there was no sensation at all going through his mind."[23]

Randolph had more luck not just with Franklin Roosevelt but with his vice president, Harry S. Truman, who moved into the White House when FDR died in 1945 and three years later ran for a full term. The issue this time was the same segregation of the military that Randolph had raised with Roosevelt. And again, Randolph played hardball, launching the Committee Against Jim Crow in Military Service and Training, threatening to rally black draftees and veterans behind a program of civil disobedience, and capitalizing on Truman's fear of blacks defecting to Progressive Party presidential nominee Henry A. Wallace. Truman already had shown his willingness to incur the wrath of powerful southerners in his Democratic Party when, in February 1948, he sent a special message to Congress urging it to approve antilynching, anti–poll tax, and other civil rights laws. Five months later, with Congress balking and pressure building from Randolph, the president signed a pair of executive orders that began the transformation of the armed forces from America's most segregated institution to its most integrated.

Randolph never seemed to run out of steam. He lobbied President Dwight D. Eisenhower to push for civil rights legislation and, after his meeting, reported that "the president was very pleasant, full of good will, but without apparent familiarity with the problems of the Negro people or readiness to do anything about them."[24] He was an architect of President Lyndon B. Johnson's War on Poverty but wanted an even bolder ten-year, $185-billion Freedom Budget, which, he said, would put all Americans to work. He encouraged blacks to register to vote, no matter that it seemed old-school; supported Israel and other causes of his longtime Jewish allies, no matter that black radicals objected; and backed President Johnson's waging of war in Vietnam, no matter that the Reverend King and other colleagues were antiwar. At age eighty-two, Randolph helped launch a campaign to organize household workers. Of all America's civil rights leaders of the Vietnam era, he was the only one who had been active back in World War I. And through the 1960s he remained the grand old man to whom younger civil rights leaders like King, Whitney Young, James Farmer, and John Lewis turned when competition prevented them from reaching a consensus or finding a spokesman.

When elements of the movement in the mid-1960s took a radical turn toward black power and the Muslim faith, and a schism formed between the newcomers and old-school NAACPers, Randolph looked to build bridges. He knew what it was like for the young rebels, having himself been dismissed as a radical in the 1920s and having taken on mainstream black leaders when he headed the National Negro Congress in 1935. Their protest echoed his in all its critical elements—from the call for racial self-reliance to its focus on economic opportunity as the key to black freedom. While he worried about militant rhetoric that at times led to the spilling of real blood, Randolph understood the passion that drove it. He especially could relate to Malcolm X, the most introspective and interesting of the new breed. Most civil rights leaders "used Malcolm as a bogeyman," said his biographer, Peter Goldman. "Only the black trade-union ancient, A. Philip Randolph, among the elders of the movement made a conscious effort to break the quarantine and reach out to Malcolm; they would meet occasionally at Randolph's office, and Malcolm would sit for hours listening to the old man's reminiscences about DuBois and Garvey and the Harlem past. 'The guy is so happy to communicate,' Randolph told Kenneth Clark; he saw, earlier than most of his colleagues, the danger in isolating Malcolm and forcing him deeper into the rigidities of his positions." Malcolm himself put it more succinctly: "All civil rights leaders are confused, but Randolph is less confused than the rest."[25]

But Randolph's legacy on civil rights is about more than longevity and inclusiveness. He recognized that blacks are disadvantaged in large measure because they are poor, and that only the government can change that. Although he relied on whites to help fund his union and civil rights work, and formed more black-white coalitions than anyone else, in the 1940s he began calling upon blacks to develop the confidence that comes from going it alone. And from bearing the costs themselves. "He who pays the fiddler," Randolph said repeatedly, "calls the tune."[26] The slogan took on substance with his March on Washington movement, the largest mass action by blacks, for blacks, since Marcus Garvey's ill-fated back-to-Africa crusade. Martin Luther King Jr. typically is credited with pioneering black protest politics, but any paternity test that reaches back far enough makes clear the real father was A. Philip Randolph.

So, too, with civil disobedience. King brought spirituality and passion to the tactic with dramatic marches like one in Selma where a national television audience watched mounted police use nightsticks and tear gas on demonstrators, and with defiant sit-ins that introduced America to Mahatma Gandhi's Indian-style passive resistance.

But Randolph was there first. Peaceful protest was the centerpiece of his marches on Washington, the real and threatened ones. His 1948 campaign against the draft was called the League for Non-Violent Civil Disobedience, and his 1947 launching of the Committee Against Jim Crow in Military Service and Training was founded on identical principles. His was a civil disobedience of the intellect more than the soul, but it was equally heartfelt. And he passed it down to young leaders he trained—from Bayard Rustin to James Peck, James Farmer to E. D. Nixon—all of whom would play critical roles in the civil rights movement.

Randolph had his critics, a small army of them, which is not surprising given how controversial his strategies were and how many decades he spent challenging the status quo. He was rightly accused of being a "political butterfly," winging from cause to cause, better at launching them than following through. While he insisted on being top man, he depended on Rustin and other lieutenants to actually run his civil rights campaigns the same way he did Webster to run the Brotherhood. And as he did with his union, he played the bluff too often to stay credible. Most cutting of all, young militants—upset when Randolph attacked "black power" as an indefensible slogan—dubbed him "Uncle Tom No. 2," according him a place of dishonor just behind Roy Wilkins of the NAACP.[27]

By then Randolph was too tired to fight back, and too distracted by the loss of his wife and best friend. He had spent ten years nursing Lucille after arthritis and a broken hip forced her into a wheelchair and largely confined her to their Harlem apartment. He read her passages from the Bible or a sonnet from Shakespeare each evening he was home, fed her the best cuts of steak, and held her hand through the night when she could not sleep. After she died in 1963, would-be suitors telephoned so often that Randolph had to get an unlisted number; rather than returning their calls, he read to himself at night, sitting in the old chair by Lucille's bed. In the summer of 1968 he was mugged at the door to his third-floor walk-up by three young assailants who had followed him from the bus stop. One grabbed him by the neck while the others rifled his pockets, finding a single dollar. They left him crumpled on the floor, pockets inside out, papers from his briefcase scattered at his side. Later that summer Randolph moved into an apartment in the Chelsea–Penn Station South district where the security was better and he did not have to climb stairs.[28]

His heart was weak and his blood pressure high, but he held on for eleven years. Death finally came on May 16, 1979, the eve of the twenty-fifth anniversary of the high court's *Brown v. Board of Education* ruling. Randolph had received his share of bouquets along with the barbs during his last years. Admiral George Dewey Square in Harlem had been renamed A. Philip Randolph Square. President Lyndon Johnson had awarded him America's highest civilian honor, the Medal of Freedom, and his picture one day would appear on a U.S. postage stamp. Still, too many of his contemporaries were gone to appropriately mourn him, and too few in the new generation understood what his legacy was. "It's so sad because there are so many young people today for whom that name means very little," NAACP president Benjamin L. Hooks said in Randolph's obituary in the *New York Times,* which appeared not where it might have been expected on the front page but on page five of the B section. "And yet, for more than 40 years, he was a tower and beacon of strength and hope for the entire black community."[29] Even his best-known civil rights contribution, the March on Washington, slipped away from him as time passed and memories faded. In August 2003, forty years after the massive demonstration on the National Mall, there were 123 anniversary stories in major U.S. newspapers—108 of which mentioned Martin Luther King Jr., while just 14 referenced A. Philip Randolph.[30]

The Reverend King never forgot Randolph's role in the march or his strength and hope. He suggested the reverence in which he held his friend by calling him "Mr. Randolph" long after the two had cemented their bond, and by listening to and taking his advice. In a letter to Randolph in 1958, King wrote, "You are truly the Dean of Negro leaders," referring to a recent article by that title in *Ebony.* "If I had to choose the ten greatest persons in America today, I would certainly include you on my list. . . . I don't know if you have ever considered writing an autobiography. I certainly hope you will. What you have done and what you have achieved should be placed in a document for generations yet unborn to read and meditate upon."[31]

E. D. Nixon, the father of the Montgomery bus boycott and a linchpin of the Brotherhood, also had looked to Randolph as a tower and beacon. "When I first heard Randolph speak," he recalled years afterward, "it was like a light. Most eloquent man I ever heard. He done more to bring me in the fight for civil rights than anybody. Before that time, I figure that a Negro would be kicked around and accept whatever the white man did. I never knew the Negro had a right to enjoy freedom like everyone else. When Randolph stood there and talked that day, it made a different man out of me. From that day on, I was determined that I was gonna fight for freedom until I was able to get some of it myself. I was just stumblin' here and there. But I been very successful in stumblin' ever since that day."[32]

C. L. DELLUMS, who took over from Randolph as president of the Brotherhood in the fall of 1968, had always split his time between union and civil rights work, just as Randolph did. Dellums ran the Oakland branches of the Brotherhood and the NAACP and oversaw nine western states for the civil rights group. This son of a barber also helped win passage of California's Fair Employment Practices Commission, then served as a member and later its chairman. He and Randolph, he said, "were the only ones generally that saw the Brotherhood as a racial movement and as part of the civil rights struggle."[33]

It was a classic Dellums boast—well-meaning, but way wide of the mark. E. D. Nixon was at least as bold as Randolph and Dellums in diving headfirst into the civil rights stew, or as he put it, stumblin' into it. Same for Milton P. Webster, who followed through on civil rights promises made by the Chief just as he had on union ones. Webster's Chicago division of the Brotherhood helped organize union drives among other workers, including janitors and dining car workers, and he was named to President Roosevelt's Fair Employment Practice Committee. Nixon and Webster, like Dellums and Randolph, saw their civil rights and union split less as a schism than as working two sides of a whole.

While its leaders were critical to the fight for black rights, the Brotherhood rank and file made an even more profound contribution. They were missionaries for the movement. They carried word of the struggle across the country, just as they did word of the latest jazz and blues releases. The Brotherhood became a school for teaching the wider community about civil rights and black manhood. "When the final history is written," said the civil rights historian Robert H. Brisbane, "the three organizations which will be at the top of the list for achievement for our fight . . . will be the NAACP, the Urban League, and, certainly, the Brotherhood."[34]

Money was the first thing that vaulted the Brotherhood onto that elite list, though it did not have a lot. There never were more than twelve thousand porters, their monthly dues were a modest dollar and a half through 1940, and when Randolph finally started drawing a real salary it was half as much as America's lowest-paid union boss.[35] The timing also was bad: the sleeping car business was fizzling and porters' jobs were being cut just as the civil rights battle was heating up. Even so, the union dug deep enough to help underwrite the Montgomery bus boycott. It gave fifty thousand dollars to the Washington march, supported Randolph as he traveled and spoke on civil rights, and paid most of the bills of organizations he spawned. Anytime blacks launched a new initiative—from protesting the 1955 lynching in Mississippi of fourteen-year-old Emmett Till, to dispatching black and white "freedom riders" across the South in 1961 to challenge segregated seating in buses and accommodations in bus stations—the first group they turned to with their hand out was the Brotherhood. And it almost always obliged. It did the same for black firemen, brakemen, and switchmen fighting expensive legal battles to keep their jobs, and for white politicians like U.S. Senator Hubert Humphrey who courageously pressed for tough civil rights laws. As for the battle to establish the national Fair

Employment Practice Committee and make sure it worked, "we spent a small fortune," said the Brotherhood's Benjamin McLaurin. "It's the porters' gift."[36]

The porters were especially generous when the Reverend King was nearly stabbed to death by a deranged black woman in Harlem in 1958. There were big bills for hospitals, hotels, and cars. Randolph and his brethren gave what they could themselves, then solicited money from sources as diverse as the American Jewish Congress and the future vice president Nelson Rockefeller. "Words are inadequate for me to express my appreciation to you for the many gracious things you did for me during my illness," King wrote Randolph. "From the moment you came in my hospital room on that dreadful Saturday afternoon to the moment I left New York City you proved to be a real source of consolation to me. Your encouraging words and your great gestures of good will served as a great spiritual lift for me and were of inestimable value in giving me the courage and strength to face the ordeal of that trying period. I can assure you that I will remember all of these things so long as the cords of memory shall lengthen."[37]

When they had no money to give, porters turned over their union halls for civil rights meetings. Then they offered up their women and kids. It was women from the Ladies' Auxiliary to the Brotherhood of Sleeping Car Porters who put up posters, handed out leaflets, and collected quarters and dollars for the March on Washington. They planned who would sleep where, where everyone would eat, and the thousand other details needed to pull off the biggest march of its kind ever. No matter that the 1940s incarnation never came off; that decision was made at higher levels, but at the grass roots these women were ready. Ladies of the auxiliary also made things happen at the Committee Against Jim Crow in Military Service and Training, the National Council for a Permanent FEPC, and other organizations their husbands dreamed up. They helped pay for the bus boycott in Montgomery, boosted antilynching and anti–poll tax bills, and sent clothing to black schoolkids in poor places like West Virginia. Watching their mothers do all that work made an impression on Pullman porters' kids, encouraging them to pitch in on everything from fund-raising to community clothes drives.[38]

As with their union work, the best place to see that civil rights activity in action was in Chicago. In the heyday of its long battle for a union, the Brotherhood ran a series of labor conferences for the wider community, with as many as three thousand people a year attending. Each conference carried clear messages: blacks deserve full civil and economic rights, they need to be self-sufficient and free of white benefactors, and it is time to issue demands rather than make requests. The Brotherhood did not just precede the civil rights movement in Chicago; it planted the seeds for it. Rather than a con-ventional labor union, it had become a school for protest politics.[39]

Brotherhood leaders and members were running similar schools as far north as Canada, and down in Florida, where Harold Reddick was one of the teachers. Reddick held the title of vice president at the Tampa Brotherhood district and the Tampa office of the NAACP. "We porters would support the local civil rights movement and keep it alive," he explained. "We'd bring in newspapers and create more information within the black community. An ignorant community can't do nothing for you, they don't know what to go for."[40] There was another kind of information porters picked up en route—about brutal acts like lynchings going on in small towns, where no one expected outsiders would find out or butt in. "I remember when a Pullman porter told NAACP leader Roy Wilkins about how these Klansmen broke open the jail in Wildwood [Florida], took this young black man out, and lynched him," said Robert W. Saunders Sr., the NAACP field secretary in Florida during the 1950s and 1960s. "I bring that incident out to show how powerful the Pullman porters were, how they cooperated. They got the news first-hand. In Wildwood, that is how the FBI was brought into the case."[41]

Not all porters were comfortable with the civil rights campaigns. Most, like workers anywhere, had more than enough to do sustain-ing a family and holding down a job. While older porters tended to see the civil rights struggle as an analogue to their fight for a union, younger ones were tiring of the war stories and unmoved by the old coalitions. To them the Brotherhood was less a cause than a service organization. Some felt their aging leaders ran the union like their private fiefdom; others resented Randolph for spending so much Brotherhood money on nonunion projects.

Happy Davis was in the middle. He revered Randolph, respected the Brotherhood, and his home base in Washington gave him an up-close look at his union's civil rights activities. But "I didn't take no part in civil rights at all," he said. "Listen, we was working so hard and when Martin Luther King and them started marching, and they came here, I had a couple porters who wanted to stay here. We didn't have the facilities. I had seven children here." Still, even with seven children and other responsibilities, Davis said his wife found the time to volunteer as a civil rights worker.[42]

As valuable as Pullman porters were as a civil rights army on wheels, they made more of an impact just by who they were and all they had accomplished. Their victory over the Pullman Company made porters a role model not only for redcaps and other railroad men but for an entire black community anxious about competing in a culture that seemed stacked in favor of whites. Porters had competed—and won. They were schooled in union bargaining and ways of the white world. Their modest numbers and segregated workforce, once seen as limits of influence and opportunity, now were badges of a proud racial monopoly. The tiny Brotherhood spoke with a stentorian voice. The once passive porter had become an inspiration to the civil rights movement and, most especially, to its young leaders.

Roy Wilkins, the longtime head of the NAACP, said there were three events that made him proudest of being black during the 1930s, when he was in his thirties. The first was during the 1936 Olympics in Nazi Berlin when black track-and-field sensation Jesse Owens won four gold medals and set Olympic and world records, giving the lie to Adolf Hitler's notions of Aryan mastery. The second was watching Joe Louis, another world-class black athlete, deck German boxer Max Schmeling in the first round of their heavyweight rematch. The third, Wilkins writes in his memoir, was "the day the Pullman Company, after a contract wrangle that had lasted more than a decade, summoned in A. Philip Randolph and the leaders of the Brotherhood of Sleeping Car Porters and said, 'Gentlemen, the Pullman Company is ready to sign.'"[43]

The congressman and civil rights activist John Lewis came of age two generations after Wilkins, but like him, Lewis drew inspiration from the porters. "It meant a great deal to me to see these well-dressed African-American males with their uniforms on," Lewis said. "They seemed to me so clean, so neat, that they represented something different, something better. For someone like me who grew up very, very poor in rural Alabama to see the image of these men, not just the job they were doing, they seemed part of some official body. They stood out as something very, very special in the African-American community."[44]

What the porters did for civil rights is easy to see. *Why* is more puzzling. Their main objectives in building a union were to work fewer hours and earn more money. The Brotherhood claimed to have done more, percentage-wise, to raise its members' wages than any other union in the United States, and given the low base they started from, it probably was true. The same claim could have been made for their reduction in hours. Porters also were determined to cement their standing in the middle class and see their children get educational and other opportunities denied them. Again, they were on the way.

So why do more? Partly because they knew too much to stay mum. They had seen more of America than anyone in the black world, tasting its good and bad. They had been tormented by Jim Crow in ways most blacks from the North would never experience, and tasted freedom in ways Dixie blacks would know only if they outlived the hollow doctrine of separate-but-equal. Porters were inspired by the wealthy, enlightened whites who rode their sleepers, and emboldened to act by the wealthy and narrow-minded. The books and journals they picked up showed them new ways of thinking, especially on race issues, and Baker Heater League sessions let them stew it over.

"I thought the civil rights movement was one of the most beautiful things we could ever have had," said Coley Mayo Mann, who grew up in Georgia and moved to Boston in the early 1940s when he went to work as a Pullman porter. Philip O. Baker, also Boston-based and on the Pullman payroll, took the day off from work to attend Randolph's 1963 March on Washington. "I felt like that was the thing to do," he said decades later. "It's just one of those things you were proud to have been a part of."[45]

There were other things particular to the porter's work that tended to radicalize him, at least when it came to skin color. The railroads were one of the most thoroughly segregated workplaces in America, and the Pullman porter had a front-row view of the unequal treatment that this produced. Then there was the less tactile but symbolically powerful link between black freedom and trains: slaves had gazed at them and dreamed of escape, escaped slaves took the underground railroad north, and the Pullman porter continued the tradition by riding his sleeping car to a better life. While a porter's all-black workforce encouraged him to see the world in racial terms, the Pullman Company's directive not to discuss politics on the job made him more eager to do it off. If he was on the fence about getting involved, A. Philip Randolph, Milton P. Webster, and other Brotherhood bosses tipped him over. Most porters respected if not worshiped their union leaders, so it was natural to emulate them by rolling up their sleeves on civil rights. Even though many wished the Chief devoted himself more fully to the Brotherhood, they knew that their status somehow was enhanced when their leader's was.

Wanting to get involved was one thing. Finding the time and energy was another. Here, too, the porter was ideally situated. He spent endless hours on the road, but once home had more free time than any other black worker, especially after the Brotherhood shortened his workweek and added vacations. And working for a Chicago-based firm insulated him from the pressure local firms put on employees to steer clear of controversial civil rights activities. The Pullman Company cared deeply about its porters' political proclivities in the days it was battling the Brotherhood, but once it recognized the union, it stopped caring.

Given all he did, it is curious that the porter plays little if any role in most tellings of the civil rights story. One reason is that too many historians date the movement as beginning with Rosa Parks and Montgomery, forgetting the decades when Randolph and his porters helped build the base. Randolph also stayed active long enough that those involved in the 1960s and 1970s thought they knew him, and saw him as an overly formal grandfatherly figure who never really mattered. They never knew the fiery-eyed bomb thrower of the 1920s, the defiant organizer of black workers through the 1930s, and the man who stood up to U.S. presidents from Coolidge through Johnson. His best days were before the television age could make him into a household personality. And he died not in the dramatic fashion of King and Malcolm X, both gunned down too young, but of a heart that stopped working at the age of ninety, in the middle of the night, with only his housekeeper bearing witness in his sparsely furnished New York apartment.

As for the porters themselves, they loved to tell stories, but only among themselves. They hid from their own children the indignities they suffered, so were not about to broadcast them to the world. They spent too long in sleeping cars fueled by discretion to feel comfortable going public, even if the topic was their own hallowed role in civil rights. Today there are too few left, and they are too ancient, to get out the word, assuming they could find anyone to listen. All of which is tragic since their story began at the true beginning of the battle for black rights, just after slavery, and it continued through the zenith of the movement in the late-1960s.

Vernon Jordan, who headed the National Urban League in the 1970s and advised President Bill Clinton in the 1990s, clearly remembers the link between porters like E. D. Nixon and the civil rights struggle—and regrets that so many have forgotten. "Nixon called me, I think it was in 1984, when [George] Wallace was still governor, and he said, 'Mr. Jordan, I am going to celebrate my fifty years in the civil rights movement and I want you to come down here and

be my speaker,'" Jordan said in an interview in his office at Rockefeller Center. "I said, 'Why should I do that, Mr. Nixon?' He said,
'You are one of the few fellas up there who really understood what I
did.' So I said I would do it, and he said, 'We will pay you an hono-
rarium.' I said, 'Look, I'm coming and you don't have to pay me a
nickel.'

"Two days later I get a call from two young black lawyers in
Montgomery, Alabama, who said to me, 'Mr. Jordan, we're calling
because we hear you're coming down to speak for Mr. E. D. Nixon.
We're calling to tell you, you can't come down here for E. D. Nixon.'
I said, 'Why is that?' They said, 'Because E. D. Nixon is an Uncle
Tom.' I said, 'Let me tell you. You are lawyers in Alabama because of
what E. D. Nixon did a long time before you were born.'"[46]

7

A Legacy That Lasts

❖

ELAINE JONES HAD the jitters. Anyone would her first week of law school, especially one as formidable as the University of Virginia to get in and stay in. But Jones faced an array of challenges that no other beginning student could even imagine. She was one of only seven women in the Class of 1970, with 184 men. She was also black. Since Thomas Jefferson founded the law school in 1826, only a handful of African-American women had applied, and a staggering total of none had been enrolled. Jones would be the first. This great-granddaughter of a slave was a role model not just for her younger brother and sister but for all the black men and women who dared dream of a life at the bar.

Having just purchased her stack of first-year textbooks, Jones retreated to one of the few settings where men were not allowed: the ladies' room in the law library. She settled into the tattered sofa, paging through the thick volumes and summoning the strength to play her role as race pioneer. Just then the dean's secretary walked in and, spying Jones, seized the opportunity to boss her. "I know you're taking your rest break now," the pink-cheeked white woman said, "but when you're finished, would you mind cleaning up the refrigerator?"

By the time Jones realized what had happened—that she had been mistaken for one of the maids, the only other black women on the law school campus—the secretary was gone. Jones was ever so alone, but she could clearly hear two voices, the way she always did in such circumstances. The first, her college-educated mother's, instructed her to "put those books down and go find that woman. Have a meeting of minds." The next was that of her father, whose higher learning consisted of nineteen years as a Pullman porter. "That's not right," he whispered. "You'll get your time."

"That second one is the one I listened to, the one I acted on," Jones recalled thirty-five years later, sitting in a conference room at the suite of offices she oversaw during her eleven years as president of the NAACP Legal Defense Fund, the nation's oldest, most esteemed civil rights law firm. "I acted on that voice a whole lot of times."

Her father's message was less of caution than biding time, of getting even rather than getting mad. It was to rise above insults and slights, to show she was better by doing better, the way her father had preached since she was a schoolgirl sitting around Sunday dinners of chicken smothered in gravy. And the way G. R. Jones had behaved himself during the nearly two decades he polished cuspidors and pacified riders on George Pullman's sleeping cars, salting away salary and tips to put three children through college and graduate school. So Elaine gave the secretary the benefit of the doubt, assuming she neither knew better nor meant harm. "She never apologized," Elaine recounted, "but there was nothing I ever needed from the dean's office that I didn't get."

Porter Jones got inside the heads of his other children the same as Elaine's, softly coaching them on how to handle being bright and black in America. For G. Daniel Jones, the middle child, that sustained him while he earned a doctorate at the mainly white Andover Newton Theological School just outside Boston, and it offers guidance as he ministers to thirteen hundred African-American congregants at Grace Baptist Church in Philadelphia. For Gwendolyn, the youngest, it helped her follow Elaine into and out of the University of Virginia School of Law, then step up as a district judge in her native Norfolk, Virginia. Elaine, meanwhile, knew her father was one of the few who would understand when she turned down a high-priced offer from a high-powered Wall Street firm after law school, instead opting for the civil rights organization that was launched by Thurgood

Marshall and that won the *Brown v. Board of Education* desegregation case.

G. R. knew little about the law, or even the ministry, but his life on the rails was example enough for his kids. They pictured him at the kitchen table being tutored in reading and writing by his schoolteacher wife, learning all he needed to pass the Pullman Company's tests of aptitude and attitude. They knew he "had to suck in a whole lot" on the sleepers but maintained his dignity despite the indignities. Off the trains, he ran a gardening business, with his own trucks and crew. The two jobs seldom kept him from Sunday dinners, presiding over a current events forum for the kids as well as a grand meal he often would cook himself. It was there, especially, that the children learned the mantras of G. R.'s life and theirs: Travel and see how other people live. Get an education, not just college but professional school. Give something back.

"Today some people see Pullman porters as Uncle Toms," Elaine Jones explained. "They were survivors. They had to survive within the limited economic framework they had so we could survive and sit here and call them 'Toms.'"

"I said at eight years old that I want to be a lawyer. Daddy said, 'Well sister, you can do whatever you want to do.' He knew somehow that you work within the system to improve it; that's what he got from Pullman. . . . We drove ourselves because our parents assumed we would do well. It's not that they demanded it. They didn't demand anything. They just assumed."[1]

So did scores of others Pullman porters, who saw their children and grandchildren, nieces and nephews, become leading litigators and scientists, lawmakers and artists. It is impossible to count them all, but it is clear by any count that there are more than anyone would have expected, or that even a gung-ho porter like G. R. Jones could have dreamed. Name an African-American who excelled in any field the last half century—from Los Angeles' Tom Bradley, the first black mayor of a major American city, to Leroy C. Richie Jr., the first black vice president at Chrysler, to Helen Jackson Claytor, the first black president of the YWCA—and there is an odds-on chance that luminary had a Pullman porter in his or her past. Not bad for a group of men who at their height made up 0.1 percent of African-Americans, and who embodied servility.

They did it partly by preaching the same lessons embraced by every generation of immigrants, and every up-by-their-bootstraps black parent: sacrificing for their children, and deferring dreams of self-improvement by a generation or even two, but never abandoning them. Pullman porters simply did it more often than anyone else. In the process they helped shape today's black middle class and intelligentsia.

PORTERS HAD PLENTY of time to contemplate their legacy during the mid-1900s, when the sleeping cars hit a fierce headwind. Fewer than 15 million passengers rode them in 1940 compared to nearly 40 million in 1920, their busiest year. Traffic picked up in the mid-1940s, thanks largely to troop transports, but crashed again by 1950, never to recover. Close to 16 million people rode sleepers that year, 11 million in 1955, and a mere 2½ million in 1965. Just as profits had risen with more passengers, they sank with fewer. Operating deficits became standard fare for Pullman starting in the mid-1940s, peaking at $35 million in 1957, and stabilizing in the $20-million range through the 1960s.[2]

It was not just passengers who were abandoning Pullman. In 1940 the U.S. Justice Department charged the company with creating an illegal monopoly that stifled competition from railroads wanting to run their own sleepers and from manufacturers wanting to build them. The main question raised by the suit was why the government had waited so long, given Pullman's uncontestable stranglehold on the market. The federal courts ruled that Pullman was indeed violating U.S. antitrust laws, and said it had to divest either its manufacturing or its operating division. Sensing the bleak future of passenger travel, the company held on to the Pullman Standard Car Manufacturing Company. It sold its operating half to a consortium of fifty-seven railroads that set up the new Pullman Company in the summer of 1947. Those machinations captivated lawyers, trust busters, and railroad buffs, but neither the traveling public nor Pullman porters noticed much change.

What they did notice was how many travel options there were after World War II. Automobile production had started to skyrocket during the First World War, with assembly lines turning out nearly 2 million cars and trucks in 1917, ten times more than in 1910. Much the way the Iron Horse had symbolized American progress in the late 1800s, so Henry Ford's Tin Lizzie embodied an America on the move in the early 1900s. The federal government fueled the trend during the 1950s when it began pumping billions of dollars into highway construction, laying down a true national network. By 1960, nearly 90 percent of Americans were traveling between cities by private car, with a patchwork of hastily constructed motels and inns displacing the old hotels on wheels.

The remaining 10 percent of travelers chose a bus, train, or plane.[3] That choice, too, was skewing against the sleeping cars. Buses were the cheapest alternative, and, with new highways to ride on and schedules rivaling the railroads, they lured away many of Pullman's middle-class riders. Day trains ate into the sleeper business in two ways: modern locomotives got there fast enough to make some night travel unnecessary, while for economy-minded overnighters there were newly spacious coach seats with leg rests and reclining backs. Even long-distance phone service proved to be competition, convincing many would-be riders to keep in touch by dialing rather than visiting.

But it was planes that hurt most. Airlines let business travelers cross the country in six hours rather than the four days a sleeper took, and ensured honeymooners and other vacationers more time at their destination. Few seemed to mind sacrificing the romance of getting there. In 1926, only 5,782 Americans flew on commercial airlines. In 1938, the number was up to 1,343,427, and by 1946, domestic flights had pulled even with Pullman in passenger loads. As for price, airlines were able to lower fares as technology improved and traffic increased, whereas Pullman had enormous labor costs that it could not shed. The sleeping car firm was left trying to market a service in the 1950s that was four times slower than its aerial rival and nearly twice as costly. By 1960, the company was back where it had been when George launched it nearly one hundred years before: as the domain of those so well heeled they could indulge in luxury and not trouble themselves about time or price.

Pullman's downturn touched porters in several ways, none good. The most obvious was hiring. The company stopped adding porters by the summer of 1939, with new openings coming only when a veteran retired or quit. The full-time workforce then stood at 7,500, down from a high of just over 12,000 in the mid-1920s, with most of the survivors old-timers who had been on the job an average of fifteen years.* Things got worse from there, with just 2,852 porters left in 1960 and 1,151 in 1968.[4]

It was ironic and unfortunate that the Pullman Company's sustained deterioration began just as its porters finally got a union and were beginning to get their due. In the 1920s, the Brotherhood of Sleeping Car Porters could make a compelling case that a company that was earning enormous profits and paying big dividends could afford to pay porters a livable wage. But what about a company whose profits were sinking, the way Pullman's did during almost the entire era after it recognized the Brotherhood, and whose major cost was the labor of its workers? Porters also were seeing their status slip within the hierarchy of the black middle class, especially in cities like Chicago. Young black men moving there from the South in the 1920s and 1930s found they could earn a good living in factories and meatpacking plants, or as police officers and firemen, none of which carried the porter's stigma of servitude or required being away from home. Add in the growing difficulty of landing a job as a

---

*Hundreds more were called up occasionally as extras. Another six hundred were full-time attendants, with fifty maids. As for college students coming on for the summer, that practice died during the antiunion blitz of the 1920s and never was resuscitated.

Pullman porter, and it is no surprise that ambitious young blacks began looking elsewhere to build their future.[5]

One place they could not look was to the airlines, which were luring away so many passengers from Pullman. U.S. carriers were notoriously discriminatory in their early years. People calling to buy tickets from neighborhoods known to be black—or who "sounded black"—were tagged with the moniker "Ruby Hart," the name of a black woman who somehow made it through such screening. Then they were told no seats were left. Blacks who did fly were often banished to the single right front seat on a DC-3, or the back of the plane, and almost never were put next to a white passenger.[6] Was such segregation in the skies legal? Not to worry, the aviation attorney Frank E. Quindry advised in 1937. "The right of a common carrier to make reasonable regulations for the conduct of its business permits it to separate white and colored persons aboard its conveyances," he wrote in the *Journal of Air Law.* Quindry, a first lieutenant in the Air Corps Reserve and district manager for Braniff, did not stop there. Airlines, he wrote, also "may refuse to accept a person for passage after another person of opposite race and color has reserved a seat on the same plane . . . provided the circumstances justify it on the ground of safety, comfort and convenience. Such circumstances exist in most sections of the south."[7]

Airlines were less direct but no less biased in selecting onboard staff and advertising their services. They picked on Negroes not as a race but through that symbol of black service, the Pullman porter. After praising the stewardess for making air travel "exceedingly pleasant," a 1942 career guide noted that "she hasn't accomplished this success by holding a whisk broom in one hand and holding the other, Gypsy like, waiting to be crossed with silver. Airline heads decided at the very beginning that they would let George, the Pullman porter, collect the quarters and the half dollars; stewardesses must not accept tips, and this rule is a strict one."[8] An equally strict rule, although it never was written down, was that the stewardess had to be white. When American Airlines hired its first black stewardess in the 1960s, it was considered a trendsetter.[9]

There was one exception to that policy of exclusion. New England & Western Air Transportation Company, a short-lived carrier whose service in 1930 included New York, Albany, and Boston, hired Pullman porters as stewards. It seemed a natural, given how often airplanes were referred to then as "Sky Pullmans," and it earned this plaudit from *Aviation* magazine: "The porters, once they overcame their nervousness about flying, were tremendously proud of their jobs and, of course, had the necessary training and background to render the right sort of service. From the novice passenger's point of view the experiment was very reassuring, for it supplied the familiar atmosphere of the Pullman car and made flying seem a lot less strange."[10]

The major airlines were not inspired by New England & Western's bold experiment, but they did see one circumstance where Pullman porters and other black men could be of service: helping arriving and departing passengers lug their bags. This new worker was called a skycap, the airport equivalent of the train station redcap, and as railroads continued to lose business more and more porters and redcaps moved to the airport. "I hated to see the railroads go down," said John Julian Jackson of Los Angeles, who went to work for the Pullman Company in 1942, at the beginning of its wartime boom, and left nineteen years later, when the situation was getting desperate. After trying work as a machinist's helper and construction laborer, he landed a job that he kept for thirty-seven years as a skycap. "When the airlines came into being, there was no work on the railroads," Jackson added, noting that planes displaced trains the same way locomotives had the stagecoach.[11]

The Pullman Company continued to hemorrhage through the 1950s, with the New Haven, Pennsylvania, and Wabash railroads opting to run their own parlor cars and New York Central severing all ties. Pullman closed or sold all but two of its repair shops, laid off three thousand workers, mothballed older heavier sleepers, and cut costs everywhere. But it could not buck the principle of entropy: railroad passenger traffic was disintegrating, and demand for sleepers was collapsing with it. The last order for a new Pullman sleeping car was filled in 1956. Rider volume fell nearly 50 percent in 1965 alone, and in 1968 losses were more than the company had earned in any year but one over its century of operations.[12]

On January 1, 1969—103 years after George Pullman gave it life—the Pullman company terminated its sleeping car services. By then most railroads understood just how bleak prospects were for passenger service generally and sleepers especially, and few still wanted to keep going with Pullman. The company had only 425 sleepers in operation at the time, down from a peak of nearly 10,000. And it employed fewer than 1,200 porters, down from a high of 12,300.

The Brotherhood of Sleeping Car Porters was undergoing a similar senescence. It continued advocating for porters in contract talks and disciplinary hearings. But its influence had waned along with its membership, and its leaders had turned their passions to civil rights and other causes less central to porters' welfare.

That shift in focus, and slow sapping of energy, was most apparent in the union's president and patriarch, A. Philip Randolph. In the Brotherhood's early days Randolph was a firebrand, rallying reluctant porters to the cause and crisscrossing the nation to build a union. By the 1960s, fatigue had replaced fire. In October of 1968 he turned over the reins of his union to one of his longtime vice presidents, C. L. Dellums. Randolph lived until 1979, long enough to watch the Brotherhood wither to fewer than a thousand members, then die in 1978. It was not called a death, but a merger with the Brotherhood of Railway and Airline Clerks, whose color bans had been such an affront two generations earlier. A year later Pullman Incorporated, the manufacturing arm of the business George founded in 1867, announced it would stop building sleeping cars.

Pullman porters were growing old alongside their company and union. With no new hires to infuse new blood, the workplace was less energized than it had been, the luxury not quite up to standards set in the 1920s and 1930s. The Brotherhood "is aged and fading," Murray Kempton wrote in the *New Republic* in 1963. "It never had more than 15,000 members and no more than 5,000 of these are working now. Porters with 30 years of service endlessly deal the brittle old playing cards in their recreation room on 125th Street in New York, awaiting their chance for an odd, infrequent extra run."[13]

Rumors had been swirling for years first about the end of railway dining services, then of the sleepers, and some porters escaped early. "I left when I saw the situation deteriorating. I left Pullman on a conditional basis; I didn't quit outright," recalled William Howard Brown, who went to work for the U.S. Post Office in the late 1950s after fifteen years as a porter. "I never did go back. But I never did really quit the Pullman Company. It quit me because they went out of business."[14]

Most stuck it out until the end, if only to see what their pension and other options might be. Those who were too young to retire, or too wed to the rails, went to work for Amtrak, the National Railroad Passenger Corporation created by Congress in 1971 to take over intercity passenger service. But although Amtrak did its best to sustain sleeping car service, it was difficult to match the reality of Pullman service—and impossible to live up to the legend. "When Pullman died, everything disappeared," said Happy Davis, who left the business when the Pullman Company did. "What happened to all that beautiful linen? The sheets and blankets they use now are disgraceful. When the railroads took over, that was the end of service, you might say."[15] Samuel Turner, meanwhile, bemoaned the way that Amtrak hired whites as waiters and porters, which "busted that solid all-black deal."[16]

Even the time-honored title of porter went. Today's incarnation has the vanilla name of attendant. Amtrak operates just 163 sleepers today, with only 257 attendants. Half the time "he" is a she, with women having crashed what under Pullman was a mainly male preserve, and neither he nor she typically knows much about the days when sleeping cars dominated cross-country travel and proud black porters were the sovereigns of the sleepers. Today's attendants come in every color of the rainbow.

While whites were breaking up the black monopoly among porters and waiters, blacks were making even greater inroads on the railroad. They were being hired in sales jobs and supervisory ones, and moving up from laborer and service posts to skilled ones. One train in December 1968 was reported to have been under the control of an all-black crew. "If any one 12-month period can be identified as the breakthrough year for the Negro, 1969 would have to be it," *Trains* magazine reported in August 1973.[17] That timing is sad as well as ironic, since the breakthrough came precisely twelve months too late for it to affect the Pullman Company.

NOT EVERYTHING DIED when the Pullman Company halted its passenger service at the beginning of 1969. It continued to maintain and service sleeping cars for U.S. railroads through August, and provided full services in Mexico for nearly two years. It worked with the railroads and the federal government to deal with pension and severance issues affecting porters and other former employees. And it kept on board sufficient staff—and money—to handle leftover legal matters, the main one being a lawsuit by Pullman porters angry about having been barred from promotion and denied conductor's pay when they performed the work of a conductor.

The Pullman Company first used a porter in place of a conductor back in the early years of sleeper service, when the conductor assigned to a run did not show up. The practice grew through the late 1920s, when there were more than seventeen hundred full-time "porters-in-charge." Conductors almost always handled the main runs to big cities, where they were responsible for between two and ten cars, and supervised the porter assigned to each car. Porters-in-charge generally worked on branch lines with a single car bound for a remote destination. With even that one car often not full, the company realized only a single staffer was needed. As for who that would be, the answer was easy: a white conductor never would be asked to do the dirty work of a black porter, although the reverse worked just fine. If race were not enough reason, there was this financial consideration: conductors earned $50 to $150 more a month than porters-in-charge.

Most porters liked running-in-charge. It gave them the authority they lacked when a conductor was on board, and by the 1960s they were paid nearly thirty-five dollars more than a standard porter, up from ten dollars in the early years. But they knew they were being exploited. A porter-in-charge did his regular work of making beds and tending to passenger needs, then did whatever the conductor who had gotten off at the main station had left undone, from collecting and selling tickets to writing out seat diagrams, wake-up cards, and reports on the condition of his sleeper. When the train stopped at small stations without clean-up crews, he took on a third job as car cleaner, for which he received at most one dollar per car. It was not the work that rankled most, but the fact that his salary was so much less than the most junior conductor's, which later translated into smaller pensions and severance payments. Although his success as a stand-in proved he could handle a conductor's responsibilities, he knew he lacked what to the Pullman Company remained the most critical qualification: milk-white skin.

Segregated systems like those were supposed to disappear with passage of the Civil Rights Act of 1964. Title VII of the act, which took effect in July 1965, made it illegal "to discriminate against any individual with respect to his compensation, terms, conditions, or privileges of employment, because of such individual's race, color, religion, sex, or national origin." It also outlawed using race as a basis for segregating or classifying workers in a way that could harm them. Both provisions spoke directly to the Pullman Company's use of porters-in-charge, but no one at the company was listening.

Earl A. Love and his lawyers found a way to get their attention. In 1968 they filed a class-action lawsuit on behalf of Love and fifteen hundred other porters-in-charge, all of whom claimed the system continued to discriminate against them after passage of the Civil Rights Act. Love had been making a similar argument for years, starting with the Civil Rights Commission in his home state of Colorado. While the commission was considering his case in 1965, the company offered Love a Hobson's choice: it would shatter its color barriers by promoting him to conductor, but he would lose

more than forty years' seniority as a porter and would be furloughed as a conductor since there was too little business to justify
taking on a new one. Love, as expected, said no. Two years later the
Pullman Company announced it was promoting twelve other porters-
in-charge to conductor. The timing was transparent, coming at a
moment when business was declining, Pullman was insisting it did
not need new conductors, and the U.S. Equal Employment Opportunity Commission was breathing down the company's neck about
Love's bias charges. "It must be concluded," the EEOC wrote in a
brief supporting the Love lawsuit, "that these promotions were
mere acts of tokenism."[18]

Martin J. Rock agreed tokenism was at work, but not the kind the
porters saw. Rock was one of the last Pullman executives left in the
1970s, and in June 1976 he took over as president of what was left of
the company. Being a porter-in-charge, Rock said, generally meant
little extra work yet it ensured at least thirty dollars more a month in
pay. The company, he added, had collected "about 300 pounds of
statistical evidence" bolstering its case—including proof that one or
two whites "snuck through" to become porters during the depression—but the judge "wouldn't even let us file that to show what it
was doing was crazy. . . . It was just a handoff to the porters."[19]

Love v. Pullman dragged on until 1976, but the court eventually
ruled in Love's favor. The Pullman Company had discriminated,
U.S. District Judge Alfred A. Arraj found, and porters who ran in-
charge after the Civil Rights Act took effect deserved to be compensated. Since the company was out of business and could not hire
them as conductors, the only remedy was money. It took another
three years for Pullman to exhaust its appeals and to challenge,
sometimes successfully, work claims and other statements by vari-
ous plaintiffs. Finally, in 1979, the company paid 1,293 former
porters-in-charge or their families nearly $5 million, with another
$500,000 for their attorneys. By the time of the payout, Pullman
was just a shell, with two full-time workers and a couple of desks
and typewriters. Love died just before the money went out—his
lawyers say it was Pullman's strategy to try and outlast him and

other aging accusers—but his heirs collected what would have been his settlement, and the hardheaded Love knew on his deathbed that he had prevailed against the once-mighty sleeping car giant.

Earl Love's lawsuit stands as an indictment of more than the porter-in-charge setup.* While its legal authority extended only to 1965, the court really was calling into doubt the entire segregated system that George Pullman instituted more than one hundred years before. "Although Pullman's president asserted that there never was a policy of discrimination," Judge Arraj wrote, "the facts seem to belie this. Porters were often told by their superintendents and by conductors that they could never be conductors."[20]

That was not the only thing conductors were telling porters. Half a century earlier the Order of Sleeping Car Conductors had correctly perceived the threat when porters were put in charge. It was not merely that the Pullman Company was supplanting conductors on hundreds of branch runs, but it was sending them a more ominous message: push too hard for money or other benefits and you can be replaced, even by black porters, which was precisely the signal Pullman had sent black porters in the 1920s when it hired Filipinos to work alongside them. And the conductors' union made clear early on that it would do whatever was necessary to put porters back in their place.

The card it played first and most often was the race one. The president of the Order of Sleeping Car Conductors wrote the Pullman Company in 1919, insisting that conductors, like riders, should not have to sleep in a berth recently used by a black porter. "All members of the Caucasian race should be entitled to this consideration whether they are conductors or passengers," W. S. Warfield penned. "To be perfectly plain, I would like to ask you if any officer of the Company would wish to occupy space which has just been

---

Love v. Pullman was "the first national class-action lawsuit," according to Earl Love's attorney, Willie L. Leftwich. Before, he said, courts were reluctant to take class-action lawsuits and had never taken a case that spanned a wide geographic area. Since Pullman was a national company and the porters were spread so thoroughly across the country, they were able to file as one unit, setting a precedent for future cases.

vacated by a porter." To be plainer still, Warfield wrote, if conductors were asked to sleep there, "they [would] undoubtedly refuse." Such blatant bigotry was not surprising given that the Order was a whites-only union, but it did suggest that the union's ongoing bid to bargain on behalf of porters as well as conductors was aimed more at controlling the black workers than representing them.[21]

What most conductors really cared about was not where porters slept but what work they did. It was fitting for them to polish and clean but not to rob a conductor of his livelihood by taking tickets and assigning berths. The Order made that case in contract talks with Pullman and repeated arguments before federal mediators and the National Railroad Adjustment Board. When those yielded only limited success, it appealed to white fears. A smear campaign across the South implied that passenger safety would be compromised if sleepers were controlled by black porters instead of white conductors. The campaign found a receptive audience in state regulators, as railroad commissions in Texas, Florida, South Carolina, and Kentucky ruled that within their borders, Pullman cars had to carry a conductor. In the end those and other assaults on the porter-in-charge system were defeated. But the Order's actions made clear that, in a strictly segregated workplace and society, most battles boiled down to black versus white.[22]

More puzzling is the Brotherhood of Sleeping Car Porters' behavior when it came to porters running-in-charge. In its formative days the Brotherhood objected to requiring porters to do a conductor's work without a conductor's pay, and it continued to pay lip service at public meetings over the decades. But it implicitly endorsed the setup by signing contracts agreeing to porters performing in-charge duties in return for modestly higher wages. It failed to push the issue as aggressively as its sister unions representing black dining car workers did with an equivalent system of waiters-in-charge, winning for them in the mid-1940s wages comparable to those of white dining car stewards and, not long after, promotion to the formerly all-white job of steward. And the Brotherhood that had represented itself as the unwavering advocate of Pullman porters steered clear of the *Love* case brought on behalf of fifteen hundred of those porters, at times demonstrating outright hostility.

His local office of the Brotherhood in Washington, D.C., told him "don't get involved in that suit; leave it alone," recalled Happy Davis, a veteran porter who often ran-in-charge, including after the Civil Rights Act of 1964 took effect.[23] Another porter, Ernest James Eley, was asked during a deposition in the *Love* case about the attitude of the new Brotherhood president, C. L. Dellums, on the matter of porters being promoted to conductors. Any time the matter was raised, Eley said, Dellums would say, "We can't do anything about that."[24]

Willie L. Leftwich, the porters' lead attorney in the *Love* case, said his interviews of more than three hundred porters and repeated dealings with the Brotherhood made clear that the union "did everything it could to put the kibosh on the case. C. L. Dellums did everything he could to kill the case. They even sent out a letter saying in effect, 'I hear tell there's a case against the Pullman Company. I advise all of you to ignore this.'" Dellums's predecessor, the venerated A. Philip Randolph, was no better, according to Leftwich: "Randolph just stood aside; he didn't fight for those men to get their conductors' pay. . . . I think Randolph had already fought his fights and thought it was over." Roma Jones Stewart, another counsel for the porters, said the Brotherhood went so far as to "send spies" into the attorneys' meetings with porters-in-charge. "I remember being shocked to find out the union was hostile to it," she added. "I would have thought they would have at least supported the suit."[25]

There was one exception among the Brotherhood brass: E. D. Nixon, the feisty head of the union's Montgomery office who masterminded the bus boycott there. "E. D Nixon," Leftwich recalled nearly twenty-five years after the case was concluded, "was first-rate. He kept the thing moving. Anything that happened, we could call on Nixon."[26]

What was the Brotherhood afraid of? It is impossible to know for sure, since none of its leaders ever said publicly. There also has been surprisingly little written on the *Love* case, considering the impact it had not just on Pullman porters but on the wider fields of class-action and race discrimination. No law review articles were published, and only limited mention was made in histories of porters and their union. That is even more surprising given all the employment records that the Pullman Company preserved for the case and eventually made public at Chicago's Newberry Library. The most exhaustive treatments of *Love v. Pullman* were by a Canadian professor, who looked at how sleeping car porters there won the right to become conductors years before their American counterparts, and by a master's student at the University of Illinois. "This whole thing has been hushed up and put under the rug," said Stewart. "It is just like it never happened."[27]

The Brotherhood probably worried that it would be dragged into the case since it had gone along with all the contracts in which porters were allowed to work as conductors. The union might even have feared being held financially liable, the way the Pullman Company was and the United Transportation Union would be in a similar suit by railroad porters.* What is certain is that the Brotherhood was in an awkward position when it came to Pullman-style segregation that prevented porters from being promoted to conductor but guaranteed them a monopoly over the job of Pullman porter. That monopoly made the Brotherhood possible and let it become a champion of black workers and the wider African-American community. Earl Love's lawsuit turned the spotlight on that Jim Crow setup—and the Brotherhood's acquiescence in it. None of this would have surprised the Pullman maids, who felt the Brotherhood's sexist sting, or the first Filipino porters, who weathered the hostility of the porters' union as it sought to preserve its black cartel. But all of this must have been embarrassing to aging civil rights warriors like Randolph and Dellums.

---

*The Pullman Company sought to absolve itself of liability by pointing the finger at the Brotherhood, but Judge Arraj did not buy that defense. "It matters not," he wrote, "whether Pullman 'maintained' these systems or merely acquiesced in union agreements prohibiting mixed or company seniority lines. The net effect is the same, since Pullman may not derive immunity from a union contract that operates discriminatorily on the basis of race or other prohibited classification." U.S. District Court of Colorado, *Love v. Pullman*, 8.

Porters were embarrassed, too. Not at the lawsuit but at the behavior they had to reveal to their lawyers. They talked about having to stay with their empty sleepers in temperatures of 40 below zero and 125 above. They told how in southern towns they were not allowed to collect tickets or even enter the train station when they were running-in-charge. "That's why porters never visited each other in their homes. They never wanted to let anything slip with their families showing their constant humiliation and degradation," said Leftwich. "They said things during our preparation of depositions that made my blood run cold. One of them said, 'Even if I lose this lawsuit, I'm not going to tell all that. I don't want my family to know what I went through.'"[28]

MOST FAMILIES KNEW more than their porter husband, father, or grandfather realized. Not the details, but enough to sense the extent of the indignities. Rather than being ashamed, they were inspired, especially since they knew they were the beneficiaries of that sacrifice. Over the years, as one after another ascended to posts of influence and esteem, they traced their success back to the sleeping car.

Sometimes that inheritance could be measured in dollars and cents. It might be living in a comfortable house, having the money for college tuition, or enjoying other material success rare in that black world of the late nineteenth to mid-twentieth centuries. "I don't ever remember *not* having a car, a television, owning our own home. I grew up knowing that I came from a family of Pullman porters, and that's why we were better off," said Ellen Story Martin, whose father, grandfather, and uncle were porters, and who went on to earn her master's from Harvard and become a manager at the Massachusetts Bay Transportation Authority. "My porter background meant I came from a family that worked, that had steady employment. I was part of the American work culture. It's just huge; I grew up with this work ethic and feeling of success."[29]

Tony Fulton's dad, a chef on the B&O, passed down an equally iron-willed work ethic. Tony was too defiant to listen then, but now he appreciates how it helped him win and keep for more than fifteen years a seat in the Maryland House of Delegates. "I was very angry as a young man growing up," he said. "I was angry that my dad was away. I was angry that he had to cook for Mr. [Howard] Simpson [president of the B&O]. I was angry that I had to work so hard. I was angry because of segregation. . . . But [now] I have a greater appreciation for life and what my dad wanted for me and why he was so tough on me. He didn't want me to be a chef cook. He didn't want me to work as hard as he had to work."[30]

The sense that life on the railroad was simply too hard—in time away from family, tense racial climate, and rigors of the job itself—became increasingly prevalent in the later years, as Pullman porters who traditionally had pushed their children to follow them onto the rails took the opposite tack. "All my children wanted to become railroad people, but I said I didn't want them to. I said, 'You and your people will get separated if you work there,'" recalled Samuel Turner, who played out his own childhood dream by working on the dining cars but attributed his two divorces to constantly being on the road.[31] Likewise John Ford, the porter who lectured at Dartmouth College, gave up on becoming a minister, but, far from letting go of his dreams, he deferred them to the next generation, saving money so his three children could attend prep school and college. Virgil Smock's three boys worked on the trains, the fourth generation of the family to do so, but none stayed long as the railroads continued their decline and the boys found jobs that suited them better.

Many times a porter's bequest to succeeding generations came in the form of practical lessons about survival and advancement in a hostile white world. "I learned a lot from my father about how to handle people. He was good with people. He used humor to make people feel comfortable," said Leroy Richie Jr., who absorbed and applied those lessons on the way to becoming valedictorian at City College of New York, graduating from New York University Law School, and serving as a regional director of the Federal Trade Commission. He went on to work at Chrysler Corporation, where for twelve years he was vice president and general counsel for automotive affairs, and for eight of them was the corporation's only senior black officer. "Being a lawyer is what I did for a living," Richie explained, "but the person that I am is my father. My personality is my father. And my personality was responsible for my successes."[32]

In William Kennard's case the lessons were enduring enough to be passed on to him even though he never knew James Kennard, his Pullman porter grandfather. It was James's travels as a porter that led his family to move from the segregated South to California, which he judged was the least racist place his sleepers stopped. And it was his insistence that his five-year-old son attend the white elementary school a few blocks away, rather than the black one across town, that compelled William's father to keep going back despite being turned away by the principal and taunted by would-be classmates. "You belong there," James told his son, and the principal and school board finally agreed.[33]

William heard that story "thousands of times" from his dad, to the point where it became a guiding principle as William rose to become the first black chairman of the Federal Communications Commission. Now he is the one passing on the tale every chance he gets, including in a commencement address in 2000 at Howard University. "My grandfather," he told the young, mainly African-American graduates, "taught my dad that when the doors of opportunity are closed, you knock. And when nobody answers, you keep knocking. And if nobody answers that door of opportunity, then you break that door down and walk on through. . . . My grandfather taught his son that when a roadblock lies in your path, you drive under it, around it, through it, over it—that you let nothing stand in the way of your dreams. That was my grandfather's lesson to my father and my father's lesson to me."[34]

Roger Wilkins got his railroad wisdom from his great-uncle Sam Williams, a porter and waiter who helped raise Roger's father, and from his grandfather Madison Jackson, who earned his law degree but made his living as a Pullman porter. Those two train veterans spawned a small battalion of black talent. There was Roger's uncle, Roy Wilkins, who ran the NAACP for twenty-two years; his mother,

Helen Jackson Claytor, the first black to preside over the YWCA; his aunt, Marvel Cooke, the first black woman to write full-time for a major white-owned newspaper;* and Roger himself, an author, professor, Pulitzer Prize winner, and the first African-American to sit on the editorial board of the *New York Times*. The common elements in those success stories, Roger said, were Williams and Jackson, who "produced stability. They produced kids who could see the value of hard work, and see that no matter how unequal society was and how much you got screwed, you could still make decent lives for yourself and your kids. That's what these porters taught. . . . They imparted a sense that a life force should be used for something beyond the accumulation of stuff."

When he was a young lawyer in the 1950s, Roger Wilkins got the chance to offer some small payback. The Brotherhood of Sleeping Car Porters was a client, and he had to accompany a porter named Jeffries to the Pullman offices to collect money due him. The Pullman manager called Jeffries by his first name, "like he was a servant," Wilkins remembered. "I said, 'He's older than you are, he works for the same company you do, and he deserves every bit as much respect as you think you're entitled to.' This guy got really pissed off. He signed the check but was totally pissed off. As we walked out, Jeffries, who was fairly old, said to me, 'Boy, you really gave it to that white man.' I said, 'You know something, I would have done this for any client, black or white, but my grandfather was a Pullman porter and I've thought about how much shit he had to take. No man doing the same job as my grandpa did is going to have to take any shit.' He said, 'What was your grandpa's name?' I told him it was Madison Jackson, and he said, 'Jack was your grandfather? Jack broke me in.' He said, 'Jack would have been very proud of you, young fella.'"[35]

---

*Cooke began her career working for three black-run publications: the *Crisis, Amsterdam News,* and *People's Voice.* She then worked for the *Compass,* a short-lived white-owned daily in New York City. She was a news and features writer, and the only black and only woman reporter. www.npc.press.org (accessed October 3, 2003).

It did not require a bond of blood to be inspired by a Pullman porter. Vernon Jordan, whose father-in-law was one, said porters "had a special status" in the public housing project in Atlanta where he grew up. "They were the envy of the community." Julian Bond, the longtime civil rights leader who now chairs the NAACP, remembered as a child being awed by porters: "They always seemed to be tall and dignified. In so many jobs the uniform is a mark of servility, but in the Pullman porter's job it was a mark of some sort of power. He was in charge. As a child, I had no idea about the struggle for a union or any of that stuff. They just were impressive-looking people."[36]

Every child or grandchild, niece or nephew, has a comparable story—of learning from their porter patriarch how to charm colleagues and disarm adversaries, and of looking to him as a model of grace and role model for advancement. Talk to enough children of porters, however, and the story begins to take a turn. The pattern is not just in lessons passed down, but in how they were applied. This, it becomes clear, was the Pullman porter's most critical contribution, his last pivotal step in a century-long climb up America's socioeconomic ladder. Since his earliest days on the sleeping car he had embraced values that were solidly middle class, from holding tight his secure job, to becoming a stalwart of church and community, to believing in his own economic and social mobility. In the 1930s, his newly won union helped win him wages that began to make that mobility a reality, letting him buy more for his family and solidify his standing in the storied American middle class. But that was not the end or even the goal. The Pullman porter's most lasting legacy was his children and grandchildren, and all that they accomplished educationally and economically, socially and politically. Which is how most porters hoped it would turn out.

That impact is apparent in their long list of distinguished descendants. The tally starts in politics, a skill every porter had to fine-tune. Fourteen-term congressman Ron Dellums, the chairman of both the influential House Armed Services Committee and the Congressional Black Caucus, was the son of a Pullman porter and the nephew of C. L. Dellums, the second president of the Brotherhood of Sleeping Car Porters. The first black mayor of Los Angeles, Tom Bradley, had a Pullman porter for a father. So did the first black mayor of Denver, Wellington E. Webb, and the first black elected as a member—then chairman—of the Boston School Committee, John O'Bryant. San Francisco's first black mayor, Willie Brown, was the son of a railroad porter, as was the first black elected to statewide office in New York, former comptroller H. Carl McCall.

Children of Pullman porters, railroad porters, and dining car workers also became big names in the worlds of law and science, arts, journalism, and sports. One was Ethel L. Payne of the *Chicago Defender,* the undisputed first lady of the black press. New York civil rights lawyer Florynce Rae Kennedy's Pullman porter father regaled her with stories of how he had used a shotgun to drive Ku Klux Klansmen off his land. Another black railroad child of note was the track star Wilma Rudolph, the first American woman to win three gold medals in one Olympics. Pullman porters' kids made their mark on jazz with the pianist Oscar Peterson and the singer Teri Thornton. Maceo Finney, an officer in the dining car union, watched his son William rise to chief of police in St. Paul.

The most famous of black railroaders' children was Justice Thurgood Marshall, who on his last day on the Supreme Court was asked by a reporter whether blacks at last were free. "Well, I'm not free," Marshall replied tersely, then used the porters, many of whom were his friends, to make a point about prejudice and pride. "Years ago, when I was a youngster, a Pullman porter told me that he'd been in every city in this country, he was sure, and he had never been in any city in the United States where he had to put his hands up in front of his face to find out that he was a Negro. I agree with him."[37]

As impressive as such bigwigs are, porters made their mark with each child they sent to college and graduate school. They watched those kids, then their grandkids, fill the ranks of black engineers and academics, doctors, business leaders, and teachers. The importance of education was drilled into porters on the sleepers, where they got an up-close look at America's elite that few black men were afforded, helping demystify the white race at the same time it made its advantages seem even more unfair and enticing. That was why they worked so hard for tips, took on second jobs at home, and bore the indignities of the race-conscious sleeping cars. There were no studies comparing porters to other occupational groups, but it was an accepted wisdom that they turned out more college graduates than anyone else. And that those kids, whether or not they made lists of the most famous, grew up believing they could do anything. The result, visible to anyone who knew those black railroad workers and watched what happened to their progeny, was that Pullman porters helped give birth to the African-American professional classes.

The anecdotal evidence was there over the years in the Pullman Company's in-house journal, and in the newsletter of the Brotherhood of Sleeping Car Porters. The two seldom agreed on anything, but both featured repeated stories of porters putting a premium on education and delighting in the success of their children. Typical is a 1922 profile in *Pullman News* of the retired porter David G. Scott of Los Angeles, who sent his two daughters to the prestigious New England Conservatory of Music. Then he helped pay for the schooling of his brother, the Reverend Isaac B. Scott of the Methodist Episcopal Church, who became the president of Wiley College in Texas and the first black bishop in Monrovia, Liberia.[38]

There is no topic porters and waiters preferred talking about more than their children, which is natural for any father, but with railroad men the focus generally was on education and accomplishment. "One of the chefs I worked for was Ollie McClelland, a striking 6-foot 4-inch black man, very fair of complexion and the father of four sons," the dining car veteran Thomas Fleming recalled in his memoir. "Like the majority of blacks working on the railroads, he had little education beyond grammar school. I discovered his illiteracy when I saw him holding a newspaper upside down and acting as though he were reading it. He'd say, 'I don't see too well, Tom. Could you read something to me?' And I would. Ollie recognized his limitations, so he pushed his kids to attend school. One son, Ollie Jr., graduated from the University of California and became a principal in a high school in Los Angeles, then superintendent of a school district. Another son, Alden, earned a law degree and practiced law in the Bay Area."[39]

That interest in education traced back to the beginnings of Pullman service. In 1892, the *New York Times* wrote about a porter, Lewis Watt, who "ha[d] for years been contributing all but a small portion of his earnings to the support of a colored school at Covington, Ga., in order that the poor boys and girls of his race might be educated."[40] More than a century later Edward Exson, looking back at his forty-seven years as a dining car worker, wondered, "How in the hell did I do it?" Then he answered his own question: "When I look at the reward that I've gotten, it's some consolation. In 1986, my son was the only student admitted to Dartmouth College from his school in Jacksonville, Florida. It was a privileged school, the best in Jacksonville, Episcopal High. There were doctors and lawyers, people of high standing, whose children applied and didn't make the grade. They accused me and my son of having known somebody, but who in the hell can a waiter know to get a child into Dartmouth?"[41]

The same thing happened in Elaine Jones's family in Virginia. G. R., her father, slaved on the sleeping cars to put his three children through the finest schools. "All he expected in return," said Elaine, the civil rights lawyer, "was that we had a duty to succeed and give back. Dad said, 'I'm doing this so they can change things.'

"He won through us."[42]

PREFACE

1. David D. Perata, *Those Pullman Blues: An Oral History of the African-American Railroad Attendant* (New York: Madison Books, 1996), 120.

I : OUT OF BONDAGE, ALL ABOARD

1. Clinton County Historical Society, *History of Clinton County, Iowa* (Clinton, Iowa: Clinton County Historical Society, 1978), 271, 452.

   The SPCSCPG was founded by George William Dulany Jr. of Clinton, Iowa, a builder of internal combustion engines for boats, member of the Clinton City Council, and president of the Clinton Chamber of Commerce. Among his charities were the Piney Woods Country Life School, a historically black boarding school in Mississippi, which Dulany contributed to "in memory of Aunt Lunky, a faithful old mammy who served our family many years."
2. Stewart H. Holbrook, *The Story of American Railroads* (New York: Crown Publishers, 1947), 337–38.
3. Liston E. Leyendecker, *Palace Car Prince: A Biography of George Mortimer Pullman* (Boulder: University of Colorado Press, 1992), 29–35.
4. August Mencken, *The Railroad Passenger Car: An Illustrated History of the First Hundred Years with Accounts by Contemporary Passengers* (Baltimore: Johns Hopkins Press, 1957), 129.
5. Richard Reinhardt, ed., *Workin' on the Railroad: Reminiscences from the Age of Steam* (Palo Alto, Calif.: American West Publishing, 1970), 295.
6. Thomas Colley Grattan, *Civilized America* (London: Bradbury and Evans, 1859), 161–62.
7. Horace Greeley, *An Overland Journey from New York to San Francisco in the Summer of 1859* (Lincoln: University of Nebraska Press, 1999), 7–8.
8. Florence Lowden Miller, "The Pullmans of Prairie Avenue: A Domestic Portrait from Letters and Diaries," *Chicago History: The Magazine of the Chicago Historical Society* 1, no. 3 (spring 1971): 142.

9. John H. White Jr., *The American Railroad Passenger Car* (Baltimore: Johns Hopkins Press, 1985), 248.

10. Charles Frederick Carter, *When Railroads Were New* (New York: Henry Holt, 1909), 177–78.

11. White, *The American Railroad Passenger Car*, 252; Ernest Poole, *Giants Gone: Men Who Made Chicago* (New York: McGraw-Hill, 1943), 193–94.

12. Andrew Carnegie, *Autobiography of Andrew Carnegie* (Boston: Houghton Mifflin, 1920), 161.

13. Holbrook, *Story*, 323; Poole, *Giants Gone*, 192–93.

14. Holbrook, *Story*, 322–23; Lucius Beebe and Charles Clegg, *Hear the Train Blow: A Pictorial Epic of America in the Railroad Age* (New York: E. P. Dutton, 1952), 369.

15. Charles Long, "Pioneer and the Lincoln Funeral Train: How 'Honest Abe' Was Used to Create a Corporate Tall Tale," *Railroad History* 186 (spring 2002); Joseph Husband, *The Story of the Pullman Car* (Chicago: A. C. McClurg, 1917); Pullman Company, *Supplement to 1969 Annual Report of the Pullman Company*, undated, Pullman Company Collection, Newberry Library.

16. Long, "Pioneer and the Lincoln Funeral Train."

17. "On the Tip of the Tongue." Interview with George Pullman, *New York Press*, December 1, 1897.

18. Ibid.

19. James D. Porterfield, *Dining by Rail: The History and Recipes of America's Golden Age of Railroad Cuisine* (New York: St. Martin's Press, 1993), 7.

20. Mencken, *The Railroad Passenger Car*, 96.

21. Lucius Beebe as quoted in Peter T. Maiken, *Night Trains: The Pullman System in the Golden Years of American Rail Travel* (Baltimore: Johns Hopkins Press, 1992).

22. Frederick Douglass, *The Life and Times of Frederick Douglass, Written by Himself* (New York: Penguin Books, 1994), 815.

23. Nat Love, *The Life and Adventures of Nat Love, Better Known in the Cattle Country as "Deadwood Dick"* (Chapel Hill: Academic Affairs Library, University of North Carolina, 1907), 7, 17.

24. B. A. Botkin and Alvin F. Harlow, eds., *A Treasury of Railroad Folklore: The Stories, Tall Tales, Traditions, Ballads, and Songs of the American Railroad Man* (New York: Bonanza Books, 1953), 402–5.; Eric Arnesen, *Brotherhoods of Color: Black Railroad Workers and the Struggle for Equality* (Cambridge, Mass.: Harvard University Press, 2001), 13.

25. Husband, *The Story of the Pullman Car*, 30.

26. *San Francisco Morning Call*, March 7, 1892.

27. Commission on Industrial Relations, *Industrial Relations: Final Report and Testimony Submitted to Congress by the Commission on Industrial Relations* (Washington, D.C.: Government Printing Office, 1916), 9553–54.

28. Porter Ernest Ford Jr., quoted in Jack Santino, *Miles of Smiles, Years of Struggle: Stories of Black Pullman Porters* (Chicago: University of Illinois Press, 1989), 140.

29. Greg LeRoy, "First Class Profits and Performances upon the Public: Pull-man Porters, 1867–1912" (paper, Illinois State History Symposium, December 3, 1982), 33–34; "Pullman Company's System of Graft," *New York Press,* September 24, 1911.

30. Love, *Life and Adventures,* 151.

31. Henry Pope Jr., "Lest We Forget," *Nashville Globe,* reprinted May 25, 1928.

32. Perata, *Those Pullman Blues,* 9, 19.

2 : ROUGH RIDES, INTIMATE ENCOUNTERS

1. L. S. Hungerford, "Instructions for Porters Employed on Cars of the Pull-man Company" (Pullman Company, 1925), 11–13.

   Some regulations were tightened over the years, as new manuals were published, while others were loosened.

2. Ibid., 19, 46.

3. Ibid., 11.

4. Ibid., 6.

5. Commission on Industrial Relations, *Industrial Relations,* 9553.

6. G. H. Gibney, "Employment of New Porters," memorandum to Pullman superintendents, district superintendents, and agents, January 27, 1941, Pullman Company Collection, Newberry Library.

7. Author interview with John R. Merritt, 2002.

8. James Burke Johnson, transcript of interview by Robert C. Hayden, Boston African-American Railroad Workers Oral History Project, 1977–91 (Archives and Special Collections Department, University of Massachusetts Boston Library), 2.

9. Pullman Company, "Porters a Great Asset to Pullman . . . ," *Pullman News,* January 1949, 18.

10. Albert Floyd Flake, transcript of interview by Robert C. Hayden, Boston African-American Railroad Workers Oral History Project, 1977–91, (Archives and Special Collections Department, University of Massachu-setts Boston Library), 6.

11. Robert E. Turner, *Memories of a Retired Pullman Porter* (New York: Exposition Press, 1954), 163–64.

12. William Hardman, *A Trip to America* (London: T. Vickers Wood, 1884), 102–3.

13. "Are Sleeping Cars Healthy?" *Independent,* January 25, 1883.

14. Herbert O. Holderness, *The Reminiscences of a Pullman Conductor, or, Character Sketches of Life in a Pullman Car* (Chicago: self-published, 1901), 27–32, 87–90, 170–77.

15. Author interview with Eugene E. Bowser, 2002.

16. Pullman Company, "Car Service Rules of the Operating Department of Pullman's Palace Car Company," manual (Chicago: C. H. Blakely, 1888), 7.

17. Author interview with Bowser.

18. Perata, *Those Pullman Blues,* 8.
19. Stanley Buder, *Pullman: An Experiment in Industrial Order and Community Planning, 1880–1930* (New York: Oxford University Press, 1967), 18.
20. Hungerford, "Instructions for Porters," 6.
21. Author interview with Leroy Graham, 2002.
22. Oscar Micheaux, *The Conquest: The Story of a Negro Pioneer* (Lincoln, Neb.: Woodruff Press, 1913), 37.
23. Pullman Company, "Death Takes 'Jim' Newsome, Chesterfield of Porters," *Pullman News,* March 1926, 360.
24. Pullman Company, "Porters in Review," *Pullman News,* April 1946, 7.
25. "Pullman Inc.," two-part series, *Fortune,* January and February 1938.
26. Benjamin E. Mays, *Born to Rebel: An Autobiography* (New York: Charles Scribner's Sons, 1971), 94–95.
27. Bruce A. MacGregor and Ted Benson, *Portrait of a Silver Lady: The Train They Called the California Zephyr* (Boulder: Pruett Publishing, 1977), 213.
28. Kerry Segrave, *Tipping: An American Social History of Gratuities* (Jefferson, N.C.: McFarland, 1944), 18.
29. Elizabeth L. Post, *Emily Post's Etiquette* (New York: Funk and Wagnalls, 1922), 145.
30. Bernard Mergen, "The Pullman Porter: From 'George' to Brotherhood," *South Atlantic Quarterly* (spring 1974): 227.
31. H. N. Hall, "The Art of the Pullman Porter," *American Mercury,* July 1931, 302.
32. Author interview with Garrard Wilson "Babe" Smock, 2002.
33. Ibid.
34. Santino, *Miles of Smiles,* 95.
35. Ibid., 95.
36. Malcolm X, *The Autobiography of Malcolm X* (New York: Ballantine Books, 1964), 85.
37. Author interview with Robert McGoings, 2002.
38. Benjamin Welles, *Sumner Welles: FDR's Global Strategist* (New York: St. Martin's Press, 1997), 1–3.
39. Taylor Gordon, *Born to Be* (New York: Covici-Friede Publishers, 1929), 85.
40. Pullman Company, "This Porter a Samaritan with a 'Pure White Soul,'" *Pullman News,* July 1924, 70.
41. Pullman Company, "Porter Dies in Saving Lives of His Passengers," *Pullman News,* July 1925, 79.
42. "Porters Seek Facts of Lynching," *Chicago Defender,* May 24, 1980; "Bandits Kill Porter, Hurt Others," *New York Times,* January 4, 1911; "Railroad's Official Report," *New York Times,* March 24, 1910.
43. Patricia C. McKissack, *The Dark-Thirty: Southern Tales of the Supernatural* (New York: Alfred A. Knopf, 1992), 35–42.
44. Claude McKay, *Home to Harlem* (New York: Harper and Brothers, 1928), 145.
45. Author interview with Babe Smock.
46. Author interview with Kenneth Judy, 2002.

47. Patricia C. McKissack and Fredrick McKissack, *A Long Hard Journey: The Story of the Pullman Porter* (New York: Walker, 1989), 15.

48. Jimmy Kearse, transcribed interview by Paula Snell, B&O Railroad Museum, May 13, 2002.

49. Author interview with Joseph Strowder, 2002.

50. Charles H. Mitchner Sr., *A Rock in a Weary Land: The Autobiography of Charles H. Mitchner Sr.* (Columbia, Md.: Doral Publications, 1999), 78–79.

51. Author interview with Lawrence "Happy" Davis, 2002.

52. George G. Bea Sr., deposition, *Earl A. Love v. Pullman Company,* August 28, 1975, 35–38, Pullman Company Collection, Newberry Library; U.S. District Court for the District of Colorado, *Earl A. Love v. Pullman Company,* Judge Alfred A. Arraj's ruling, February 9, 1976, Pullman Company Collection, Newberry Library.

53. G. H. Gibney, "Employment of New Porters."

54. Author interview with Dean Denniston, 2003.

55. Pullman Company, "Car Service Rules," 9.

56. Holderness, *Reminiscences,* 16.

57. Micheaux, *The Conquest,* 50.

58. Commission on Industrial Relations, *Industrial Relations,* 9631.

59. Author interview with Marshall Keiley, 2002.

60. Perata, *Those Pullman Blues,* 6.

61. "Thirty Pullman Porters Trapped as Bootleggers," *Chicago Defender,* November 18, 1922.

62. Arthur D. Dubin, "A Pullman Postscript," *Trains,* November 1969, 23; Carroll Harding, "George M. Pullman and the Pullman Company" (New York, San Francisco, and Montreal: Newcomen Society of North America, 1951), 24; William Adelman, *Touring Pullman: A Study in Company Paternalism; A Walking Guide to the Pullman Community in Chicago, Illinois* (Chicago: Illinois Labor History Society, 1972), 2.

63. Lucius Beebe, *Mr. Pullman's Elegant Palace Car* (Garden City, N.Y.: Doubleday, 1961), before the table of contents.

64. E. B. White, "Progress and Change," in *One Man's Meat* (New York: Harper and Row, 1944), 28.

65. Beebe and Clegg, *Hear the Train Blow,* 368.

66. Arthur D. Dubin, *Pullman Paint and Lettering Notebook* (Brookfield, Wis.: Kalmbach Books, 1997); Dubin, "A Pullman Postscript," 22.

67. Buder, *Pullman: An Experiment in Industrial Order and Community Planning,* 34–35.

68. William Smith, *A Yorkshireman's Trip to the United States and Canada* (London: Longmanns, Green, 1892), 223.

69. Poole, *Giants Gone,* 195.

70. Adelman, *Touring Pullman,* 6.

71. Arnesen, *Brotherhoods of Color,* 30.

72. Emmett Dedmon, *Fabulous Chicago* (Toronto: McClelland and Stewart, 1981), 245–46.

1. Taped interview by David Perata with Babe Smock, 1986.
2. Perata, *Those Pullman Blues,* 11.
3. Author interview with Ollis Fellows, 2002.
4. Bob Withers, *The President Travels by Train: Politics and Pullmans* (Lynchburg, Va.: TLC Publishing, 1996), 134–35.
5. Author interview with McGoings.
6. Taped interview by David Perata with Samuel Turner, 1986.
7. Mark V. Tushnet, ed. *Thurgood Marshall: His Speeches, Writings, Arguments, Opinions, and Reminiscences* (Chicago: Lawrence Hill Books, 2001), 415; Roy Wilkins, *Standing Fast: The Autobiography of Roy Wilkins* (New York: Viking Press, 1982), 41.
8. Mays, *Born to Rebel,* 38–39.
9. Redcaps in Arnesen, *Brotherhoods of Color,* 155; Phi Beta Kappa in William H. Harris, *Keeping the Faith: A. Philip Randolph, Milton P. Webster, and the Brotherhood of Sleeping Car Porters* (Urbana: University of Illinois Press, 1977), 15; Costin in Pullman Company, "Here Are Pullman Porters in Review: The Pullman Traveler Knows Him Well," *Pullman News,* April 1946, 5.
10. Perata interview with Turner.
11. "Pullman Porter Wins as College Lecturer," *New York Times,* April 13, 1924.
12. Pullman Company, "Pullman Service Means Education, Says Porter," *Pullman News,* May 1924, 5.
13. Snell interview with Kearse.
14. James R. Grossman, "Blowing the Trumpet: The *Chicago Defender* and Black Migration During World War I," *Illinois Historical Journal* 78, no. 25 (summer 1982): 82–96.
15. Ibid.; James R. Grossman, *Land of Hope: Chicago, Black Southerners, and the Great Migration* (Chicago: University of Chicago Press, 1989), 74–78; Martin Jackson Terrell, "A Study of the *Chicago Defender*'s 'Great Northern Drive'" (master's thesis, Ohio University College of Communication, 1991), 25–37.
16. Author interview with Harold Reddick, 2002.
17. Author interview with Virgil Orite Smock, 2002.
18. Author interview with Babe Smock.
19. Snell interview with Kearse.
20. Author interview with Babe Smock.
21. Edward Berman, "The Pullman Porters Win," *Nation,* August 21, 1935, 4; H. R. Lary for Pullman Company, "Method of Computing Time and Pay of Porters Between 1-1-1916 and Federal Control Period Commencing 1-1-1918," July 14, 1937, Pullman Company Collection, Newberry Library.
22. Charles Frederick Anderson, *Freemen Yet Slaves Under "Abe" Lincoln's Son, or, Service and Wages of Pullman Porters* (Chicago: Enterprise Printing House, 1904), 27.

23. Turner, *Memories of a Retired Pullman Porter,* 115.
24. Author interview with Davis.
25. Pullman Company, "Car Service Rules" manual, 10.
26. Lary, "Computing Time and Pay," 9.
27. George Copeland, "Pullman Porters Ask for a New Deal," *New York Times,* March 4, 1934.
28. Author interview with Lester Arnold, 2002.
29. Author interview with Leroy Parchman, 2002.
30. U.S. Railroad Administration, *Report of the Railroad Wage Commission to the Director General of Railroads,* April 30, 1918, 151.
31. "Puts Risk on Employees," *Chicago Tribune,* October 7, 1903.
32. Author interviews with Parchman and Virgil Smock.
33. William R. Scott, *The Itching Palm: A Study of the Habit of Tipping in North America* (Philadelphia: Penn Publishing, 1916), 105.
34. California Railroad Commission, *In the Matter of the Investigation on the Commission's Own Motion of the Rules, Regulations and Practices of the Pullman Company,* report, April 25, 1914, 879–80, 883.
35. Melvin James Segal, "The Status of the Pullman Porter" (master's thesis, University of Illinois, 1935), 21–26.
36. Berman, "The Pullman Porters Win," 3.
37. Commission on Industrial Relations, *Industrial Relations,* 9667–80.
38. H. R. Lary, "Memorandum to Mr. Vroom," July 21, 1938, Pullman Company Collection, Newberry Library.
39. "Pullman Porters Will Sing for Passengers," *New York Times,* April 22, 1922.
40. Arnesen, *Brotherhoods of Color,* 90.
41. Author interview with Reddick.
42. Author interview with Bowser.
43. Author interview with Reddick.
44. Author interview with Jimmy Kearse, 2002.
45. Author interview with John Thomas Harrison, 2002.
46. Opie Read, "Caste of Negro Porters Defies Time and Change," *New York Tribune,* January 6, 1918.
47. Clinton County Historical Society, *History,* 271.
48. Leyendecker, *Palace Car Prince,* 203.
49. Author interview with Babe Smock.
50. Author interview with Virgil Smock.
51. Author interview with McGoings.
52. Wilkins, *Standing Fast,* 41.
53. Author interview with William Howard Brown, 2002.
54. Beebe, *Mr. Pullman's Elegant Palace Car,* 459.
55. Laura Hillenbrand, *Seabiscuit: An American Legend* (New York: Random House, 2001), xviii, 131; Beebe, *Mr. Pullman's Elegant Palace Car,* 352.
56. Lynn Haines, "Probing the Pullman Company, Including Many New and Interesting Facts About Sleeping Cars," *American Magazine,* May–October 1910, 114–16.

57. "Get 422 Per Cent Pullman Profits, Richest Melon Grown in General Corporate Field," *Chicago Tribune*, February 14, 1910; Harry Thurston Peck, *Twenty Years of the Republic* (New York: Dodd, Mead, 1929), 377.

58. Benjamin Stolberg, "The Pullman Peon: A Study in Industrial Race Exploitation," *Nation*, April 7, 1926, 365–67; LeRoy, "First Class Profits," 7; Greg LeRoy, "Scandalized, Analyzed, Paternalized, Fraternalized, Nationalized, and Company-Unionized, But Nowhere near Recognized: Pullman Porters, 1913–1924" (paper, Illinois Historical Society, Chicago, October 9, 1981), 20.

59. LeRoy, "First Class Profits," 25–27.

60. "Pullman Porters May Go Out on Strike Owing to Decrease of Tips," *St. Louis Post-Dispatch*, August 2, 1901.

61. Anderson, *Freemen Yet Slaves*, 45–46.

62. McKissack and McKissack, *A Long Hard Journey*, 49.

63. Louis R. Harlan and Raymond W. Smock, eds., *The Booker T. Washington Papers*, vol. 13: *1914–1915* (Urbana and Chicago: University of Illinois Press, 1984), 80–84.

64. LeRoy, "Scandalized," 17–18; Arnesen, *Brotherhoods of Color*, 60–65.

65. "Sleeping-Car Company Spotters: Innocent Conductors and Porters Discharged on Their Lying Reports," *Chicago Tribune*, June 5, 1887; "Sleeping-Car Porters: Some More Facts About Spotters and Their Ways," *Chicago Tribune*, June 15, 1887.

66. Holderness, *Reminiscences*, 211–14.

67. "Service Record, Garrard David Smock," Pullman Company Collection, Newberry Library; "Service Record, Garrard Wilson Smock," Pullman Company Collection, Newberry Library; "Service Record, Virgil Orite Smock," Pullman Company Collection, Newberry Library.

68. LeRoy, "First Class Profits," 22.

69. Author interview with William Howard Brown.

70. Pullman Porters Benefit Association, Minutes of annual convention of Pullman Porters Benefit Association, 1927–28, Pullman Company Collection, Newberry Library; LeRoy, "Scandalized," 25.

71. "Picnic for Pullman Porters," *New York Times*, July 29, 1910.

72. Claude A. Barnett to E. F. Carry, July 30, 1925, memorandum, Claude Barnett Papers, Chicago Historical Society.

73. C. L. Dellums, interview by Joyce Henderson, Earl Warren Oral History Project (University of California, Berkeley, 1973), 19.

74. Taped interview by David Perata with Jewel Brown, 1987.

75. Author interview with Parchman.

76. Author interview with Reddick.

77. John S. Goff, *Robert Todd Lincoln: A Man in His Own Right* (Norman: University of Oklahoma Press, 1969), 70–71, 119–20, 234.

78. Ibid, 220–21; Lloyd Lewis, *Myths After Lincoln* (New York: Harcourt, Brace, 1929), 266–87.

    Robert Todd's worries were not abstract. There had been several bids to rob his father's tomb, and one—in 1876—almost succeeded.

79. "A Reply to Pullman Propaganda," *Messenger*, October 1926, 292.

80. Ibid.
81. Commission on Industrial Relations, *Industrial Relations,* 9667–68.
82. Ibid., 9551–52.

4 : SAINT PHILIP AND THE BATTLE
FOR BROTHERHOOD

1. Precisely who branded Randolph "the most dangerous Negro in America" is a matter of debate. Eric Arnesen (*Brotherhoods of Color,* 89) and William H. Harris (*Keeping the Faith,* 30) say it was Wilson's attorney general, A. Mitchell Palmer. Stephen B. Oates (*Let the Trumpet Sound: The Life of Martin Luther King, Jr.* [New York: Harper and Row, 1982], 120) says it was the Wilson administration, and *Time* magazine agrees in a story titled "The Most Dangerous Negro" (May 28, 1979). Manning Marable (*From the Grassroots: Essays Toward African-American Liberation* [Boston: South End Press, 1980], 61) says it was President Wilson himself. Others say it was the Lusk Committee of the New York State Legislature that came up with the description, or maybe a journalist. Whatever the source, there was a consensus that the label fit, and that Randolph wore it as a badge of honor.
2. A. Philip Randolph, "The Reminiscences of A. Philip Randolph" (New York: Oral History Research Office, Columbia University, 1973), 234–41; Oswald Garrison Villard, "Phylon Profile XIII: A. Philip Randolph," *Phylon,* July–September, 1947, 226.
3. Jervis Anderson, *A. Philip Randolph: A Biographical Portrait* (Berkeley: University of California Press, 1972), 169.
4. Randolph, "Reminiscences," 234–35.
5. "Pullman Porters to Demand Pay Rise," *New York Times,* August 26, 1925; "200 Sleeping Car Porters Organize in Brotherhood," *New York Herald Tribune,* August 26, 1925.
6. James H. Hogans, "Things Seen, Heard, and Done Among Pullman Employees," *New York Age,* August 29, 1925; "500 Enthusiastic Porters Loudly Cheer Proposed Porters' Union," *New York Amsterdam News,* September 2, 1925.
7. James B. Crooks, "Jacksonville in the Progressive Era: Responses to Urban Growth," *Florida Historical Quarterly,* July 1986, 68–70.
8. Anderson, *Randolph: A Biographical Portrait,* 41.
9. Randolph, "Reminiscences," 70.
10. Lester Velie, *Labor USA* (New York: Harper and Brothers, 1958), 208; A. Philip Randolph, "If I Were Young Today," *Ebony,* July 1, 1963, 81; Randolph, "Reminiscences," 26, 73.
11. "Over-earnest" in Edwin R. Embree, *13 Against the Odds* (New York: Viking Press, 1944), 215. Embree does not identify the friend. "Impeccable English" in Anderson, *Randolph: A Biographical Portrait,* 46.
12. Randolph, "Reminiscences," 55.
13. Randolph, "If I Were Young," 81.
14. Anderson, *Randolph: A Biographical Portrait,* 48.

15. Ibid., 56.
16. Ibid., 62.
17. Ibid., 66.
18. Theodore Kornweibel Jr., *No Crystal Stair: Black Life and the "Messenger," 1917–1928* (Westport, Conn.: Greenwood Press, 1975), 27; Randolph, "Reminiscences," 157.
19. Anderson, *Randolph: A Biographical Portrait,* 78.
20. Kornweibel, *No Crystal Stair,* 132–70; Manning Marable, "A. Philip Randolph and the Foundations of Black American Socialism," *Radical America* 14 (March–April 1980): 17; Anderson, *Randolph: A Biographical Portrait,* 136–37.
21. "The March of Soviet Government," *Messenger,* May–June 1919, 8; Frederick G. Detweiler, *The Negro Press in the United States* (Chicago: University of Chicago Press, 1922), 169.
22. Kornweibel, *No Crystal Stair,* 53, 78; Patrick S. Washburn, *A Question of Sedition: The Federal Government's Investigation of the Black Press During World War II* (New York: Oxford University Press, 1986), 26–27; U.S. Department of Justice, *Investigation Activities of the Department of Justice,* report to the U.S. Senate, November 17, 1919, 172, 184.
23. Kornweibel, *No Crystal Stair,* 4; Anderson, *Randolph: A Biographical Portrait,* 119; Langston Hughes, *The Big Sea: An Autobiography* (New York: Hill and Wang, 1940), 233, 236.
24. Kornweibel, *No Crystal Stair,* 53, 55; Paula Pfeffer, *A. Philip Randolph, Pioneer of the Civil Rights Movement* (Baton Rouge: Louisiana State University Press, 1990), 15.
25. Randolph, "Reminiscences," 242.
26. Cary Wintz, ed., *African American Political Thought, 1890–1930* (Armonk, N.Y.: M. E. Sharpe, 1996), 306–8.
27. Anderson, *Randolph: A Biographical Portrait,* 178–79.
28. Greg LeRoy, "The Founding Heart of A. Philip Randolph's Union: Milton P. Webster and Chicago's Pullman Porters Organize, 1925–1937," *Labor's Heritage,* July 1991, 35; Melinda Chateauvert, *Marching Together: The Women of the Brotherhood of Sleeping Car Porters* (Urbana: University of Illinois Press, 1998), 47–50; Benjamin McLaurin, *The Reminiscences of Benjamin F. McLaurin* (New York: Oral History Research Office, Columbia University, 1962), 252, 254.
29. Anderson, *Randolph: A Biographical Portrait,* 184; LeRoy, "Founding Heart," 25–28; Beth Tompkins Bates, *Pullman Porters and the Rise of Protest Politics in Black America* (Chapel Hill: University of North Carolina Press, 2001), 45–48.
30. Bates, *Pullman Porters,* 43–44; Perry Howard, "Open Letter to Pullman Porters," *Spokesman,* November 1925, 16.
31. "Pullman Porters Win a Million More Pay," *New York Times,* February 11, 1926.
32. Anderson, *Randolph: A Biographical Portrait,* 185; Harris, *Keeping the Faith,* 43–44; Roi Ottley, *The Lonely Warrior: The Life and Times of Robert S. Abbott* (Chicago: Henry Regnery, 1955), 266; Brailsford R. Brazeal, *The*

Brotherhood of Sleeping Car Porters: Its Origin and Development (New York: Harper and Brothers, 1946), 50–56; Horace R. Cayton and George S. Mitchell, *Black Workers and the New Unions* (College Park, Md.: McGrath Publishing, 1939), 396; Andrew Buni, *Robert L. Vann of the Pittsburgh Courier: Politics and Black Journalism* (Pittsburgh: University of Pittsburgh Press, 1974), 170.

33. Claude Barnett, two memorandums to James Keeley, Pullman Company, 1925; Barnett letter to James Keeley, Pullman Company, April 26, 1926, Barnett Papers, Chicago Historical Society, 2–3.

34. "Fooler" in Bates, *Pullman Porters,* 55; *Defender* in Ottley, *Lonely Warrior,* 262–63; *Whip* in Brazeal, *Brotherhood,* 51.

35. McLaurin *Reminiscences,* 5–8, 106–7.

36. F. L. Simmons, attachment to memorandum to G. A. Kelly, "Service Record of Milton Price Webster," February 2, 1933, Pullman Company Collection, Newberry Library; O. W. Snoddy memorandum to O. P. Powell on Dellums's termination, November 10, 1927, Pullman Company Collection, Newberry Library.

37. Barbara Posadas, "The Hierarchy of Color and Psychological Adjustment in an Industrial Environment: Filipinos, the Pullman Company, and the Brotherhood of Sleeping Car Porters," *Labor History* (summer 1982): 355.

38. Ibid., 362.

39. Ibid., 355–57.

40. "Convicted of Assault and Attempt to Kill Ashley L. Totten, Officer of Brotherhood, Man Gets 3 Months," *New York Age,* August 3, 1929.

41. Pullman Company, "List of Colored Employees Who Are Entitled to Special Consideration," undated memorandum, Pullman Company Collection, Newberry Library.

42. A. Philip Randolph, "A Reply to Joe D. 'Blibb,' 'Idiot-Or' of the Chicago 'Flip,' Mis-Named the 'Whip,'" *Messenger,* December 1925, 378.

43. "The Pullman Porters' Organization," *Chicago Defender,* November 19, 1927; "Porters Get Inside Data on Wage Tilt," *Chicago Defender,* November 19, 1927.

44. Black Klan, undated letters, Pullman Company Collection, Newberry Library.

45. LeRoy, "Founding Heart," 37.

46. Joseph F. Wilson, *Tearing Down the Color Bar: A Documentary History and Analysis of the Brotherhood of Sleeping Car Porters* (New York: Columbia University Press, 1989), 118, 279–80; Turner, *Memories of a Retired Pullman Porter,* 137.

47. Buni, *Robert L. Vann,* 163–65.

48. Ibid., 166–69; A. Philip Randolph, "Randolph Replies to Vann," *Messenger,* May–June 1928, 114; Robert L. Vann, "Randolph's Ravings No Answer to Open Letter of Courier," *Pittsburgh Courier,* April 28, 1928.

49. Buni, *Robert L. Vann,* 169–71; Harris, *Keeping the Faith,* 134–40.

50. Philip S. Foner and Ronald L. Lewis, eds., *Black Workers: A Documentary History from Colonial Times to the Present* (Philadelphia: Temple University Press, 1989), 394, 396.

51. "The Pullman Porters' Case," *Chicago Defender,* August 20, 1927.

52. Anderson, *Randolph: A Biographical Portrait,* 194.

53. Ibid., 200–201; Henderson interview with Dellums, 65–66; Harris, *Keeping the Faith,* 112.

54. Brazeal, *Brotherhood,* 78–79; William H. Harris memorandum to author, September 4, 2003.

55. Rienzi B. Lemus, "Re: Mr. A. Philip Randolph," *New York Age,* July 14, 1928; Anderson, *Randolph: A Biographical Portrait,* 204; Mark Solomon, *The Cry Was Unity: Communists and African-Americans, 1917–1936* (Jackson: University Press of Mississippi, 1998), 63.

56. Harris, *Keeping the Faith,* 143.

57. McLaurin, *Reminiscences,* 168; William H. Harris, "A. Philip Randolph as a Charismatic Leader, 1925–1941," *Journal of Negro History* (autumn 1979): 304.

58. Anderson, *Randolph: A Biographical Portrait,* 203.

59. Sterling D. Spero and Abram L. Harris, *The Black Worker: The Negro and the Labor Movement* (New York: Columbia University Press, 1931), 460.

60. Dad Moore to Milton P. Webster, April 16, 1928, Pullman Company Collection, Newberry Library.

61. Anderson, *Randolph: A Biographical Portrait,* 212; McLaurin, *Reminiscences,* 120–21.

62. Ibid., 160.

63. Henderson interview with Dellums, 29.

64. Anderson, *Randolph: A Biographical Portrait,* 224.

65. Author interview with Roger Wilkins, 2003.

66. Chateauvert, *Marching Together,* 2; Melinda Chateauvert memorandum to author, August 1, 2003.

67. Chateauvert, *Marching Together,* 87.

68. Ibid., 60.

69. Ibid.

70. Abram Harris, *The Negro Worker: A Problem of Vital Concern to the Entire Labor Movement,* Progressive Labor Library, Pamphlet 3 (New York: National Executive Committee of the Conference for Progressive Labor Action, 1930), 10; Ira De A. Reid, "Lily-White Labor," *Opportunity,* June 1930, 189.

71. A. Philip Randolph to Milton P. Webster, August 20, 1928.

72. "The Porter Who Carried Hope to His Race," *Reader's Digest,* May 1959, 123; Velie, *Labor USA,* 207; Murray Kempton, *Part of Our Time: Some Ruins and Monuments of the Thirties* (New York: Simon and Schuster, 1955), 246.

73. G. James Fleming, "Pullman Porters Win Pot of Gold," *Crisis,* November 1937, 333.

74. "Pullman Porters Win Recognition," *New York Times,* July 2, 1935.

75. Anderson, *Randolph: A Biographical Portrait,* 225; James Farmer, *Lay Bare the Heart: An Autobiography of the Civil Rights Movement* (New York: Arbor House, 1985), 156–57.

76. Author interview with Reddick.

77. Perata interview with Jewel Brown.
78. Author interview with Denniston.
79. Kempton, *Part of Our Time*, 246.
80. "The Pullman Porter's Victory," *Opportunity: Journal of Negro Life*, August 1935, 231.
81. Perata interview with Jewel Brown.

5 : BEHIND THE MASK

1. John Gould, "A Train That Filled Our Field with Dreams," *Christian Science Monitor*, April 10, 1998; author interview with Gould, 2003.
2. Ibid.
3. Emma Goldman, *Living My Life: An Autobiography of Emma Goldman* (New York: Alfred A. Knopf, 1931), 710.
4. Mergen, "The Pullman Porter," 226.
5. Sinclair Lewis, *Babbitt* (New York: Harcourt Brace Jovanovich, 1922), 120.
6. Octavus Roy Cohen, *Epic Peters: Pullman Porter* (New York: D. Appleton, 1924), 4, 71.
7. James Weldon Johnson, *The Autobiography of an Ex-Coloured Man* (New York: Alfred A. Knopf, 1927), 62–64, 84–85.
8. Ann Banks, ed., *First-Person America* (New York: Alfred A. Knopf, 1980), 250.
9. Studs Terkel, *Hard Times: An Oral History of the Great Depression* (New York: Pantheon Books, 1970), 117.
10. Leroy Spriggs, interview by Frank Byrd, March 6, 1939, in *American Life Histories: Manuscripts from the Federal Writers' Project, 1936–1940* (New York).
11. Alice Walker, *The Temple of My Familiar* (New York: Pocket Books, 1989), 35.
12. James Alan McPherson, *Hue and Cry* (New York: HarperCollins, 1968), 41–42.
13. Karen English, *Francie* (New York: Farrar Straus Giroux, 1999), 7, 175.
14. Preston Sturges, "The Palm Beach Story," in *Four More Screenplays by Preston Sturges* (Berkeley: University of California Press, 1995).
15. Eugene O'Neill, *The Emperor Jones*, text of play, www.eoneill.com (accessed January 18, 2003), 3.
16. Kempton, *Part of Our Time*, 240.
17. James A. Bridges, transcript of interview by Robert C. Hayden, Boston African-American Railroad Workers Oral History Project, 1977–91 (Archives and Special Collections Department, University of Massachusetts Boston Library), 2.
18. Robert McG. Thomas Jr., "Eddie Anderson, 71, Benny's Rochester," *New York Times*, February 29, 1977.
19. Harry Warren and Al Dubin, "Shuffle off to Buffalo," American sheet music version, www.harrywarren.net (accessed September 15, 2003).
20. Botkin and Harlow, *Treasury of Railroad Folklore*, 457.

21. Steve Goodman, "The City of New Orleans," words and history of song, www.geocities.com (accessed October 1, 2003).
22. "The Man Called George," *Trains,* August 1973, 22.
23. Howard W. Odum and Guy B. Johnson, *Negro Workaday Songs* (Chapel Hill: University of North Carolina Press, 1926), 186–87.
24. "Pullman Porter's Dream Hits 'Numbers' Men Hard," *New York Times,* January 13, 1935; "Ex-Porter Charters a Pullman Car," *New York Times,* September 3, 1960.
25. Paul Scheffer, "The United States and War Debts: The Political Aspect," *International Affairs,* July 1932, 451.
26. Richard Thruelsen, "Pullman Porter," *Saturday Evening Post,* May 21, 1949.
27. Information on Matthew Henson from www.matthewhenson.com; www.turnerlearning.com; www.people.fas.harvard.edu.
28. Lawrence W. Levine, *Black Culture and Black Consciousness: Afro-American Folk Thought from Slavery to Freedom* (New York: Oxford University Press, 1977), 266; William Howland Kenney, *Chicago Jazz: A Cultural History, 1904–1930* (New York: Oxford University Press, 1993), 123; W. C. Handy, *Father of the Blues: An Autobiography* (New York: Macmillan, 1941), 208; Perry Bradford, *Born with the Blues: Perry Bradford's Own Story* (New York: Oak Publications, 1965), 48.
29. Author interview with Strowder.
30. "Porter Served Presidents on the Move," *Minneapolis Tribune,* June 26, 1983.
31. Author interview with Edward Roland Exson, 2002.
32. Author interview with McGoings.
33. McLaurin, *Reminiscences,* 167.
34. "Rare Books for Negroes," *New York Times,* November 13, 1921; "George Young Dead; Had Book Exchange," *New York Times,* April 19, 1935.
35. Jack Salzman, David Lionel Smith, and Cornel West, eds., *Encyclopedia of African-American Culture and History* (New York: Simon and Schuster, 1996), 438.
36. Claude McKay, *A Long Way from Home* (New York: Lee Furman, 1937), 30.
37. McKay, *Home to Harlem,* 174–75.
38. McLaurin, *Reminiscences,* 266.
39. Author interview with Reddick.
40. Author interview with William Howard Brown.
41. Santino, *Miles of Smiles,* 51.
42. Perata interview with Turner.
43. Santino, *Miles of Smiles,* 126.
44. Author interview with Maggie Hudson, 2002.
45. Author interview with Exson.
46. Author interview with Kearse.
47. Taped interview by David Perata with George Henry Smock, 1987.
48. Author interview with Arnold.

49. Author interview with Ernest Porter, 2002.

50. Author interview with Strowder.

51. Malcolm X, *Autobiography*, 87.

52. Author interview with Samuel Turner, 2002.

53. Santino, *Miles of Smiles*, 127.

54. Turner, *Memories of a Retired Pullman Porter*, 143.

55. Perata interview with George Smock.

56. Author interview with Merritt.

57. Author interview with Roger Wilkins.

58. Author interview with Davis.

59. White, *American Railroad Passenger Car*, 246, 264.

60. H. Roger Grant, *We Took the Train* (DeKalb: Northern Illinois University Press, 1990), 144.

61. Author interview with Philip Henry Logan, 2002.

62. Author interview with Graham.

63. Author interview with Strowder.

64. Wallace C. Speers, letter to the editor, *New York Times,* July 29, 1943.

65. Author interview with Parchman.

66. Snell interview with Kearse.

67. Author interview with Fellows.

68. Author interview with Virgil Smock.

6 : TRAIN TO FREEDOM

1. Henry Hampton and Steve Fayer, *Voices of Freedom: An Oral History of the Civil Rights Movement from the 1950s through the 1980s* (New York: Bantam Books, 1990), 21.

2. Howell Raines, *My Soul Is Rested: Movement Days in the Deep South Remembered* (New York: G. P. Putnam's Sons, 1977), 48.

3. Ibid., 48–49.

4. Milton Viorst, *Fire in the Streets: America in the 1960s* (New York: Simon and Schuster, 1979), 51.

5. Raines, *My Soul Is Rested,* 50.

6. Ibid., 50–51.

7. Martin Luther King Jr., *Stride Toward Freedom: The Montgomery Story* (New York: Harper and Row, 1958), 39, 46, 57.

8. Lerone Bennett Jr., *Before the Mayflower: A History of the Negro in America, 1619–1966* (Chicago: Johnson Publishing, 1966), 295.

9. Alan Dundes, *Mother Wit from the Laughing Barrel: Readings in the Interpretation of Afro-American Folklore* (New York: Garland Publishing, 1981), 200.

10. Bates, *Pullman Porters,* 125–47; Anderson, *Randolph: A Biographical Portrait,* 229–40.

11. John Hope Franklin and Alfred A. Moss Jr., *From Slavery to Freedom: A History of African-Americans* (New York: McGraw-Hill), 1994, 434–35.

12. Wilson, *Tearing Down the Color Bar,* 178.

13. Robert A. Hill, ed. *The FBI's RACON: Racial Conditions in the United States During World War II* (Boston: Northeastern University Press, 1995), 25–26.
14. Anderson, *Randolph: A Biographical Portrait,* 256–57.
15. Kempton, *Part of Our Time,* 252.
16. "A. Philip Randolph, Leader," *New York Amsterdam Star-News,* July 12, 1941, 14.
17. Theophilus Lewis, "Plays and a Point of View," *Interracial Review,* July 1942, 111; Herbert Garfinkel, *When Negroes March: The March on Washington Movement in the Organizational Politics for FEPC* (New York: Atheneum, 1969), 92–96.
18. Juan Williams, *Eyes on the Prize: America's Civil Rights Years, 1954–1965* (New York: Viking Publishing, 1987), 197; Arthur M. Schlesinger Jr., *A Thousand Days: John F. Kennedy in the White House* (Boston: Houghton Mifflin, 1965), 969, 972.
19. Hampton and Fayer, *Voices of Freedom,* 169.
20. Williams, *Eyes on the Prize,* 201–2.
21. "Meany, in Fiery Debate, Denounces Negro Unionist," *New York Times,* September 24, 1959; A. H. Raskin, "Labor to Tighten Racial Bias Curb," *New York Times,* September 25, 1959.
22. Doris Kearns Goodwin, *No Ordinary Time: Franklin and Eleanor Roosevelt: The Home Front in World War II* (New York: Simon and Schuster, 1994), 351–53.
23. Anderson, *Randolph: A Biographical Portrait,* 247.
24. "Negroes' Leader a Man of Dignity," *New York Times,* August 29, 1963.
25. Peter Goldman, *The Death and Life of Malcolm X* (Urbana: University of Illinois Press, 1973), 94; Anderson, *Randolph: A Biographical Portrait,* 13.
26. Rayford W. Logan, ed., *What the Negro Wants* (Chapel Hill: University of North Carolina Press, 1944), 146.
27. Phyl Garland, "A. Philip Randolph: Labor's Grand Old Man," *Ebony,* May 1969, 31.
28. Anderson, *Randolph: A Biographical Portrait,* 17–20.
29. "Tributes to Randolph Led by Carter and Mondale," *New York Times,* May 18, 1979.
30. Online survey by author and his researchers using a LexisNexis search engine that covers more than fifty major American newspapers, from the *Boston Globe* and *New York Times* to the *Chicago Tribune, Miami Herald,* and *Los Angeles Times.*
31. Martin Luther King Jr. letter to A. Philip Randolph, November 8, 1958, Boston University Archives.
32. Terkel, *Hard Times,* 119.
33. Henderson interview with Dellums, 140.
34. Wilson, *Tearing Down the Color Bar,* 152.
35. Anderson, *Randolph: A Biographical Portrait,* 268.
36. McLaurin, *Reminiscences,* 65.
37. King letter to Randolph, November 8, 1958.

38. Chateauvert, *Marching Together,* 163–68; Arnesen, *Brotherhoods of Color,* 104.

39. Bates, *Pullman Porters,* 101–5, 125–27.

40. Author interview with Reddick.

41. Author interview with Robert W. Saunders Sr., 2002.

42. Author interview with Davis.

43. Wilkins, *Standing Fast,* 164.

44. Author interview with John Lewis, 2003.

45. Coley Mayo Mann and Philip O. Baker, transcripts of interviews by Robert C. Hayden, Boston African-American Railroad Workers Oral History Project, 1977–91 (Archives and Special Collections Department, University of Massachusetts Boston Library), 20 (Mann) and 11 (Baker).

46. Author interview with Vernon Jordan, 2002.

7 : A LEGACY THAT LASTS

1. Author interview with Elaine Jones, 2002.

2. There are many ways to look at the Pullman Company's profitability, or lack thereof, in its later years. Some suggest the company continued making money, but that was only after its railroad owners covered its substantial deficits. The figures used here are more indicative of the actual problems the sleeping car company faced, and come from data it supplied to the U.S. District Court of Colorado in the *Earl A. Love v. Pullman Company* lawsuit.

3. White, *American Railroad Passenger Car,* 266.

4. U.S. District Court for the District of Colorado, *Earl A. Love v. Pullman Company,* Judge Alfred A. Arraj's ruling, February 9, 1976, Pullman Company Collection, Newberry Library, 6.

5. Bates, *Pullman Porters,* 25–26.

6. Robert J. Serling, *Eagle: The Story of American Airlines* (New York: St. Martin's/Marek, 1985), 288. Discrimination was so widespread, Serling said, that "one wealthy black businessman used to send his white chauffeur to pick up his ticket."

7. Frank E. Quindry, "Airline Passenger Discrimination," *Journal of Air Law,* October 1932, 511, 513–14.

8. Ben B. Follett, *Careers in Aviation* (Boston: Waverly House, 1942), 101.

9. Serling, *Eagle,* 288; Charles Gilbert Hall and Rudolph A. Merkle, *The Sky's the Limit! Jobs in Commercial Aviation and How to Get Them* (New York: Funk and Wagnalls, 1943), 132.

10. C. B. Allen, "The Airline Attendant's Job," *Aviation,* April 1931, 245.

11. Author interview with John Julian Jackson, 2003.

12. White, *American Railroad Passenger Car,* 266; "Pullman Conductor All But Disappears with End of 1968," *New York Times,* December 31, 1968.

13. Murray Kempton, "A. Philip Randolph: The Choice, Mr. President . . . ," *New Republic,* July 6, 1963, 15.

14. Author interview with William Howard Brown.

15. Author interview with Davis.

16. Author interview with Samuel Turner.
17. "The Man Called George," *Trains*, August 1973, 26.
18. Equal Employment Opportunity Commission, amicus curiae brief in case of *Earl A. Love v. Pullman Company*, December 5, 1975, 9.
19. Author interview with Martin J. Rock, 2003.
20. U.S. District Court of Colorado, *Earl A. Love v. Pullman Company*, 5.
21. Jennifer Baniewicz, "The Pullman Porter-in-Charge" (paper for History 552 class, University of Illinois at Chicago), 12; W. S. Warfield to L. S. Taylor, October 4, 1919, Pullman Company Collection, Newberry Library.

    Taylor was the federal manager at the Pullman Company. In a note to a colleague, he said he had explained to Warfield, "Each man had his individual bedding and clean linen and . . . I feel the so called hardship was largely imaginary." Warfield, Taylor added, "seemed to accept my idea of this matter and also my suggestion that the least said about it the better for all concerned." See L. S. Taylor memorandum to O. P. Powell, October 28, 1919, Pullman Company Collection, Newberry Library.
22. Baniewicz, "Pullman Porter-in-Charge," 12–18; Brazeal, *Brotherhood*, 145.
23. Author interview with Davis.
24. Ernest James Eley, deposition, *Earl A. Love v. Pullman Company*, September 18, 1965, 117.
25. Author interviews with Willie L. Leftwich and Roma Jones Stewart, 2002.
26. Author interview with Leftwich.
27. Agnes Calliste, "Struggle for Employment Equity by Blacks on American and Canadian Railroads," *Journal of Black Studies* 25, no. 3 (January 1995); Baniewicz, "Pullman Porter-in-Charge"; author interview with Stewart.
28. Ernest Holsendolph, "Court Decides Pullman Porters Long Were Victims of Job Bias," *New York Times*, February 23, 1976, 17.
29. Author interview with Ellen Story Martin, 2003.
30. Tony Fulton, transcribed interview with Paula Snell, B&O Railroad Museum, March 18, 2002.
31. Author interview with Samuel Turner.
32. Author interview with Leroy C. Richie Jr., 2002.
33. Author interview with William Kennard, 2002.
34. William Kennard, Commencement Address, Howard University, May 13, 2000.
35. Author interview with Roger Wilkins.
36. Author interviews with Jordan, and with Julian Bond (2002).
37. Aaron Epstein, "Marshall Was the Conscience of the Court," *Houston Chronicle*, January 25, 1993.
    Marshall's father worked on a dining car.
38. Pullman Company, "Here Is the World's Most Perfect Servant," *Pullman News*, December 1922, 233–34.
39. Thomas C. Fleming, *Thomas Fleming's 20th Century: In the Black World* (self-published, 2001), 26.
40. "A Pullman Porter's Good Work," *New York Times*, January 23, 1892.
41. Author interview with Exson.
42. Author interview with Elaine Jones.

Adams, Julius J. *The Challenge: A Study in Negro Leadership*. New York: Wendell Malliet, 1949.

Ade, George. *Chicago Stories*. Chicago: Henry Regnery, 1963.

Adelman, William. *Touring Pullman: A Study in Company Paternalism; A Walking Guide to the Pullman Community in Chicago, Illinois*. Chicago: Illinois Labor History Society, 1972.

Album of Genealogy and Biography: Cook County, Illinois. Chicago: Calumet Book and Engraving, 1895.

Allen, C. B. "The Airline Attendant's Job." *Aviation*, April 1931.

Alvarez, Eugene. *Travel on Southern Antebellum Railroads, 1828–1860*. Tuscaloosa, Ala.: University of Alabama Press, 1974.

American Labor. "A. Philip Randolph," August 1968.

Anderson, C. *A Sleeping Car Porter's Experience: Training in Brief Ordinary Life Founded on Actual Experience*. Self-published, November 27, 1916.

Anderson, Charles Frederick. *Freemen Yet Slaves Under "Abe" Lincoln's Son, or, Service and Wages of Pullman Porters*. Chicago: Enterprise Printing House, 1904.

Anderson, Jervis. *A. Philip Randolph: A Biographical Portrait*. Berkeley: University of California Press, 1972.

Andreas, Alfred Theodore. *History of Chicago*. Vol. 3. New York: Arno Press, 1975.

Arlington National Cemetery Web site. www.arlingtoncemetery.org (accessed July 10, 2003).

Arnesen, Eric. *Brotherhoods of Color: Black Railroad Workers and the Struggle for Equality*. Cambridge, Mass.: Harvard University Press, 2001.

Baker, Ray Stannard. *Following the Color Line: An Account of Negro Citizenship in the American Democracy*. New York: Doubleday, Page, 1908.

Baltimore Afro-American. "Pullman Workers," February 24, 1940.

B&O Railroad Museum oral history project. Interviews by Paula Snell of: Tony Fulton (March 18, 2002) and James Kearse (May 13, 2002).

Baniewicz, Jennifer. "The Pullman Porter-in-Charge." Paper for History 552 class, University of Illinois at Chicago, May 2, 1996.

Banks, Ann, ed. *First-Person America.* New York: Alfred A. Knopf, 1980.

Bardolph, Richard. *The Negro Vanguard.* New York: Rinehart, 1959.

Barger, Harold. *The Transportation Industries, 1889–1946: A Study of Output, Employment, and Productivity.* New York: National Bureau of Economic Research, 1951.

Barnes, Catherine. *Journey from Jim Crow: The Desegregation of Southern Transit.* New York: Columbia University Press, 1983.

Barnett, Claude. Letter to L. S. Hungerford, June 17, 1924. Claude Barnett Papers, Chicago Historical Society.

———. Letter to James Keeley, Pullman Company, April 26, 1926. Barnett Papers, Chicago Historical Society.

———. Letter and attachments to James Keeley, Pullman Company, May 10, 1927. Barnett Papers, Chicago Historical Society.

———. Memorandum to E. F. Carry, president of Pullman Company, July 30, 1925. Barnett Papers, Chicago Historical Society.

———. Memorandum to James Keeley, Pullman Company, 1923. Barnett Papers, Chicago Historical Society.

———. Two memorandums to James Keeley, Pullman Company, 1925. Barnett Papers, Chicago Historical Society.

Bartling, Hugh Edward. "Company Towns and the Corporate State." Ph.D. diss., University of Kentucky at Lexington, 1999.

Bates, Beth Tompkins. *Pullman Porters and the Rise of Protest Politics in Black America.* Chapel Hill: University of North Carolina Press, 2001.

Bea, George G., Sr. Deposition, *Earl A. Love v. Pullman Company.* August 28, 1975. Pullman Company Collection, Newberry Library.

Beberdick, Frank. *The Pullman Time Line, 1831–1998.* Self-published, 2000.

———, and the Historic Pullman Foundation. *Chicago's Historic Pullman District.* Chicago: Arcadia Publishing, 1998.

Beebe, Lucius. *Mr. Pullman's Elegant Palace Car.* Garden City, N.Y.: Doubleday, 1961.

———, and Charles Clegg. *Hear the Train Blow: A Pictorial Epic of America in the Railroad Age.* New York: E. P. Dutton, 1952.

Bennett, Lerone, Jr. *Before the Mayflower: A History of the Negro in America, 1619–1966.* Chicago: Johnson Publishing, 1966.

———. *Confrontation: Black and White.* Baltimore: Penguin Books, 1965.

———. *Wade in the Water: Great Moments in Black History.* Chicago: Johnson Publishing, 1979.

Berman, Edward. "The Pullman Porters Win." *Nation,* August 21, 1935.

Berman, William C. *The Politics of Civil Rights in the Truman Administration.* Columbus: Ohio State University Press, 1970.

Bernstein, Irving. *Turbulent Years: A History of the American Worker, 1933–1941.* Boston: Houghton Mifflin, 1970.

Berry, C. B. *The Other Side: How It Struck Us.* London: Griffith and Farran, 1880.

Best Talent of the Northwest. *Biographical Sketches of the Leading Men of Chicago.* Chicago: Wilson and St. Clair Publishers, 1868.

Black Klan. Undated letters. Pullman Company Collection, Newberry Library.

Black Worker. "Brother E. D. Nixon," March 1954.

———. "The Brotherhood and the Filipinos," February 1, 1930.

———. "Chinese Workers Pulled off Portland, Ore.," May 1, 1930.

———. "The Job of the Pullman Porter," December 1939.

———. "Nixon Runs Good Race," May 1954.

———. "The Porter Growls," June 1, 1930.

———. "Some Don'ts for Porters," December 1947.

Blake, Mary E. *On the Wing: Rambling Notes of a Trip to the Pacific.* Boston: Lee and Shepard Publishers, 1883.

Boddam-Whetham, J. W. *Western Wanderings: A Record of Travel in the Evening Land.* London: Richard Bentley and Son, 1874.

Bontemps, Arna. "The Most Dangerous Negro in America." *Negro Digest,* September 1961.

———: *100 Years of Negro Freedom.* New York: Dodd, Mead, 1961.

Boston African-American Railroad Workers Oral History Project. Interviews by Robert C. Hayden, 1977–91, of: Philip O. Baker, James A. Bridges, Theron Brown, Wesley Overton Crawford, Albert Floyd Flake, Otis A. Gates Jr., Julius B. Hinton, James Burke Johnson, Coley Mayo Mann, Henry Smith, Lewis Henry Wade, and George Arthur Walker. Archives and Special Collections Department, University of Massachusetts Boston Library.

Boston Evening Transcript. "Porters Demand More Pay," December 16, 1910.

Boston Globe. "John O'Bryant, Ex-School Panel Chairman, Dies," July 4, 1992.

Botkin, B. A., and Alvin F. Harlow, eds. *A Treasury of Railroad Folklore: The Stories, Tall Tales, Traditions, Ballads, and Songs of the American Railroad Man.* New York: Bonanza Books, 1953.

Boyd, F. "Previous Struggles of the Pullman Porters to Organize." *Messenger,* September 1926.

Bradford, Perry. *Born with the Blues: Perry Bradford's Own Story.* New York: Oak Publications, 1965.

Branch, Taylor. *Parting the Waters: America in the King Years, 1954–63.* New York: Simon and Schuster, 1988.

Brazeal, Brailsford R. *The Brotherhood of Sleeping Car Porters: Its Origin and Development.* New York: Harper and Brothers, 1946.

Brinkley, Douglas. *Rosa Parks.* New York: Viking, 2000.

Brooks, Thomas R. *Walls Come Tumbling Down: A History of the Civil Rights Movement, 1940–1970.* Englewood Cliffs, N.J.: Prentice-Hall, 1974.

Buder, Stanley. *Pullman: An Experiment in Industrial Order and Community Planning, 1880–1930.* New York: Oxford University Press, 1967.

Buni, Andrew. *Robert L. Vann of the Pittsburgh Courier: Politics and Black Journalism.* Pittsburgh: University of Pittsburgh Press, 1974.

Bureau of Information of the Eastern Railways. *Wages and Labor Relations in the Railroad Industry, 1900–1941.* New York: Bureau of Information of Eastern Railways, 1942.

Byrd, Frank. *See* Federal Writers' Project.

California Railroad Commission. *In the Matter of the Investigation on the Commission's Own Motion of the Rules, Regulations and Practices of the Pullman Company.* Report. April 25, 1914.

Calliste, Agnes. "Struggle for Employment Equity by Blacks on American and Canadian Railroads." *Journal of Black Studies* 25, no. 3 (January 1995).

Card Games Home Page, www.pagatcom. "Rules of Card Games: Bid Whist" (accessed February 23, 2003).

Carnegie, Andrew. *Autobiography of Andrew Carnegie.* Boston: Houghton Mifflin, 1920.

Carter, Charles Frederick. *When Railroads Were New.* New York: Henry Holt, 1909.

Cayton, Horace R., and George S. Mitchell. *Black Workers and the New Unions.* College Park, Md.: McGrath Publishing, 1939.

Chateauvert, Melinda. *Marching Together: The Women of the Brotherhood of Sleeping Car Porters.* Urbana: University of Illinois Press, 1998.

Chicago Commission on Race Relations. *The Negro in Chicago: A Study of Race Relations and a Race Riot.* Chicago: University of Chicago Press, 1922.

Chicago Defender. "'George' Dies Quiet Death on Pullmans," January 1, 1927.

———. "Mays Charges Randolph with Misrepresenting Pullman Case," March 27, 1926.

———. "Porters Demand Pullman Reforms, Stage Huge Parade of Protest in New York," June 10, 1933.

———. "Porters Get Inside Data on Wage Tilt," November 19, 1927.

———. "Porters Seek Facts of Lynching," May 24, 1980.

———. "Pullman Porters in Liquor Business," September 4, 1920.

———. "The Pullman Porters' Case," August 20, 1927.

———. "The Pullman Porters' Organization," November 19, 1927.

———. "Pullman Porters Win Increase," September 4, 1937.

———. "Randolph's Ravings No Answer to Open Letter of *Courier*," August 20, 1927.

———. "The South at the Crossroads: The Boycott Story and Montgomery," May 26, 1956.

———. "Spends Fifty Years Inside Pullman Cars," May 8, 1926.

———. "Thirty Pullman Porters Trapped as Bootleggers," November 18, 1922.

———. "U.S. Mediation Board Drops Pullman Porters' Wrangle," August 20, 1927.

Chicago Sunday Tribune. "Car Porters in Revolt: Declare Joke Writers Have Ruined Their Biz," August 4, 1901.

———. "Spies on Pullman Cars," August 14, 1904.

Chicago Tribune. "Biggest Tip Yet: Company Gives Nearly $200,000 to Conductors and Porters," February 4, 1908.

———. "Car Porters' Union Is Quiet," August 8, 1901.

———. "Cleaners Strike: Cars Are Grimy," April 9, 1902.

———. "Get 422 Per Cent Pullman Profits, Richest Melon Grown in General Corporate Field," February 14, 1910.

———. "Hard Luck of the Car Porters: Joke Writers Keep Jingling Silver Tips out of Their Pockets," May 14, 1897.

———. "He Bosses the Pullman: That Modern Autocrat, the Porter of the Sleeping Car," November 6, 1889.

———. "Must Have Safes on Sleeping Cars," February 20, 1897.

———. "Puts Risk on Employe[e]s," October 7, 1903.

———. "Pullman Explains His Absence," February 14, 1895.

———. "Sleeping-Car Company Spotters: Innocent Conductors and Porters Discharged on Their Lying Reports," June 5, 1887.

———. "Sleeping-Car Porters: How Their Present Treatment by the Sleeping Car Companies Inconveniences the Traveling Public," June 18, 1887.

———. "Sleeping-Car Porters: Some More Facts About Spotters and Their Ways," June 15, 1887.

Clarke, Thomas Curtis, et al. *The American Railway: Its Construction, Development, Management, and Appliances.* New York: Charles Scribner's Sons, 1897.

Clinton County Historical Society. *History of Clinton County, Iowa.* Clinton, Iowa: Clinton County Historical Society, 1978.

Cohen, Octavus Roy. *Epic Peters: Pullman Porter.* New York: D. Appleton, 1924.

Cohn, Ruby. "Black Power on Stage: Emperor Jones and King Cristophe." *Yale French Studies* 46 (1971).

Columbia University Oral History Research Office. "The Reminiscences of A. Philip Randolph," transcription of interview by Wendell Wray of A. Philip Randolph, 1973.

———. "The Reminiscences of Benjamin F. McLaurin," transcription of interview by William T. Ingersol of Benjamin F. McLaurin, 1962.

Commission on Industrial Relations. *Industrial Relations: Final Report and Testimony Submitted to Congress by the Commission on Industrial Relations.* Washington, D.C.: Government Printing Office, 1916.

Cook, Frederick Francis. *Bygone Days in Chicago: Recollections of the "Garden City" of the Sixties.* Chicago: A. C. McClurg, 1910.

Copeland, George. "Pullman Porters Ask for a New Deal." *New York Times,* March 4, 1934.

Crooks, James B. "Jacksonville in the Progressive Era: Responses to Urban Growth." *Florida Historical Quarterly,* July 1986.

Curtis, Benjamin Robbins. *Dottings 'round the Circle.* Boston: James R. Osgood, 1876.

Cwiklik, Robert. *A. Philip Randolph and the Labor Movement.* Brookfield, Conn.: Millbrook Press, 1993.

Dartmouth. "Pullman Porter Talks to Economics Class," March 26, 1924.

———. "Train Porter Speaks to Economics Class," March 25, 1924.

Davis, Daniel S. *Mr. Black Labor: The Story of A. Philip Randolph, Father of the Civil Rights Movement.* New York: E. P. Dutton, 1972.

De A. Reid, Ira. "Lily-White Labor." *Opportunity,* June 1930.

———. *Negro Membership in American Labor Unions.* New York: Department of Research and Investigations of the National Urban League, 1930.

Dedmon, Emmett. *Fabulous Chicago.* Toronto: McClelland and Stewart, 1981.

Deedes, Henry. *Sketches of the South and West, or, Ten Months' Residence in the United States.* London: William Blackwood and Sons, 1915.

DeSantis, Alan Douglas. "Selling the American Dream: The *Chicago Defender* and the Great Migration of 1915–1919." Ph.D. diss., Indiana University at Bloomington, 1993.

Detweiler, Frederick G. *The Negro Press in the United States.* Chicago: University of Chicago Press, 1922.

Dickens, Charles. *American Notes for General Circulation and Pictures from Italy.* London: Mandarin Paperbacks, 1842.

Diven, Bill. "Pullman Porter Yarns." Letter to author, 2002.

Douglass, Frederick. *The Life and Times of Frederick Douglass, Written by Himself.* New York: Penguin Books, 1994.

Drake, St. Clair, and Horace R. Cayton. *Black Metropolis: A Study of Negro Life in a Northern City.* New York: Harcourt, Brace and World, 1945.

Dubin, Arthur D. *Pullman Paint and Lettering Notebook.* Brookfield, Wis.: Kalmbach Books, 1997.

———. "A Pullman Postscript." *Trains,* November 1969.

DuBois, W. E. B. "The American Federation of Labor and the Negro." *Crisis,* July 1929, 241.

———. *Darkwater: Voices from Within the Veil.* New York: AMS Press, 1920.

Dundes, Alan. *Mother Wit from the Laughing Barrel: Readings in the Interpretation of Afro-American Folklore.* New York: Garland Publishing, 1981.

Dunn, Robert W. "Pullman 'Company Union' Slavery." *Labor Age,* March 1926.

Durham, John Stephens. "The Labor Unions and the Negro." *Atlantic Monthly,* February 1898.

Earl Warren Oral History Project, University of California, Berkeley. Interview by Joyce Henderson of C. L. Dellums, 1973.

Ebony. "New Look in Negro Labor," September 1956.

Eley, Ernest James. Deposition, *Earl A. Love v. Pullman Company.* September 18, 1965.

Embree, Edwin R. *13 Against the Odds.* New York: Viking Press, 1944.

English, Karen. *Francie.* New York: Farrar Straus Giroux, 1999.

Epstein, Aaron. "Marshall Was the Conscience of the Court." *Houston Chronicle,* January 25, 1993.

Equal Employment Opportunity Commission. Amicus curiae brief, *Earl A. Love v. Pullman Company.* December 5, 1975.

Farmer, James. *Lay Bare the Heart: An Autobiography of the Civil Rights Movement.* New York: Arbor House, 1985.

Federal Writers' Project. Interview by Frank Byrd of Leroy Spriggs, March 6, 1939, in "American Life Histories: Manuscripts from the Federal Writers' Project, 1936–1940."

Fleming, G. James. "Pullman Porters Win Pot of Gold." *Crisis,* November 1937.

Fleming, Thomas C. *Thomas Fleming's 20th Century: In the Black World.* Self-published, 2001.

Follett, Ben B. *Careers in Aviation.* Boston: Waverly House, 1942.

Foner, Philip S. *Organized Labor and the Black Worker, 1619–1981.* New York: International Publishers, 1974.

———, and Ronald L. Lewis, eds. *Black Workers: A Documentary History from Colonial Times to the Present.* Philadelphia: Temple University Press, 1989.

Footsteps: African-American History. "Blacks and the Railroads," January–February 2002.

Fortune. "Pullman, Inc." Part 1, January 1938.

———. "Pullman, Inc. (cont.)." Part 2, February 1938.

Franklin, John Hope, and Alfred A. Moss Jr. *From Slavery to Freedom: A History of African-Americans.* New York: McGraw-Hill, 1994.

Franklin, V. P. *Black Self-Determination: A Cultural History of the Faith of the Fathers.* Westport, Conn.: Lawrence Hill, 1984.

Frazier, E. Franklin. *The Negro Family in Chicago.* Chicago: University of Chicago Press, 1932.

Gairey, Harry. *A Black Man's Toronto, 1914–1980: The Reminiscences of Harry Gairey.* Ed. Donna Hall. Toronto: Multicultural History Society of Ontario, 1981.

Garfinkel, Herbert. *When Negroes March: The March on Washington Movement in the Organizational Politics for FEPC.* New York: Atheneum, 1969.

Garland, Phyl. "A. Philip Randolph: Labor's Grand Old Man." *Ebony,* May 1969.

George, Charles B. *Forty Years on the Rail: Reminiscences of a Veteran Conductor.* Chicago: R. R. Donnelley, 1887.

Gibney, G. H. "Employment of New Porters." Memorandum to Pullman superintendents, district superintendents, and agents, January 27, 1941. Pullman Company Collection, Newberry Library.

Goff, John S. *Robert Todd Lincoln: A Man in His Own Right.* Norman: University of Oklahoma Press, 1969.

Goldman, Emma. *Living My Life: An Autobiography of Emma Goldman.* New York: Alfred A. Knopf, 1931.

Goldman, Peter. *The Death and Life of Malcolm X.* Urbana: University of Illinois Press, 1973.

Goodman, Steve. "The City of New Orleans." Words and history of song. www.geocities.com (accessed October 1, 2003).

Goodwin, Doris Kearns. *No Ordinary Time: Franklin and Eleanor Roosevelt: The Home Front in World War II.* New York: Simon and Schuster, 1994.

Gordon, Sarah H. *Passage to Union: How the Railroads Transformed American Life, 1829–1929.* Chicago: Ivan R. Dee, 1996.

Gordon, Taylor. *Born to Be.* New York: Covici-Friede Publishers, 1929.

Gould, John. "A Train That Filled Our Field with Dreams." *Christian Science Monitor,* April 10, 1998.

Grant, H. Roger. *We Took the Train.* DeKalb: Northern Illinois University Press, 1990.

Grattan, Thomas Colley. *Civilized America.* London: Bradbury and Evans, 1859.

Greeley, Horace. *An Overland Journey from New York to San Francisco in the Summer of 1859.* Lincoln: University of Nebraska Press, 1999.

Greene, Lorenzo, and Carter G. Woodson. *The Negro Wage Earner.* New York: Russell and Russell, 1969.

Griffler, Keith P. *What Price Alliance: Black Radicals Confront White Labor, 1918–1938.* New York: Garland Publishing, 1995.

Grizzle, Stanley G. *My Name's Not George: The Story of the Brotherhood of Sleeping Car Porters in Canada.* Toronto: Umbrella Press, 1998.

Grossman, James R. "Blowing the Trumpet: The *Chicago Defender* and Black Migration During World War I." *Illinois Historical Journal* 78, no. 25 (summer 1982).

———. *Land of Hope: Chicago, Black Southerners, and the Great Migration.* Chicago: University of Chicago Press, 1989.

Haines, Lynn. "Probing the Pullman Company, Including Many New and Interesting Facts About Sleeping Cars." *American Magazine,* May–October 1910.

Haizlip, Shirlee Taylor. *The Sweeter the Juice.* New York: Simon and Schuster, 1994.

Hale, Edward E. *GTT; or, The Wonderful Adventures of a Pullman.* Boston: Roberts Brothers, 1877.

Hall, Charles Gilbert, and Rudolph A. Merkle. *The Sky's the Limit! Jobs in Commercial Aviation and How to Get Them.* New York: Funk and Wagnalls, 1943.

Hall, H. N. "The Art of the Pullman Porter." *American Mercury,* July 1931.

Hampton, Henry, and Steve Fayer. *Voices of Freedom: An Oral History of the Civil Rights Movement from the 1950s Through the 1980s.* New York: Bantam Books, 1990.

Handy, W. C. *Father of the Blues: An Autobiography.* New York: Macmillan, 1941.

Hankey, David, and John Hankey. *See* Maryland Historical Society Oral History Office.

Harding, Carroll. "George M. Pullman and the Pullman Company." New York, San Francisco, and Montreal: Newcomen Society of North America, 1951.

Hardman, William. *A Trip to America.* London: T. Vickers Wood, 1884.

Hardy, Lady Duffus. *Through Cities and Prairie Lands: Sketches of an American Tour.* New York: R. Worthington, 1881.

Harlan, Louis R., and Raymond W. Smock, eds. *The Booker T. Washington Papers,* vol. 13: 1914–1915. Urbana and Chicago: University of Illinois Press, 1984.

Harris, Abram. *The Negro Worker: A Problem of Vital Concern to the Entire Labor Movement.* Progressive Labor Library, Pamphlet 3. New York: National Executive Committee of the Conference for Progressive Labor Action, 1930.

Harris, William H. "A. Philip Randolph as a Charismatic Leader, 1925–1941." *Journal of Negro History* (autumn 1979).

———. *The Harder We Run: Black Workers Since the Civil War.* New York: Oxford University Press, 1982.

———. *Keeping the Faith: A. Philip Randolph, Milton P. Webster, and the Brotherhood of Sleeping Car Porters.* Urbana, Ill.: University of Illinois Press, 1977.

Hayden, Robert C. *See* Boston African-American Railroad Workers Oral History Project.

Hedgeman, Anna Harold. *The Trumpet Sounds: A Memoir of Negro Leadership.* New York: Holt, Rinehart and Winston, 1964.

Heebie Jeebies 2, no. 24, May 8, 1926.

Henderson, Joyce. *See* Earl Warren Oral History Project.

Hendrickson, Paul. "The Ladies Before Rosa: They Too Wouldn't Give up Their Seats; Let Us Now Praise Unfamous Women." *Washington Post,* April 12, 1998.

Hill, Herbert. *Black Labor and the American Legal System: Race, Work, and the Law.* Washington, D.C.: Bureau of National Affairs, 1977.

Hill, Robert A., ed. *The FBI's RACON: Racial Conditions in the United States During World War II.* Boston: Northeastern University Press, 1995.

Hillenbrand, Laura. *Seabiscuit: An American Legend.* New York: Random House, 2001.

Hirsch, Jerrold. "Review of *Miles of Smiles, Years of Struggle: Stories of Black Pullman Porters,* by Jack Santino." *Journal of Southern History* 57, no. 2 (May 1991).

Hirsch, Susan. "Rethinking the Sexual Division of Labor: Pullman Repair Shops, 1900–1969." *Radical History,* April 1986.

Hogan, Lawrence D. *A Black National News Service: The Associated Negro Press and Claude Barnett, 1919–1945.* Rutherford, N.J.: Fairleigh Dickinson University Press, 1984.

Hogans, James H. "Things Seen, Heard, and Done Among Pullman Employees." *New York Age,* August 29, 1925.

Holbrook, Stewart H. *The Age of the Moguls.* Garden City, N.Y.: Doubleday, 1954.

———. *The Story of American Railroads.* New York: Crown Publishers, 1947.

Holderness, Herbert O. *The Reminiscences of a Pullman Conductor, or, Character Sketches of Life in a Pullman Car.* Chicago: Self-published, 1901.

Holsendolph, Ernest. "Court Decides Pullman Porters Long Were Victims of Job Bias." *New York Times,* February 23, 1976.

Howard, Perry. "Open Letter to Pullman Porters." *Spokesman,* November 1925.

———. "Perry Howard Replies to Randolph." *Pittsburgh Courier,* October 24, 1925.

———. "Perry W. Howard Replies to Randolph on Pullman Issue." *Chicago Defender,* October 31, 1925.

Hughes, Langston. *The Big Sea: An Autobiography.* New York: Hill and Wang, 1940.

Hungerford, Edward. "Eating on the Train," *Harper's Weekly,* March 21, 1914.

———. *The Modern Railroad.* Chicago: A. C. McClurg, 1911.

Hungerford, L. S. "Instructions for Porters Employed on Cars of the Pullman Company," 1925. Pullman Company Collection, Newberry Library.

Husband, Joseph. *The Story of the Pullman Car.* Chicago: A. C. McClurg, 1917.

Hutchinson, William T. *Lowden of Illinois: The Life of Frank O. Lowden.* Chicago: University of Chicago Press, 1957.

Independent. "Are Sleeping Cars Healthy?" January 25, 1883.

Ingersoll, William T. *See* Columbia University Oral History Research Office.

Isay, David. *Holding On.* New York: W. W. Norton, 1996.

Jackson, Alan A. *The Wordsworth Railway Dictionary.* Hertfordshire, England: Wordsworth Editions, 1997.

Jackson, Murray. "Three Tone Poems for Unc Art Stelle." *Callaloo* 0, no. 32 (summer 1987).

Jaynes, Gerald David. *Branches Without Roots: Genesis of the Black Working Class in the South, 1862–1882.* New York: Oxford University Press, 1986.

Jet. "The Man Who Turned Down a Million Dollars," February 21, 1952.

Johnson, Charles S. "Negroes in the Railway Industry, Part II." *Phylon,* April–June, 1942.

Johnson, James Weldon. *The Autobiography of an Ex-Coloured Man.* New York: Alfred A. Knopf, 1927.

Kempton, Murray. "A. Philip Randolph: The Choice, Mr. President . . ." *New Republic,* July 6, 1963.

———. *Part of Our Time: Some Ruins and Monuments of the Thirties.* New York: Simon and Schuster, 1955.

Kennard, William. Commencement Address, Howard University. May 13, 2000.

Kenney, William Howland. *Chicago Jazz: A Cultural History, 1904–1930.* New York: Oxford University Press, 1993.

King, Martin Luther, Jr. Letter to A. Philip Randolph. November 8, 1958. One in a series of letters to and from A. Philip Randolph. Boston University Archives.

———. *Stride Toward Freedom: The Montgomery Story.* New York: Harper and Row, 1958.

Kisor, Henry. *Zephyr: Tracking a Dream Across America.* New York: Random House, 1994.

Kolm, Suzanne Lee. "Women's Labor Aloft: A Cultural History of Airline Flight Attendants in the United States." Ph.D. diss., Brown University, 1995.

Kornweibel, Theodore, Jr. "Jim Crow Cars: A Brief History and Census." *National Railway Bulletin* 62, no. 4 (1997).

———. *No Crystal Stair: Black Life and the "Messenger," 1917–1928.* Westport, Conn.: Greenwood Press, 1975.

Lary, H. R. "Memorandum to Mr. Vroom," July 21, 1938. Pullman Company Collection, Newberry Library.

———. "Method of Computing Time and Pay of Porters Between 1-1-1916 and Federal Control Period Commencing 1-1-1918," July 14, 1937. Pullman Company Collection, Newberry Library.

Lemus, Rienzi B. "Re: Mr. A. Philip Randolph." *New York Age,* July 14, 1928.

LeRoy, Greg. "First Class Profits and Performances upon the Public: Pullman Porters, 1867–1912." Paper presented to Illinois State History Symposium, December 3, 1982.

———. "The Founding Heart of A. Philip Randolph's Union: Milton P. Webster and Chicago's Pullman Porters Organize, 1925–1937." *Labor's Heritage,* July 1991.

———. "Scandalized, Analyzed, Paternalized, Fraternalized, Nationalized, and Company-Unionized, But Nowhere near Recognized: Pullman Porters, 1913–1924." Paper presented to Illinois Historical Society, Chicago, October 9, 1981.

Leuthner, Stuart. *The Railroaders.* New York: Random House, 1983.

Levine, Lawrence W. *Black Culture and Black Consciousness: Afro-American Folk Thought from Slavery to Freedom.* New York: Oxford University Press, 1977.

Levine, Michael. *African Americans and Civil Rights: From 1619 to the Present.* Phoenix, Ariz.: Oryx Press, 1996.

Lewis, David L. *King: A Critical Biography.* New York: Praeger Publishers, 1970.

Lewis, Lloyd. *Myths After Lincoln.* New York: Harcourt, Brace, 1929.

Lewis, Sinclair. *Babbitt.* New York: Harcourt Brace Jovanovich, 1922.

Lewis, Theophilus. "Plays and a Point of View." *Interracial Review,* July 1942.

Leyendecker, Liston E. *Palace Car Prince: A Biography of George Mortimer Pullman.* Boulder: University of Colorado Press, 1992.

Licht, Walter. *Working for the Railroad: The Organization of Work in the Nineteenth Century.* Princeton: Princeton University Press, 1983.

Lochard, Metz T. P. "The Negro Press in Illinois." *Journal of Illinois State Historical Society* (autumn 1963).

Logan, Rayford W. *The Negro in American Life and Thought: The Nadir, 1877–1901*. New York: Dial Press, 1954.

———, ed. *What the Negro Wants*. Chapel Hill: University of North Carolina Press, 1944.

Long, Charles. "Pioneer and the Lincoln Funeral Train: How 'Honest Abe' Was Used to Create a Corporate Tall Tale." *Railroad History* 186 (spring 2002).

Love, Nat. *The Life and Adventures of Nat Love, Better Known in the Cattle Country as "Deadwood Dick."* Chapel Hill: Academic Affairs Library, University of North Carolina, 1907.

Lowenthal, Max. *The Federal Bureau of Investigation*. Westport, Conn.: Greenwood Press, 1950.

Lowry, Helen Bullitt. "Pity the Poor Pullman Porter." *New York Times,* October 24, 1920.

MacGregor, Bruce A., and Ted Benson. *Portrait of a Silver Lady: The Train They Called the California Zephyr*. Boulder: Pruett Publishing, 1977.

Mackay, Charles. *Life and Liberty in America, or, Sketches of a Tour in the United States and Canada in 1857–8*. New York: Harper and Brothers, 1859.

Maiken, Peter T. *Night Trains: The Pullman System in the Golden Years of American Rail Travel*. Baltimore: Johns Hopkins Press, 1992.

Malcolm X. *The Autobiography of Malcolm X*. New York: Ballantine Books, 1964.

Marable, Manning. "A. Philip Randolph and the Foundations of Black American Socialism." *Radical America* 14 (March–April 1980).

———. *From the Grassroots: Essays Toward African-American Liberation*. Boston: South End Press, 1980.

———. *Race, Reform, and Rebellion: The Second Reconstruction in Black America, 1945–1982*. Jackson: University of Mississippi Press, 1991.

Marshall, Walter Gore. *Through America: or, Nine Months in the United States*. Freeport, N.Y.: Books for Libraries Press, 1882.

Maryland Historical Society Oral History Office. "Daniel Peters: B&O Dining Car Chef," transcription of interview by David Hankey and John Hankey of Daniel Peters, August 22, 1975.

Mayer, Martin. "The Lone Wolf of Civil Rights." *Saturday Evening Post,* July 11–18, 1964.

Mays, Benjamin E. *Born to Rebel: An Autobiography*. New York: Charles Scribner's Sons, 1971.

McKay, Claude. *Harlem: Negro Metropolis*. New York: Harvest Books, 1940.

———. *Home to Harlem*. New York: Harper and Brothers, 1928.

———. *A Long Way from Home*. New York: Lee Furman, 1937.

McKinney, Ernest Rice. "The Pullman Porter." Preston News Service, 1925. Claude Barnett Papers, Chicago Historical Society.

McKissack, Patricia C. *The Dark-Thirty: Southern Tales of the Supernatural*. New York: Alfred A. Knopf, 1992.

———, and Fredrick McKissack. *A Long Hard Journey: The Story of the Pullman Porter*. New York: Walker, 1989.

McPherson, James Alan. *Hue and Cry*. New York: HarperCollins, 1968.

Mencken, August. *The Railroad Passenger Car: An Illustrated History of the First Hundred Years with Accounts by Contemporary Passengers.* Baltimore: Johns Hopkins Press, 1957.

Mergen, Bernard. "The Pullman Porter: From 'George' to Brotherhood." *South Atlantic Quarterly* (spring 1974).

Messenger. "The March of Soviet Government," May–June 1919.

Micheaux, Oscar. *The Conquest: The Story of a Negro Pioneer.* Lincoln, Neb.: Woodruff Press, 1913.

Miller, Florence Lowden. "The Pullmans of Prairie Avenue: A Domestic Portrait from Letters and Diaries." *Chicago History: The Magazine of the Chicago Historical Society* 1, no. 3 (spring 1971).

Minneapolis Tribune. "Porter Served Presidents on the Move," June 26, 1983.

Minnesota History: The Quarterly of the Minnesota Historical Society. "The Brotherhood of Sleeping Car Porters in St. Paul," spring 1997.

Minton, Bruce, and John Stuart. *Men Who Lead Labor.* New York: Modern Age Books, 1937.

Missouri Folklore Class of 1994. "The Shoes Still Shine." Collection of stories from fifth-grade students in St. Louis. Meramec College, 1994.

Mitchner, Charles H., Sr. *A Rock in a Weary Land: The Autobiography of Charles H. Mitchner Sr.* Columbia, Md.: Doral Publications, 1999.

Mobile Daily Register. "The Civil Rights Rut and the Pullman Sleeping Cars," March 25, 1875.

Moedinger, William M. "It's Gonna Be One of Those Trips, Captain." *Trains,* May 1972.

———. "The Life of a Pullman Conductor Was Not All Bad." *Trains,* October 1972.

———. "A Million Miles-Plus in the Uniform of George M." *Trains,* February 1970.

———. "Pullman—From the Peak of Troop Travel to the Impact of the Jet." *Trains,* March 1970.

Moore, Dad. Letter to Milton P. Webster, April 16, 1928. Pullman Company Collection, Newberry Library.

Morel, Julian. *Pullman: The Pullman Car Company—Its Services, Cars, and Traditions.* London: David and Charles, 1983.

Morrison, Allan. "A. Philip Randolph: Dean of Negro Leaders." *Ebony,* November 1958.

Murray, Pauli. *Song in a Weary Throat: An American Pilgrimage.* New York: Harper and Row, 1987.

Myrdal, Gunnar. *An American Dilemma: The Negro Problem and Modern Democracy,* vol. 2. New York: Harper and Brothers, 1944.

Nation. "Palace Cars," December 6, 1877.

———. "The Pullman Porters," June 9, 1926.

Negro Labor Committee. Negro Labor Committee Record Group, 1925–69. September 1971. New York Public Library, Schomburg Collection of Negro Literature and History.

Nevins, Allan. *American Social History: As Recorded by British Travelers.* New York: Henry Holt, 1923.

New York Age. "Convicted of Assault and Attempt to Kill Ashley L. Totten, Officer of Brotherhood, Man Gets 3 Months," August 3, 1929.

———. "Owen and Randolph Get into Trouble," September 7, 1918.

———. "The Pullman Company and Employing Negro Labor," February 4, 1928.

———. "Pullman Porter News," September 29, 1923.

———. "Re: Mr. A. Philip Randolph," July 14, 1928.

New York Amsterdam News. "A. Philip Randolph, Leader," July 12, 1941.

———. "Do You Know the Password?" December 18, 1929.

———. "500 Enthusiastic Porters Loudly Cheer Proposed Porters' Union," September 2, 1925.

New York City Tribune. "Caste of Negro Porters Defies Time and Change," January 6, 1918. Tuskegee Institute News Clipping File.

New York Herald Tribune. "200 Sleeping Car Porters Organize in Brotherhood," August 26, 1925.

New York Press. "On the Tip of the Tongue." Interview with George Pullman, December 1, 1897.

———. "Pullman Company's System of Graft," September 24, 1911.

New York Telegram and Evening Mail. "A Pullman Porter's Lecture," March 27, 1924.

New York Times. "Bandit Holds Up Train at Chicago," December 14, 1947.

———. "Bandits Kill Porter, Hurt Others," January 4, 1911.

———. "Children Ride the Rails," August 3, 1958.

———. "Dartmouth to Hear Parlor Car Porter," March 24, 1924.

———. "Dining Car Tips Banned on Chinese Rail System." January 6, 1935.

———. "Eddie Anderson, 71, Benny's Rochester," March 1, 1977.

———. "Ex-Porter Charters a Pullman Car," September 3, 1960.

———. "A French View of Resurgent America," August 20, 1933.

———. "Four Robbed in Train Hold-Up," November 20, 1912.

———. "George Young Dead; Had Book Exchange," April 19, 1935.

———. "Green Is Heckled by Negro Radicals," July 1, 1929.

———. "Immortal George, Thus Is the Pullman Porter Dubbed Knight after Him of the Dragon and of Mount Vernon," June 8, 1924.

———. "Meany, in Fiery Debate, Denounces Negro Unionist," September 24, 1959.

———. "Mrs. Roosevelt: A Leader in Tipping on Dining Cars," February 2, 1939.

———. "Negroes' Leader a Man of Dignity," August 29, 1963.

———. "Pay Rise to Pullman Porters," August 26, 1937.

———. "Picnic for Pullman Porters," July 29, 1910.

———. "Pullman Conductor All But Disappears with End of 1968," December 31, 1968.

———. "Pullman Porter Strangely Slain," April 6, 1930.

———. "Pullman Porter Tells of Erlanger's Tour," November 7, 1931.

———. "Pullman Porter Wins as College Lecturer," April 13, 1924.

———. "Pullman Porter's Dream Hits 'Numbers' Men Hard," January 13, 1935.

———. "Pullman Porters Get Pay Increase," February 21, 1924.

———. "A Pullman Porter's Good Work," January 23, 1892.

————. "Pullman Porters Issue Strike Call," June 25, 1963.

————. "Pullman Porters See Intimidation," July 21, 1929.

————. "Pullman Porters to Demand Pay Rise," August 26, 1925.

————. "The Pullman Porter's Whisk," December 7, 1909.

————. "Pullman Porters Will Sing for Passengers," April 22, 1922.

————. "Pullman Porters Win a Million More Pay," February 11, 1926.

————. "Pullman Porters Win Recognition," July 2, 1935.

————. "Pullman Porters Win Union Status," July 2, 1935.

————. "Railroad's Official Report," March 24, 1910.

————. "Rare Books for Negroes," November 13, 1921.

————. "Snob as Ideal Draws Criticism," June 9, 1929.

————. "Spies on Pullman Cars," February 6, 1886.

————. "Tips Are Smaller But Tipping Persists," December 31, 1933.

————. "Tips Really Don't Go to Tiptakers," May 5, 1914.

————. "Tributes to Randolph Led by Carter and Mondale," May 18, 1979.

New York Times Magazine. "Tippers—They Are Either 'Stiffs' or 'Sports,'" October 4, 1936.

Nichols, T. L. *Forty Years of American Life.* London: Longmans, Green, 1874.

Northrup, Herbert R. *Organized Labor and the Negro.* New York: Harper and Brothers, 1971.

Novak, Daniel A. *The Wheel of Servitude: Black Forced Labor After Slavery.* Lexington: University of Kentucky Press, 1978.

Oates, Stephen B. *Let the Trumpet Sound: The Life of Martin Luther King, Jr.* New York: Harper and Row, 1982.

O'Connor, Flannery. *Wise Blood.* New York: Farrar Straus Giroux, 1949.

Odum, Howard W., and Guy B. Johnson. *Negro Workaday Songs.* Chapel Hill: University of North Carolina Press, 1926.

O'Neill, Eugene. *The Emperor Jones.* Text of play. www.eoneill.com (accessed January 18, 2003).

Opportunity: Journal of Negro Life. "The Pullman Porter's Victory," August 1935.

O'Reilly, Kenneth. *Racial Matters: The FBI's Secret Files on Black America, 1960–1972.* New York: Free Press, 1989.

Osborn, M. B. "Instructions for Employees on Cars of the Pullman Company." Manual, 1926. Pullman Company Collection, Newberry Library.

Osofsky, Gilbert. *The Burden of Race: A Documentary History of Negro-White Relations in America.* New York: Harper and Row, 1967.

Ottley, Roi. *The Lonely Warrior: The Life and Times of Robert S. Abbott.* Chicago: Henry Regnery, 1955.

————. *New World A-Coming.* Boston: Houghton Mifflin, 1943.

————, and William J. Weatherby, eds. *The Negro in New York: An Informal Social History.* New York: New York Public Library, 1967.

Owen, Chandler. "The Neglected Truth." *Messenger,* January 1926.

Painter, Leonard. *Through Fifty Years with the Brotherhood Railway Carmen of America.* Kansas City: Brotherhood Railway Carmen of America, 1941.

Palmer, Edward Nelson. "Negro Secret Societies." *Social Forces,* December 1944.

Patterson, Frederick. *Chronicles of Faith: The Autobiography of Frederick D. Patterson.* Ed. Martia Graham Goodson. Tuscaloosa: University of Alabama Press, 1991.

Pearson, Richard. "Marvel Cooke Dies at 99." *Washington Post,* December 2, 2000.

Peck, Harry Thurston. *Twenty Years of the Republic.* New York: Dodd, Mead, 1929.

Peck, James. *Freedom Ride.* New York: Simon and Schuster, 1962.

Peeks, Edward. *The Long Struggle for Black Power.* New York: Charles Scribner's Sons, 1971.

Perata, David D. *Those Pullman Blues: An Oral History of the African-American Railroad Attendant.* New York: Madison Books, 1996.

———. Taped interviews of Pullman porters and other black railroad workers: Alex Ashley (1987), Norman Bookman (1986), Jewel Brown (1987), Jimmy Clark (1987), George McLain (1987), Julius Payne (1987), Garrard Wilson "Babe" Smock (1986), George Henry Smock (1987), Virgil Orite Smock (1986), James Steele (1986), Samuel Turner (1986), and W. A. Wilson (1986).

Peterson, Oscar. *A Jazz Odyssey: The Life of Oscar Peterson.* New York: Continuum Press, 2002.

Pfeffer, Paula. *A. Philip Randolph, Pioneer of the Civil Rights Movement.* Baton Rouge: Louisiana State University Press, 1990.

———. "The Evolution of A. Philip Randolph and Bayard Rustin from Radicalism to Conservatism." In *Black Conservatism: Essays in Intellectual and Political History,* edited by Peter Eisenstadt. New York: Garland Publishing, 1999.

———. "The Women Behind the Union." *Labor History* (fall 1995).

Pittsburgh Courier. "Porters Hear of Raise at Confab," September 4, 1937.

Poole, Ernest. *Giants Gone: Men Who Made Chicago.* New York: McGraw-Hill, 1943.

Pope, Henry, Jr. "Lest We Forget." *Nashville Globe,* reprinted May 25, 1928.

Porterfield, James D. *Dining by Rail: The History and Recipes of America's Golden Age of Railroad Cuisine.* New York: St. Martin's Press, 1993.

Posadas, Barbara. "The Hierarchy of Color and Psychological Adjustment in an Industrial Environment: Filipinos, the Pullman Company, and the Brotherhood of Sleeping Car Porters." *Labor History* (summer 1982).

Post, Elizabeth L. *Emily Post's Etiquette.* New York: Funk and Wagnalls, 1922.

Powledge, Fred. *Free at Last: The Civil Rights Movement and the People Who Made It.* Boston: Little, Brown, 1991.

Pullman Company. "Agreement Between the Pullman Company and Porters, Attendants and Maids." October 1, 1937. Pullman Company Collection, Newberry Library.

———. "Car Service Rules of the Operating Department of Pullman's Palace Car Company." Company manual. Chicago: C. H. Blakely, 1888. Pullman Company Collection, Newberry Library.

———. "Death Takes 'Jim' Newsome, Chesterfield of Porters." *Pullman News,* March 1926.

———. "First Pullman Conductor Dies." *Pullman News,* January 1923.

———. "From Slavery to the Seat, and Then the Pullman." *Pullman News,* May 1923.

———. "Hand Maidens for Travelers." *Pullman News,* January 1923.

———. "Here Are Pullman Porters in Review: The Pullman Traveler Knows Him Well," *Pullman News,* April 1946.

———. "Here Is the World's Most Perfect Servant." *Pullman News,* December 1922.

———. *Life on a Pullman; Pullman Progress: 1859 Wood, 1907 Steel, 1933 Aluminum;* and *Pullman Facts No. 1-12: Service You Get with Your Pullman Ticket.* Undated promotional pamphlets. Pullman Company Collection, Newberry Library.

———. "List of Colored Employees Who Are Entitled to Special Consideration." Undated memorandum. Pullman Company Collection, Newberry Library.

———. Personnel files of Garrard David Smock. Pullman Company Collection, Newberry Library.

———. "Porter Dies in Saving Lives of His Passsengers." *Pullman News,* July 1925.

———. "Porters a Great Asset to Pullman . . ." *Pullman News,* January 1949.

———. "Porters in Review." *Pullman News,* April 1946.

———. *Porters' Rates of Pay.* Undated report. Pullman Company Collection, Newberry Library.

———. "Pullman Company Commissary Department: Beverage Service." Pullman Company manual, 1937.

———. Pullman Company service records and termination notes on C. L. Dellums and other Brotherhood organizers. Pullman Company Collection, Newberry Library.

———. Pullman Company statement of wage rates for porters and maids, with memorandum attached from H. R. Lary and P. D. Vroom, Pullman Company managers, December 31, 1915. Pullman Company Collection, Newberry Library.

———. "Pullman Service Means Education, Says Porter." *Pullman News,* May 1924.

———. "Regulations for the Care and Handling of Pullman Linen and Blankets." Company manual, 1923.

———. "Service Record, Garrard David Smock." Pullman Company Collection, Newberry Library.

———. "Service Record, Garrard Wilson Smock." Pullman Company Collection, Newberry Library.

———. "Service Record, Virgil Orite Smock." Pullman Company Collection, Newberry Library.

———. "Service Record of Porters and Maids in the Service of the Pullman Company." Undated memorandum. Pullman Company Collection, Newberry Library.

———. *Statistics—Porters.* Report, June 20, 1927. Pullman Company Collection, Newberry Library.

———. *Supplement to 1969 Annual Report of the Pullman Company.* Undated. Pullman Company Collection, Newberry Library.

———. "This Porter a Samaritan with a 'Pure White Soul.'" *Pullman News,* July 1924.

Pullman Porters Benefit Association. Minutes of annual convention of Pullman Porters Benefit Association, 1927–28. Pullman Company Collection, Newberry Library.

Quindry, Frank E. "Airline Passenger Discrimination." *Journal of Air Law,*
October 1932.

Rae, W. F. *Westward by Rail: The New Route to the East.* New York:
D. Appleton, 1871.

Railway Age. "A Bit of Sleeping Car History." Letter to the editor, April 10,
1879.

Railway Age Gazette. "The Decision in the Pullman Rate Case: Interstate
Commerce Commission Ruling," April 15, 1910.

———. "Industrial Relations Commission at Washington," May 7, 1915.

Railway Age's Comprehensive Railroad Dictionary. Omaha: Simmons-
Boardman Books, 1984.

Raines, Howell. *My Soul Is Rested: Movement Days in the Deep South
Remembered.* New York: G. P. Putnam's Sons, 1977.

Randall, Ruth Painter. *Lincoln's Sons.* New York: Little, Brown, 1955.

Randolph, A. Philip. "A. Philip Randolph Answers New Questions for Perry
Howard." *Messenger,* December 1925.

———. "The Crisis of Negro Railroad Workers." *American Federationist,*
August 1939.

———. "If I Were Young Today." *Ebony,* July 1, 1963.

———. Letter to Martin Luther King Jr., December 16, 1958. Manuscript
Division, Library of Congress.

———. Letter to Milton P. Webster, August 20, 1928.

———. Letters to President Dwight D. Eisenhower, 1956–57. Frederick Morrow
Collection, Boston University.

———. "Porters Get Inside Data on Wage Tilt." *Chicago Defender,* November
19, 1927.

———. "The Pullman Company and the Pullman Porter." *Messenger,* September
1925.

———. "Randolph Replies to Vann." *Messenger,* May–June 1928.

———. "A Reply to Joe D. 'Blibb,' 'Idiot-Or' of the Chicago 'Flip,' Mis-Named
the 'Whip.'" *Messenger,* December 1925.

———. "A Reply to Pullman Propaganda." *Messenger,* October 1926.

———. "The Story of the Struggle of Pullman Porters for Economic Justice."
Chicago Defender, December 29, 1928.

———. "The Truth About the Brotherhood of Sleeping Car Porters." *Messenger.*

Raskin, A. H. "Labor to Tighten Racial Bias Curb." *New York Times,*
September 25, 1959.

———. "Meany, in Fiery Debate, Denounces Negro Unionist." *New York
Times,* September 24, 1959.

Read, Opie. "Caste of Negro Porters Defies Time and Change." *New York
Tribune,* January 6, 1918.

Reader's Digest. "The Porter Who Carried Hope to His Race," May 1959.

Reddick, Harold. "Harold Nathaniel Reddick: The Courageous Life of a Florida
Civil Rights Leader." Self-published, n.d.

Reddick, L. D. *Crusader Without Violence: A Biography of Martin Luther King,
Jr.* New York: Harper and Brothers, 1959.

Redding, J. Saunders. *The Lonesome Road: The Story of the Negro's Part in
America.* Garden City, N.Y.: Doubleday, 1958.

Reed, Christopher Robert. *All the World Is Here! The Black Presence at White City*. Bloomington, Ind.: University of Indiana Press, 2000.

Reiff, Janice, and Susan Hirsch. "Pullman and Its Public: Image and Aim in Making and Interpreting History." *Public Historian* 2, no. 4 (fall 1989).

Reinhardt, Richard. *Out West on the Overland Train*. Palo Alto, Calif.: American West Publishing, 1967.

————, ed. *Workin' on the Railroad: Reminiscences from the Age of Steam*. Palo Alto, Calif.: American West Publishing, 1970.

Risher, Howard W. *The Negro in the Railroad Industry*. Philadelphia: University of Pennsylvania Press, 1971.

Robinson, Jo Ann Gibson. *The Montgomery Bus Boycott and the Women Who Started It: The Memoir of Jo Ann Gibson Robinson*. Ed. David J. Garrow. Knoxville, Tenn: University of Tennessee Press, 1987.

Rock, Martin J. "1966 Suit 1523—*Earl A. Love v. The Pullman Company*." Letter, with attached witness sheet, to David C. Miller, October 6, 1975. Pullman Company Collection, Newberry Library.

Rogers, J. A. *From "Superman" to Man*. New York: J. A. Rogers Publications, 1917.

Rustin, Bayard. *Down the Line: The Collected Writings of Bayard Rustin*. Chicago: Quadrangle Books, 1971.

Salzman, Jack, David Lionel Smith, and Cornel West, eds. *Encyclopedia of African-American Culture and History*. New York: Simon and Schuster, 1996.

San Francisco *Morning Call*, March 7, 1892.

Santino, Jack. *Miles of Smiles, Years of Struggle: Stories of Black Pullman Porters*. Chicago: University of Illinois Press, 1989.

Scheffer, Paul. "The United States and War Debts: The Political Aspect." *International Affairs*, July 1932.

Schlesinger, Arthur M., Jr. *A Thousand Days: John F. Kennedy in the White House*. Boston: Houghton Mifflin, 1965.

Schuyler, George S. *Black and Conservative: The Autobiography of George S. Schuyler*. New Rochelle, N.Y.: House Publishers, 1966.

Scott, William R. *The Itching Palm: A Study of the Habit of Tipping in North America*. Philadelphia: Penn Publishing, 1916.

Segal, Melvin James. "The Status of the Pullman Porter." Master's thesis, University of Illinois, 1935.

Segrave, Kerry. *Tipping: An American Social History of Gratuities*. Jefferson, N.C.: McFarland, 1944.

Serling, Robert J. *Eagle: The Story of American Airlines*. New York: St. Martin's/Marek, 1985.

Shaffer, Frank E. "Pullman Prolificacy." *Trains*, October 1967.

Simmons, F. L. "Service Record of Milton Price Webster." Attachment to memorandum to G. A. Kelly, February 2, 1933. Pullman Company Collection, Newberry Library.

Sladen, Douglas. *On the Cars and Off: Being the Journey of a Pilgrimage Along the Queen's Highway to the East, from Halifax in Nova Scotia to Victoria in Vancouver's Island*. London: Ward, Lock and Bowden, 1895.

Smith, William. *A Yorkshireman's Trip to the United States and Canada.*
London: Longmans, Green, 1892.

Snell, Paula. *See* B&O Railroad Museum oral history project.

Solomon, Mark. *The Cry Was Unity: Communists and African-Americans,
1917–1936.* Jackson: University Press of Mississippi, 1998.

Snoddy, O. W. Memorandum to O. P. Powell on Dellums's termination,
November 10, 1927. Pullman Company Collection, Newberry Library.

Spear, Allan H. *Black Chicago: The Making of a Negro Ghetto, 1890–1920.*
Chicago: University of Chicago Press, 1967.

Speers, Wallace C. Letter to the editor, *New York Times,* July 29, 1943.

Spero, Sterling D., and Abram L. Harris. *The Black Worker: The Negro and the
Labor Movement.* New York: Columbia University Press, 1931.

St. Louis Argus. "Brotherhood Sleeping Car Porters Lose," August 19, 1927.

St. Louis Post-Dispatch. "Pullman Porters May Go Out on Strike Owing to
Decrease of Tips," August 2, 1901.

Stearns, Marshall W. *The Story of Jazz.* New York: Oxford University Press, 1956.

Stevenson, Janet. *The Montgomery Bus Boycott: December, 1955.* New York:
Focus Books, 1971.

Stevenson, Robert Louis. *From Scotland to Silverado.* Cambridge, Mass.:
Belknap Press of Harvard University Press, 1966.

Stolberg, Benjamin. "The Pullman Peon: A Study in Industrial Race Exploitation." *Nation,* April 7, 1926.

Stover, John F. *American Railroads.* Chicago: University of Chicago Press, 1961.

Strouse, Richard. "Notes on Tips, Tippers, and Tipees." *New York Times
Magazine,* July 17, 1949.

Sturges, Preston. "The Palm Beach Story." In *Four More Screenplays by Preston
Sturges.* Berkeley: University of California Press, 1995.

Swift, Edward M., and Charles S. Boyd. *The Pullman Porter Looks at Life.*
Washington, D.C.: Howard University School of Medicine, n.d.

Tarry, Ellen. *The Third Door: The Autobiography of an American Negro
Woman.* Westport, Conn.: Negro Universities Press, 1971.

Taylor, L. S. Memorandum to O. P. Powell, October 28, 1919. Pullman
Company Collection, Newberry Library.

Tennant, Diane. "Sisters Savor the Struggle." *Virginian-Pilot* (Norfolk, Va.),
April 11, 1999.

Terkel, Studs. *Hard Times: An Oral History of the Great Depression.* New York:
Pantheon Books, 1970.

Terrell, Martin Jackson. "A Study of the *Chicago Defender*'s 'Great Northern
Drive.'" Master's thesis, Ohio University College of Communication, 1991.

Thomas, Robert McG., Jr. "Eddie Anderson, 71, Benny's Rochester." *New York
Times,* February 29, 1977.

Thornton, J. Mills, III. *Dividing Lines: Municipal Politics and the Struggle for
Civil Rights in Montgomery, Birmingham, and Selma.* Tuscaloosa: University
of Alabama Press, 2002.

Thruelsen, Richard. "Pullman Porter." *Saturday Evening Post.* May 21, 1949.

Time. "The Most Dangerous Negro," May 28, 1979.

Totten, A. L. "Pullman Soothing Slave." *Messenger.* Undated.

Towner, Ausburn. *Seven Days in a Pullman Car.* New York: J. S. Ogilvie Publishers, 1883.

Trollope, Anthony. *North America.* New York: Alfred A. Knopf, 1951.

Turner, Robert E. *Memories of a Retired Pullman Porter.* New York: Exposition Press, 1954.

Tushnet, Mark V., ed. *Thurgood Marshall: His Speeches, Writings, Arguments, Opinions, and Reminiscences.* Chicago: Lawrence Hill Books, 2001.

Tuttle, William M. *Race Riot: Chicago in the Summer of 1919.* New York: Atheneum, 1970.

Tye, Larry. Author interviews with Pullman porters, waiters, chefs, and other black railroad workers: Lester Arnold (2002), Johnnie Bickers (2002), Eugene E. Bowser (2002), Theron Brown (2003), William Howard Brown (2002), Kenneth C. Crawford (2002), Wesley Overton Crawford (2003), Lawrence "Happy" Davis (2002), Dean Denniston (2003), Clarence Edwards (2002), Edward Roland Exson (2002), Ollis Fellows (2002), Otis A. Gates Jr. (2002), Leroy Graham (2002), Maurice Gray (2002), William F. Gund (2002), John Thomas Harrison (2002), Maggie Hudson (2002), Charles Jackson (2002), John Julian Jackson (2003), George E. Johnson (2003), Kenneth Judy (2002), James Kearse (2002), Philip Henry Logan (2002), Robert McGoings (2002), John R. Merritt (2002), Leroy Parchman (2002), Clarence Perkins (2002), Ernest Porter (2002), Harold Reddick (2002), Garrard Wilson "Babe" Smock (2002, 2003), Virgil Orite Smock (2002, 2003), Joseph Strowder (2002), Samuel Turner (2002, 2003), William "Mose" Turner (2002), and Jimmy Watkins (2002).

———. Author interviews with families of porters and other black railroad workers: Majora Carter (2003), Pamela Caruthers (2002, 2003), Fred Crawford (2002), Dean Denniston Jr.(2003), Tony Fulton (2002), Annie Maude Gates (2002), William Gates (2002), Robert A. Harris (2002), Georgette Hicks (2002), Irene Hill (2002), James Hill (2002), Elaine Jones (2002), G. Daniel Jones (2003), Vernon Jordan (2002), William Kennard (2002), C. Bruce Lee (2003), Ellen Story Martin (2003), Tina Marie Perry (2002), Doris Ross Reddick (2002), Leroy C. Richie Jr. (2002), Barbara Jean Robinson (2002), Elaine Robinson (2002), Kevin Robinson (2002), Thelma Russell (2002), Delores Shackleford (2002), Bea Smock (2002), Dera Tomkins (2002), and Roger Wilkins (2003).

———. Author interviews with Pullman conductors: Marshall Keiley (2002), Carroll B. Long (2002), and William J. Wengler (2002).

———. Other author interviews: Eric Arnesen (2002), Julian Bond (2002), John H. Boucree (2002), Byron Boyd (2002), Taylor Branch (2002), Martha Briggs (2002, 2003), Melinda Chateauvert (2003), Bill Diven (2002, 2003), Bill Fletcher (2002), Ron Goldfeder (2002), John Gould (2003), James Green (2002), Jack Greenberg (2002), James Grossman (2002), Robert C. Hayden (2002), Norman Hill (2002), Susan Hirsch (2002), Bill Howes (2002, 2003), Willie L. Leftwich (2002), Greg LeRoy (2002), John Lewis (2003), Nancy Pope (2003), Janice Reiff (2002), Martin J. Rock (2003), Mildred Roxborough (2003), Robert W. Saunders Sr. (2002), Roma Jones Stewart(2002), Paul Valteau (2002), and Larry Wright (2002).

U.S. Department of Justice. *Investigation Activities of the Department of Justice.* Report to the U.S. Senate, November 17, 1919.

U.S. District Court for the District of Colorado. *Earl A. Love v. Pullman Company.* Judge Alfred A. Arraj's ruling. February 9, 1976. Pullman Company Collection, Newberry Library.

U.S. News and World Report. "The March—Gains and Losses," September 9, 1963.

———. "The March—What Negroes Expected . . . What They Want Next," September 9, 1963.

U.S. Railroad Administration. *Report of the Railroad Wage Commission to the Director General of Railroads.* April 30, 1918.

Valien, Preston. "The Brotherhood of Sleeping Car Porters." *Phylon,* July–September 1940.

Vann, Robert L. "Randolph's Ravings No Answer to Open Letter of *Courier.*" *Pittsburgh Courier,* April 28, 1928.

Velie, Lester. *Labor USA.* New York: Harper and Brothers, 1958.

Viekman, William K. "The Man Called George." *Trains,* August 1973.

Villard, Oswald Garrison. "Phylon Profile XIII: A. Philip Randolph." *Phylon,* July–September 1947.

Viorst, Milton. *Fire in the Streets: America in the 1960s.* New York: Simon and Schuster, 1979.

Walker, Aaron C. *Red Star Calculator and Porter's Guide for Porters, Attendants, and Maids.* Pullman Company. 1937.

Walker, Alice. *The Temple of My Familiar.* New York: Pocket Books, 1989.

Wall Street Journal. "Pullman Porters Lose," March 10, 1928.

Warfield, W. S. Letter to L. S. Taylor, October 4, 1919. Pullman Company Collection, Newberry Library.

Warren, Harry, and Al Dubin. "Shuffle off to Buffalo." American sheet music version. www.harrywarren.net (accessed September 15, 2003).

Washburn, Patrick S. *A Question of Sedition: The Federal Government's Investigation of the Black Press During World War II.* New York: Oxford University Press, 1986.

Waskow, Arthur I. *From Race Riot to Sit-in, 1919 and the 1960s: A Study in the Connection Between Conflict and Violence.* Garden City, N.Y.: Doubleday, 1966.

Webster, Milton P. Letter to A. Philip Randolph, November 11, 1927. Pullman Company Collection, Newberry Library.

Welles, Benjamin. *Sumner Welles: FDR's Global Strategist.* New York: St. Martin's Press, 1997.

Weybright, Victor. "Pullman Porters on Parade." *Survey Graphic,* November 1935.

White, E. B. *One Man's Meat.* New York: Harper and Row, 1944.

White, John H., Jr. *The American Railroad Passenger Car.* Baltimore: Johns Hopkins Press, 1985.

White, Walter. *A Man Called White: The Autobiography of Walter White.* Athens: University of Georgia Press, 1995.

Wilkins, Roy. *Standing Fast: The Autobiography of Roy Wilkins.* New York: Viking Press, 1982.

Wilkinson, William. *Memorials of the Minnesota Forest Fires in the Year 1894.* Minneapolis: Norman E. Wilkinson, 1895.

Williams, Juan. *Eyes on the Prize: America's Civil Rights Years, 1954–1965.* New York: Viking Publishing, 1987.

Williamson, Ellen. *When We Went First Class.* Garden City, N.Y.: Doubleday, 1977.

Wilson, Joseph F. *Tearing Down the Color Bar: A Documentary History and Analysis of the Brotherhood of Sleeping Car Porters.* New York: Columbia University Press, 1989.

Wintz, Cary, ed. *African American Political Thought, 1890–1930.* Armonk, N.Y.: M. E. Sharpe, 1996.

Withers, Bob. *The President Travels by Train: Politics and Pullmans.* Lynchburg, Va.: TLC Publishing, 1996.

Wolf, Jake, and Weldon Melick. "A Pullman Porter Speaks His Mind." *Coronet,* April 1948.

Wood, Allan James, ed. Player Statistics. www.1918redsox.com (accessed September 15, 2003).

Wray, Wendell. *See* Columbia University Oral History Research Office.

Yelverton, Therese. *Viscountess Avonmore: Teresina in America.* London: Richard Bentley and Son, 1875.

ACKNOWLEDGMENTS

ANY BOOK PROJECT produces anxiety. This one was full-throttle angst, since it spurred me to leave the journalism career I had loved for twenty years. But my bosses at the *Boston Globe* had graciously granted me book and fellowship leaves for three of the previous six years, and when I signed a contract for this book I knew I should go for good. I relished having time to track down surviving porters and tell their story. Working from home offered the prospect of shaving only when I wanted, staying in pajamas half the day, and swimming at Walden Pond anytime temperatures allowed. It also meant losing my safety net—no job waiting, no newspaper identity to fall back on—which is why I am more grateful than normal to friends and family who held my hand these last two years.

That list, as all things for me bookwise, starts with Jill Kneerim. This special agent once again believed in my idea, helping me sharpen my proposal and my thinking. She convinced me that the time to launch a new career is when you still like your old one. And, when my original editor at Henry Holt left shortly after reviewing this manuscript, Jill made sure I stayed in great hands. That first editor, Deborah Brody, is the kind authors and journalists covet: one who demonstrates interest without applying pressure, reminds you of deadlines while letting you bend them, and makes edits that substantially improve your book. Deb's last gift was helping find an extraordinary editor to take over when she left. Vanessa Mobley treated my book with at least as much care and concern as if she had been there from the start. She pored through the manuscript, twice, and made suggestions that clarified critical concepts and smoothed rough edges. She brainstormed with me about the picture layout, helped craft an inventive marketing plan, and got me over anxieties about changing editors. Two more staffers at Holt were pivotal: Daniel Reid, Vanessa's deputy, who answered my incessant inquiries, and Christopher O'Connell, a gifted production editor. Also thanks to Vicki Haire, the copy editor who sorted out my grammar and punctuation and found just the right words and ideas when I was unable.

Speaking of editing, as a longtime medical reporter I was used to the peer-review process where fellow researchers critique articles before publication. It works so well that I borrowed it for this book. William H. Harris, the retired president of historically black Texas Southern and Alabama State universities as well as Paine College, wrote the definitive biography of the Brotherhood of Sleeping Car Porters. He applied his understanding of the union and African-American history in reviewing my manuscript. Bill Howes did the same from his perch as one of America's leading scholars of the rails, an expertise amassed as head of passenger operations at the Baltimore & Ohio and Chesapeake & Ohio railroads, a director of the Pullman Company, and president of the venerable Railway and Locomotive Historical Society.

Don MacGillis, Andy Savitz, and Sally Jacobs also read an early draft, offering advice candid enough to make me squirm and thoughtful enough to make it better. All are as good editors as friends.

While a book like mine is about people and ideas, it takes money to make it happen. Much of that came from my publisher, but the researchers I hired and the year I spent crisscrossing the country talking to porters were expensive. So was paying travel costs for the ace photographer who worked with me, Lee Wexler. For that I thank the Alicia Patterson Foundation. There is no more generous funder of journalists and ex-journalists, and foundation firebrand Margaret Engel and her selection committee bolstered my confidence by believing in my project. So did the Rockefeller Foundation, which gave me a month at its Bellagio Study and Conference Center on Lake Como in Italy. I traipsed up and down the mountain listening to tapes of Pullman porters, built lasting friendships with my fellow fellows, and outlined the book from my study overlooking the Swiss and Italian Alps. Two other benefactors were critical. Chicago's Newberry Library has all the Pullman Company papers and not only sponsored me during a productive month of research there but let me ask endless questions of Martha Briggs, James Grossman, and other wise staffers. The Gilder Lehrman Institute of American History did the same in New York, where I sifted through collections at the New York Public Library and Columbia University.

When you are new to a field of research, you lean on the experts to help navigate. Greg LeRoy knew the Pullman porters intimately from working as an Amtrak attendant and studying them as a labor historian. He shared his papers, time, and insights. Eric Arnesen did, too, and he knows more than anyone else about the roots of black railroad workers. David Perata, author of *Those Pullman Blues: An Oral History of the African American Railroad Attendant,* made me copies of fifty hours of his taped interviews that helped me understand how porters saw their jobs and lives. He also provided pictures he had collected and impressions he had formed. Other authors and scholars generous with feedback were Melinda Chateauvert, James Green, Robert C. Hayden, and Susan Hirsch. Thanks as well to Clifford Black and Dan Stessel at Amtrak, and to Paula Snell and Dave Fischvogt at the B&O Railroad Museum.

I hired a stream of student-researchers, in Boston, Washington, and Chicago, to help with library searches, porter searches, and other inquiries. The four who stayed longest and put up most with my perpetual pestering were Carolyn D'Aquila, John Gamber Jr., Leah Kaminski, and Adrianne Kocinski. Your work, and that of each of the others, was critical and appreciated. Ken Whitney, thanks for keeping my computers running on time, and Marc Shechtman, thanks for your library acumen.

My family and friends were more tolerant than they should have been of my endless traveling, writing, and being unavailable. That's you, Mom, Uncle Ray, siblings Suzanne and Norman, Donald and

Ariela, and their great kids Rachel, Andrea, Elan, and, the newest addition to the family, Zach. As for my ten-year-old nephew Eitan, you showed me that the porters' story could be interesting even to elementary schoolers. My second family, the Warburg-Rosenblums, moved back to Boston just as I was finishing my book, which gave me more joy than they know and less time to welcome them than they deserved. Alison Arnett, Anne Bernays, Billy and Sally Connolly, Justin Kaplan, Penny Savitz, Marylou Sudders, and Marianne Sutton were there holding me up, as always. So were Beryl Ann Cowan, Carolyn Hine, Lizzie Kahn, Steve Kurkjian, Dick Lehr, Morgan McVicar, Tom Palmer, Judy Rakowsky, Richard Saltus, and Don Skwar. Old Nieman friends, led by Bill and Lynne Kovach, continue to sustain me, as do new Bellagio ones, led by Harriet and Sheldon Segal. Lee Wexler made the picture part of this project a pleasure, and his wife Susan and kids Ben and Rebecca were gracious as I imposed on his time not just to travel the country taking brilliant pictures but, once back, to do painstaking editing and restoration of old photos collected from museums, libraries, and other collections.

Andrew Dreyfus, my boss at the Blue Cross Blue Shield of Massachusetts Foundation, has been terrific in accommodating my book schedule as I direct the foundation's Health Coverage Fellowship for medical journalists. This year's fellows and last, along with foundation staffers Barbara Bergman, Sarah Iselin, Celeste Reid Lee, Angela McCoy, and Jessica Seabury, have made the program fun and nearly trouble-free. All of them, along with Andrew, now are friends as well as colleagues.

Lastly, I want to acknowledge the waiters, cooks, attendants, and especially the Pullman porters who—with their kids and grandkids, nieces and nephews—opened their doors and lives to a total stranger. I am grateful.

INDEX

Pullman Standard Car Manufacturing
Company, 232
Pullman (town), 110
blacks and porters banned from, 26
built, 68–70
manufacturing and repair shops, 65
strike of 1894 and, 70–71

Quindry, Frank E., 235

race heroes, Randolph's, 118–19
"race men," 82
race riots of 1919, 129
racial justice. *See also* civil rights
movement
BSCP's campaign for, 159–60, 205
integration of train attendants and
job opportunities and, 238–39
Randolph's fight for, 204–5, 213–14
reasons porters fight for, 224–26
racial relations, xiii
FDR's Order 8802 as milestone in,
209
Negro professionals and, in early
1900s, 81
rules of, changed by WW I, 96–97
rules of, suspended during travel,
45
sexual advances and, 51–52
tipping and, 49–50
racism and racial discrimination, 93.
See also civil rights movement;
Jim Crow; racial justice; racial
relations; segregation
AFL and, 158–59
airlines and, 235
American Railway Union and,
70–71
conductors and, 62–63, 242–43
dining-car workers and, 61–62
George Pullman and, 26–27
Jacksonville and, 117–18
juries and, 213–14
labor unions and, 102, 166–67
Montgomery buses and, 201
NAACP vs. NNC and, 206
names for porters and, 96
passengers and mask of porters and,
187–94, 196
porters as entertainers and, 93
Racial Monopoly pamphlet and,
111

Randolph fights, 125–26, 128
segregation of railroads and, 43–44
in South, and porters, 59–60
touching between porters and
passengers and, 44–45
town of Pullman and, 70
used to divide labor force, 242–43
used to exploit porters, 114
white railroad workers and, 21
WW II and, 197
"radical desegregation," 201
radical trade unionism movement, 128
Railroad Administration, 88
railroads
accidents, 67–68, 89
all-Pullman lines, 97
black workers as strikebreakers for,
21
Civil War and, 10
clearances widened by, for Pullman,
13–14
"colored labor" and, before Civil
War, 20–21
early, 6–7
financial arrangements of, with
Pullman, 65–66
first sleeping car service, 7–8
link between black freedom and,
225
segregation of passengers by,
43–44
strike of 1937 and, 162
toilets in, 39
transcontinental, 10
workers segregated by color and
height by, 61n
Railway Labor Act (RLA), 147–49
Railway Men's International
Benevolent Industrial
Association, 101, 102
Rainey, Ma, 183
Randolph, Asa Philip, xvi
AFL and, 158–59, 161
awards and honors and, 218
black community and, in 1930s,
159–160
black radicals of 1960s and,
215–16
brother James and, 120–21, 152
BSCP organized by, 131–35
BSCP organizers choose, as leader,
113–16

About the Author

LARRY TYE was a longtime reporter for the *Boston Globe*, where he won numerous awards. He now directs a Boston-based training program for medical journalists. A former Nieman Fellow at Harvard University, Tye is also the author of *The Father of Spin* and *Home Lands*. He can be reached online at www.larrytye.com.